Canning &
Preserving

FOR

DUMMIES®

Canning & Preserving

FOR DUMMIES®

by Karen Ward

WILEY

Wiley Publishing, Inc.

Canning & Preserving For Dummies®

Published by
Wiley Publishing, Inc.
111 River Street
Hoboken, NJ 07030
www.wiley.com

About the Author

Karen Ward is a life-long home canner, as well as a cookbook author, culinary teacher, and home economist. In addition to judging preserved food at the San Diego County Fair each year, Karen teaches canning and preserving to men and women of all ages, to foster the knowledge, skill, and techniques of these ancient and modern-day arts.

Karen is the author of *Pickles, Peaches, and Chocolate* (C and K Enterprises) and has been featured on Home and Garden Television's *Smart Solutions* as well as being a return guest on QVC. She is a member of the Southern California Culinary Guild and the International Association of Culinary Professionals for which she co-chaired the Host City Event for their 24th annual conference held in San Diego, California, in April 2002. Karen is a native-born Southern Californian. She makes her home in San Diego with her husband, Chris.

Dedication

To Chris, with love, for your never-wavering support and encouragement.

Author's Acknowledgments

No one writes a cookbook alone. It boggles my mind when I think of the number of people involved. And the one thing that makes putting a book like this together so much fun is sharing my food with family and friends.

Thanks to Senior Editor Linda Ingroia for welcoming this idea, and Erin Connell, Assistant Editor, for embracing the concept. When they took on other assignments, Pam Mourouzis stepped in to safely and perfectly process this project to completion.

Special thanks to my Project Editor, Elizabeth Kuball, for being there day and night; Tere Drenth, coach extraordinaire; Emily Nolan, recipe tester and technical editor; illustrator Elizabeth Kurtzman; and the rest of the Wiley team for sharing their knowledge and expertise in making this book a success.

Thanks to my husband, friend, and most truthful critic, Chris, for holding one of my hands while I stirred my jams and jellies with the other. You supported me through writing, recipe testing, lots of tasting, computer frustrations, and more tasting.

Thanks to my parents, George and Martha Bistagne, for their love and broad shoulders to lean on; and to my sister Diana Bistagne, for having faith in my abilities and sharing her knowledge and experience.

Thanks to my pal, Judy Carlson, who kept (and keeps) growing a seemingly endless supply of tomatoes, squash, and other goodies that kept my imagination boiling with new recipe ideas; Judy's husband, Craig, for his manual labor in readying the garden; and all of my friends and colleagues who kept "checking in" and offered the moral support I needed to complete this project.

Publisher's Acknowledgments

We're proud of this book; please send us your comments through our Dummies online registration form located at www.dummies.com/register/.

Some of the people who helped bring this book to market include the following:

Acquisitions, Editorial, and Media Development

Project Editor: Elizabeth Kuball

Acquisitions Editor: Pam Mourouzis

Technical Editor and Recipe Tester: Emily Nolan

Editorial Manager: Michelle Hacker

Editorial Assistant: Elizabeth Rea

Cover Photos: © Dodds Photography/ StockFood

Cartoons: Rich Tennant, www.the5thwave.com

Production

Project Coordinator: Dale White

Layout and Graphics: LeAndra Johnson, Stephanie D. Jumper, Jacque Schneider, Julie Trippetti, Jeremey Unger

Special Art: Elizabeth Kurtzman

Proofreaders: Laura Albert, Andy Hollandbeck, Charles Spencer, TECHBOOKS Production Services

Indexer: TECHBOOKS Production Services

Special Help

Tere Drenth

Publishing and Editorial for Consumer Dummies

Diane Graves Steele, Vice President and Publisher, Consumer Dummies

Joyce Pepple, Acquisitions Director, Consumer Dummies

Kristin A. Cocks, Product Development Director, Consumer Dummies

Michael Spring, Vice President and Publisher, Travel

Brice Gosnell, Associate Publisher, Travel

Suzanne Jannetta, Editorial Director, Travel

Publishing for Technology Dummies

Andy Cummings, Vice President and Publisher, Dummies Technology/General User

Composition Services

Gerry Fahey, Vice President of Production Services

Debbie Stailey, Director of Composition Services

Contents at a Glance

Recipes at a Glance

Pickled Dishes

Preserves and Conserves

Sauces, Salsas, Syrups, and Pastes

Soups and Stocks

Table of Contents

Introduction

. . . .

You're not alone if you've thought about canning and preserving your own food but you haven't tried it because you're afraid it's too involved. Today's methods and procedures for home-canning, freezing, and drying food are simple and easy. Many of the techniques may be similar to those your grandmother used, but you'll find they've been perfected. In this book, I give you all the information you need to can and preserve food safely.

About This Book

Allow me to introduce you to the wonderful world of canning and preserving. I've organized three preserving methods in an easy-to-understand format. I walk you step by step through each technique and won't leave you hanging in any portion of this book. Look for the illustrations of different techniques and equipment along with my tips for making your journey fun and rewarding. I also include many of my favorite recipes for your enjoyment.

Conventions Used in This Book

The recipes in this book include preparation times, cooking times, processing times, and the yield you should expect from your efforts. Here are some details that apply to all of the recipes but aren't repeated each time:

- ✔ Use a vinegar with 5 percent acidity.
- ✔ Use pure salt with no additives. (Canning or pickling salt is best.)
- ✔ Cook all food in heavy-bottomed pots and pans.
- ✔ Use nonreactive equipment and utensils (items made from glass, stainless steel, or enamel-coated steel or iron).
- ✔ Use glass jars and two-piece caps approved for home-canning.
- ✔ Always use new lids for canning.

  ✔ Start counting your water-bath processing time when the water reaches a full rolling boil.

  ✔ Begin counting your pressure-canner processing time after releasing air in the canner and achieving the required pressure.

Also, all temperatures are Fahrenheit. All recipes and processing times are developed for altitudes at sea level to 1,000 feet above sea level. (For higher altitudes, refer to the altitude adjustment charts in Chapters 4 and 9.)

Foolish Assumptions

You don't need any previous canning or preserving experience in order to start, or continue, your endeavor to become a first-class food preserver. You'll find basic kitchen skills helpful in moving through the food preparation steps.

If I have a quick tip for a technique, I include it to save you time and increase your knowledge of working in your kitchen. Don't worry if you don't know how to use the canning and preserving equipment; I include illustrations of the equipment and discuss the steps for use where it's appropriate.

How This Book Is Organized

This book is organized into parts. The first part gives you basic information about canning and preserving, filling you in on terminology, equipment, and food safety. In the next four parts, I show you the techniques for different preserving methods. Each of these parts includes tried-and-true, tested recipes and preserving tips offering you a lot of practice for each technique. Motivation for trying each technique won't be a problem.

Part 1: Getting Started

With so many misconceptions about canning and preserving, I begin by explaining each method and dispelling your fears for each technique. This is a good starting point if you're new to canning and preserving. If you've been away from any of these techniques, review each method. You'll find information on specialty equipment and utensils for each method. Don't overlook the chapter on food safety. It's important to know what dangers may occur — and how to recognize them — if you skip any processing step, make adjustments to your recipe, change a processing method or time.

Part II: Water-Bath Canning

If you like sweet spreads, relishes, or pickled food, start with this part. Water-bath canning is the most popular food-preserving method and the easier of the two approved canning methods. I lead you step by step through the process while I explain what foods are suitable for this preserving method. You can try dozens of recipes, from jam and jelly to chutney and relish.

Part III: Pressure Canning

Pressure canning is the approved method for processing food that's naturally low in acid, like vegetables and meat. These foods contain more heat-resistant and hard-to-destroy bacteria than food that's safely water-bath processed. I carefully describe the procedures and steps for canning these foods, whether it's vegetables or meals of convenience like White Chili or Simmering Split Pea Soup.

Part IV: Freezing

In this part, you'll discover that your freezer is more than a place for leftovers and ice cream. Utilize this cold area for planning and preparing your meals with a minimum of time and effort. You'll understand why the proper freezer containers and packaging methods combined with correct thawing prevent damage to your food while preserving its quality, flavor, and color.

Part V: Drying

This is the oldest and slowest method for preserving food. Drying preserves food by removing moisture. And you won't want to miss the part on making fruit leathers. Who doesn't like to unroll the dried sheets of puréed fruit? This is one time your kids can play with their food and get away with it.

Part VI: The Part of Tens

This part includes short chapters highlighting canning problems that you may encounter and fun places to shop online or by catalog to satisfy your canning and preserving needs.

Appendix

Near the back of the book, I've included a metric equivalent chart that's a handy reference guide for converting any measurements.

Icons Used in This Book

The following four icons appear throughout this book. I use them to point out specific points or remind you of items you'll want to be sure not to miss.

This icon points out tips or shortcuts I've picked up over the years. I share them with you to make your work easier and more hassle-free.

This icon means, "Okay, you've heard this stuff before, but the information is important and bears repeating."

When you see this icon, pay special attention. I'm warning you about a potential problem, and I let you know how to overcome the dilemma.

These bits of technical information are interesting, but it's okay to skip them if you want to. Of course, paying attention to this icon will make you seem like you've been canning and preserving since you've been walking.

Where to Go from Here

This book covers four techniques for preserving food: water-bath canning, pressure canning, freezing, and drying. Although you can start in any portion of this book, don't skip Chapter 3. It describes safe processing methods and tells you how to identify spoiled food. If you have any doubts about canning and preserving safety, this chapter will put your fears at ease.

Review the first chapter in Parts II, III, IV, and V before selecting a recipe in one of these sections; they describe the technique used in that part. For example, if you'd like to make the Mixed Pickled Veggies in Chapter 8, check out Chapter 4 for the basics on water-bath canning. If you still can't decide where to start, review the recipes and start with one that sounds good to you!

Part I
Getting Started

The 5th Wave
By Rich Tennant

"...and here's what we canned from the garden this year. Beets, carrots, cucumbers...oh, there's that glove I couldn't find."

In this part . . .

Welcome to the fun and rewarding world of canning and preserving. In this part, I provide you with an overview to jump-start your skills or enhance your wisdom and experience. Knowing what equipment and tools are necessary for these methods and what you may already have in your kitchen gets you on the road to an organized and well-prepared beginning. I walk you through the terms and procedures you'll practice, and I discuss potential spoilers and procedures for preventing them.

When your family and friends say, "This is the best *(fill in your favorite canned or preserved item)* I've ever tasted. Have you ever thought about selling it?" you'll know you've arrived as a successful home canner and preserver.

Chapter 1

Everything You've Wanted to Know about Canning and Preserving, but Didn't Know Who to Ask

● ●

In This Chapter

▶ Discovering the world of canning and preserving

▶ Understanding the *why*s and *how*s of canning and preserving

▶ Preparing yourself for safely canning and preserving your foods

▶ Becoming a successful food canner and preserver

● ●

*O*ver the years, because of our busy lifestyles and the convenience of refrigeration and supermarkets, the art of canning and preserving has declined and almost been forgotten. But today, many people have a renewed interest in learning these arts. In the pages that follow, I introduce you to the ancient and modern-day techniques that will help you can and preserve with ease.

Producing canned and preserved food in your kitchen is fun and easy. You'll have no doubts about preparing safe home-canned and -preserved food after you discover what each method does, which method is best for different foods, the rules for the technique you choose, and safe food-handling techniques.

In this chapter, I give you an overview of the four canning and preserving techniques I present in this book: water-bath canning, pressure canning, freezing, and drying.

If you're new to canning and preserving, don't be overwhelmed or scared off by the rules. I walk you through easy, step-by-step instructions for each technique. After you understand the basic procedures for a method, like water-bath canning, it's just a matter of concentrating on preparing your recipe.

Knowing the Benefits of Canning and Preserving Your Own Food

One of life's luxuries is offering fresh-tasting, home-canned food to your family and friends throughout the year. Home-canning and -preserving instantly rewards your efforts when you follow the proper steps for handling and processing your food. As you complete each step, you'll observe your food making the transformation from fresh fruit, like strawberries, into a rich, red, delicious jam.

What is canning and preserving?

Canning and preserving are methods used for protecting food from spoilage so it may be used at a later time. Some preserving methods, like drying, date back to ancient times. Canning is the most popular preserving method used today. The most commonly canned foods are jam, jelly, fruit spreads, vegetables, and tomato sauce.

Put by or *putting up* are terms that describe canning years ago, before there was refrigeration. They meant, "Save something perishable for use later when you'll need it."

Who is canning today?

Although home-canning has skipped one or two generations, one thing is for sure: It's on the rise. Men and women of all ages practice the art of home-canning. It no longer matters whether you live in the country or in the city or if you grow your own food. Fresh ingredients are available just about everywhere.

Exact statistics regarding home-canning vary, but according to the largest manufacturer of home-canning products, Alltrista, approximately one out of four households in the United States cans food. Today, most home-canned products are used in the home where they're produced.

Why would you want to can?

Do you love fresh ingredients? Do you enjoy specialty foods from gourmet stores but dislike the high prices? Does working in the kitchen and handling food provide you with a sense of relaxation? Do you like to know what goes into your food? If you've answered "yes" to one of these questions and you're willing to spend the time, then canning and preserving are for you.

Home-canning is a safe and economical way to preserve large or small quantities of high-quality food. Taking the time to select your recipe, choosing and preparing your food, and packaging and processing it for safety is fulfilling and a source of pride for you, the home-canner.

Meeting Your Techniques: Canning, Freezing, and Drying

The techniques I discuss in this book are safe for home use and produce superior results when you follow all the steps for each method. You compromise the quality and safety of your food if you make your own rules. An example of this is shortening your processing period or not timing it correctly. Either of these adjustments can cause food spoilage because the food doesn't heat long enough to destroy all of the microorganisms in it.

Review the basic techniques for your type of food preserving before you begin — and if you're already familiar with the techniques, review them annually just to refresh your memory. You'll experience fewer interruptions in your food-preserving process.

About canning food

Don't let anyone tell you that home-canning is complicated and unsafe. It's simply not true. Canning is the process of applying heat to food that's sealed in a jar to destroy any microorganisms that can cause food spoilage.

Although you may hear of many canning methods, only two are approved by the United States Department of Agriculture (USDA). These are water-bath canning and pressure canning.

- ✔ **Water-bath canning:** This method uses a large kettle of boiling water. Filled jars are submerged in the water and heated to an internal temperature of 212 degrees for a specific period of time. Use this method for processing high-acid foods, such as fruit, items made from fruit, pickles, pickled food, and tomatoes. Chapter 4 explains this method in detail.

- ✔ **Pressure canning:** Pressure canning uses a large kettle that produces steam in a locked compartment. The filled jars in the kettle reach an internal temperature of 240 degrees under a specific pressure (stated in pounds) that's measured with a dial gauge or weighted gauge on the pressure-canner cover. Use a pressure canner for processing vegetables and other low-acid foods, such as meat, poultry, and fish. For more information about pressure canning, see Chapter 9.

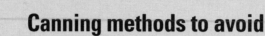

Canning methods to avoid

Older canning methods are unreliable and, for that reason, aren't used or recommended today for home-canning. Occasionally, these methods are "revived" as being faster and easier than water-bath or pressure canning, but using any of the following methods is like playing Russian roulette with your food safety. Just because your grandmother used one of the following methods doesn't make it safe to use today. If you see instructions that require you to use any of the following methods, do yourself a favor and pass by that recipe.

✔ **Oven method:** In this method, filled jars are placed in a hot oven. The method is unsafe because your food's internal temperature most likely won't become hot enough to destroy microorganisms and other bacteria that cause spoilage. There's just no guarantee that the food in the jars will reach the temperature you set your oven at. There's also a chance that your jars may explode from the sudden temperature change when your oven door is opened.

✔ **Open-kettle method:** In this method, food is cooked in an open pot and transferred to sterilized jars. The two-piece caps are quickly added in hopes of sealing the jars as the food cools. This process produces a low vacuum seal that may be broken as gas from spoiling food builds up in the jar. This occurs because your food isn't heated to

destroy microorganisms. There's also a chance your food may become contaminated when transferring it into the jars.

✔ **Steam method:** This method uses a shallow, covered pan with a rack in the bottom. After the filled jars are placed in the pan, steam circulates around the jars. This method is unsafe because the jars aren't evenly heated and the steam isn't pressurized to superheat the food and destroy microorganisms. Don't confuse this method with pressure canning.

✔ **Microwave oven:** All microwave ovens heat differently. Because of this, there's no way to set standards for processing times that achieve a high temperature to penetrate the jars and destroy microorganisms that cause food spoilage.

✔ **Dishwasher:** This is another appliance where you can't control the temperature. A dishwasher is inadequate for sterilizing filled or unfilled jars because the temperature in the unit isn't constant.

✔ **Aspirin:** Don't laugh at this, but at one time, aspirin was used as a substitute for heat processing. It does contain a germicidal agent that acts as a preservative, but this agent doesn't destroy the enzyme that causes deterioration in food and causes food spoilage.

In both of these methods, your filled jars of food are heated to a high temperature that destroys microorganisms and produces an airtight, vacuum seal. Produce a safe product by using the correct method for your type of food, following your recipe instructions to the letter, and completing each processing step.

Don't confuse a pressure canner with a pressure cooker, which is used to cook food fast.

About freezing food

Food for freezing must be absolutely fresh. The quality won't get better just because you throw it in the freezer. Properly packaging food in freezer paper or freezer containers prevents any deterioration in its quality. Damage occurs when your food comes in contact with the dry air of a freezer. Preserve the flavor, texture, color, and nutritive value of your food by quickly freezing it at a temperature of 0 degrees or lower.

About drying food

Drying is the oldest method known for preserving food. This process removes moisture from your food by exposing it to a low temperature. Good air circulation assists in evenly drying the food.

An electric dehydrator is the best and most efficient unit for drying, or dehydrating, food. This specialty appliance produces a steady flow of air with an evenly regulated temperature. You can also dry food in your oven or by using the heat of the sun, but your results will be inferior to food dried in a dehydrator.

Finding Out What's Involved in Successful Canning and Preserving

Canning and preserving methods are simple and safe, and they produce food that's nutritious, delicious, and just plain satisfying to your taste buds. Becoming a successful food preserver takes time, effort, and knowledge of the rules. Follow these tips for achieving success as a home canner and preserver:

- ✔ **Start with the freshest, best products available.** Preserving doesn't improve food quality. If you put garbage in, you get garbage out.

- ✔ **Know the rules and techniques for your canning or preserving method before you start your work.** Don't try to learn a technique during or after you've started your processing.

- ✔ **Work in short sessions to prevent fatigue and potential mistakes.** Process no more than two items in one day.

- ✔ **Stay up-to-date on new or revised guidelines for your preserving method.**

- ✔ **Use the correct processing method and processing time to destroy microorganisms.**

- ✔ **Know the elevation you're working at.** Adjust your processing time or pressure when you're at an altitude over 1,000 feet above sea level.

- ✔ **Put together a plan before you start your preserving session.** Have the proper equipment and correct ingredients on hand to prevent last-minute shortages and inconvenient breaks.

In addition to the previous tips, read your recipe more than once. Make a list of what you'll need and check off items as you gather them. Get out your equipment and make sure everything you need is present and accounted for. If you're using a pressure canner or an electric dehydrator, test out the equipment to ensure everything's working properly.

Use recipes from reliable sources or ones that you've made successfully. Follow your recipe to the letter. Don't substitute ingredients, adjust quantities, or make up your own food combinations. Improvisation and safe food preservation aren't compatible.

Now you're ready to take your food to its final destination in the preservation process. Whether you choose canning, freezing, or drying, proceed down your canning and preserving road with confidence.

Chapter 2

Walk the Walk, Talk the Talk: The Language and Gear of Canning and Preserving

- -

In This Chapter

▶ Checking out your everyday kitchen utensils and equipment

▶ Exploring and using canning and preserving gear

▶ Viewing your options for packaging food for your freezer

▶ Tracking down gear for drying

▶ Achieving the proper headspace

- -

*H*ow many times have you heard the phrase "Use the right tool for the job"? At no time is this truer than when you're canning and preserving. The majority of the items I discuss in this chapter won't break the bank, but they'll make your canning and preserving tasks more efficient. The faster you process your fresh ingredients, the better the quality and flavor of your final product.

Terms and words used for canning and preserving may be familiar to you, but they can take on different meanings for canning and preserving methods. In this chapter, I list the tools and utensils you need to complete your tasks. Some tools, like a jar lifter or a lid wand, are only used for canning. Other tools, like pots, pans, and knives, are used throughout the year for everyday tasks. Purchase good-quality tools and equipment; their quality and durability will pay for themselves many times over.

If your local stores aren't familiar with the canning and preserving items you're looking for, or you're having trouble locating them, Chapter 18 lists sources for canning and preserving supplies.

Assorted Basic Tools

I've separated basic tools into two sections: items that your kitchen shouldn't be without and other tools that you can do without but that make jobs like peeling and seeding cucumbers or mashing a pot of cooked fruit a breeze.

Must-have basic tools

If you're serious about any work in the kitchen, these basic tools are indispensable. Purchase the best quality you can afford. Good-quality items will grow old with you.

✔ **Knives:** I don't know what I'd do without my three basic knives — a paring knife, a multipurpose knife with a 6-inch blade, and my 8-inch (some people prefer a 10-inch) chef's knife.

Properly caring for your knives protects your investment. Keep your knives razor-sharp. Store them in a block or a storage rack in a drawer so they don't touch each other. Select knives that are balanced and the knife will do the work for you.

✔ **Measuring cups:** Accuracy in measuring ingredients is essential to achieve the correct balance of ingredients for canning. There are two types of measuring cups: those for measuring dry ingredients and those for measuring liquid ingredients (see Figure 2-1):

Figure 2-1:
Measuring cups for dry and liquid food products.

liquid measure cup   dry measure cups

- Dry measuring cups come in graduated sizes ranging from ¼ cup to 1 cup. For an accurate measure, fill the cup to the top with your ingredient. Level it off with a spatula or other straight-edged item. Use these cups for flour, sugar, or solid fats.

- Liquid measuring cups have a pouring spout on one side and a handle on the other. Lines on the side of the cup indicate quantity levels. These cups range in size from 1 to 4 cups and are made from glass, plastic, or metal. I prefer glass measuring cups because I can easily see the amount of liquid in the cup.

- **Measuring spoons (see Figure 2-2):** These come in graduated sizes from ⅛ teaspoon to 2 tablespoons. I have two sets, one to measure dry ingredients and the other for wet ingredients. With two sets of spoons, I don't have to stop and clean them when I measure the same amount of wet and dry ingredients.

- **Cooking spoons:** Have more than one large spoon made from nonreactive metal (like stainless steel).

- **Wooden spoons (refer to Figure 2-2):** Collect an assortment of different spoons and you'll always have the size you need.

Figure 2-2: Miscellaneous kitchen tools: wooden spoon, box grater, timer, measuring spoons, rubber spatula, and lemon juicer.

- **Rubber spatulas (refer to Figure 2-2):** These are available in a variety of colors and sizes, from flat to spoon-shaped. Use heat-resistant ones for cooking items containing sugar.

- **Tongs:** Tongs are handy for all types of kitchen chores, especially moving large pieces of food into and out of hot water. I prefer the spring-loaded variety in different lengths. Don't overlook a locking mechanism. It keeps the tongs closed when you're not using them.

- **Ladle:** Use a ladle that's heatproof with a good pouring spout.

- **Potholders:** Protect your hands from hot items. Don't use wet potholders because the heat quickly transfers through the potholder (in the form of steam), causing a severe burn.

- **Kitchen towels and paper towels:** Use these for cleaning your jar rims and as a pad for your cooling jars.

- ✓ **Graters:** I have two favorite types of graters, a box grater (refer to Figure 2-2) and a microplane grater (see Figure 2-3). A box grater gives you four or more options for shredding and grating. A microplane grater is an updated version of a *rasp* (a woodworking tool) that's perfect for removing the zest from citrus fruit.

- ✓ **Zester (refer to Figure 2-3):** Before the microplane grater, a zester was the tool for removing citrus fruit *zest* (just the skin without the bitter white part). It's still an asset when you need a small amount of zest (a teaspoon or less), but for larger amounts, use a microplane grater.

Figure 2-3:
Microplane grater and zester.

- ✓ **Scissors:** Purchase a set to keep in your kitchen. Use scissors instead of knives to open food packages.

- ✓ **Timer (refer to Figure 2-2):** I'd be lost without my timer. Choose one that's easy to read, easy to set, and loud enough to hear if you leave the room.

- ✓ **Waterproof pens and markers:** Select ones that don't rub off.

- ✓ **Labels:** You can make labels from masking or freezer tape, customize your own on your home computer, or order small quantities from a company like My Own Labels (see Chapter 18).

- ✓ **Cutting board:** A good cutting board protects your knives while providing you with a movable work surface.

- ✓ **Candy thermometer:** A candy thermometer accurately registers the temperature of candy and sugar. In canning, it's used to check the temperature of cooked items. Some candy thermometers have marks indicating the gel point for jelly (220 degrees).

Purchase a candy thermometer that's easy to read with a base to support the thermometer so the bulb portion doesn't touch the bottom of your pan. If this occurs, your temperature reading won't be accurate.

Nice-to-have basic tools

If you don't already have these items in your kitchen, add them as you find the need for them. They don't take up a lot of room, and you'll find yourself constantly reaching for them.

- ✔ **Vegetable peeler:** Use this for peeling carrots, potatoes, and apples.

- ✔ **Potato masher:** This makes quick work of smashing your cooked fruits or vegetables.

- ✔ **Lemon juicer (see Figure 2-2):** This tool works on any citrus fruit and allows you to extract the juice in a hurry. Just cut your fruit in half, insert the juicer point into the fruit, and press away.

  Measure your juice and keep seeds and pulp out by squeezing your fruit into a mesh strainer resting on the edge of a measuring cup.

- ✔ **Melon baller:** Easily removes the seeds from a halved cucumber (check out Figure 8-2) without your seeds ending up all over your kitchen.

- ✔ **Corer:** This tool removes apple cores without damaging the fruit. This is a real timesaver when you're handling pounds of apples.

- ✔ **Cherry/olive pitter:** There's nothing better for removing cherry and olive pits. Purchase the size of pitter that holds your fruit size.

Pots, pans, mixing bowls, and more

I can't imagine a kitchen without an assortment of pots, pans, and mixing bowls. You don't need to purchase everything at one time. Start with a good basic assortment and add pieces as you find a need for them.

Pots

Pots have two looped handles (one on each side of the pot), range in size from 5 to 8 quarts, are deep, and allow ample space for the expansion of your food during a hard-rolling boil. A good-quality, heavy-bottomed pot provides even heat distribution for cooking jams, jellies, or other condiments.

Saucepans

Saucepans range in size from 1 to 3 quarts. They have a long handle on one side of the pan and usually come with a fitted lid.

Mixing bowls

Keep a variety of mixing bowl sizes in your kitchen. I prefer sets in graduated sizes that stack inside each other for easy storage. Bowls made from glass and stainless steel are the most durable.

Purchase mixing bowls with flat, not curved, bases. They won't slide all over your kitchen counter while you work.

Colander

Colanders aren't just for draining pasta. They're perfect for washing and draining fruits and vegetables. Simply fill your colander with food and immerse it in a sink full of water. Remove the colander from the water and let your food drain while you move on to other tasks.

Wire basket

A collapsible wire or mesh basket with a lifting handle makes blanching a breeze. Place your filled basket of food into your pot of boiling water. When the blanching time is up, lift the food-filled basket out of the boiling water.

Making Work Easier with Specialty Equipment

I find all these items indispensable for my canning chores. There's not one I'd want to be without because they all save me loads of time.

Food processor

Purchase the best-quality food processor you can afford. It should be heavy and sturdy so that it doesn't bounce around on your kitchen counter as it's processing away. Figure 2-4 is one example of a food processor.

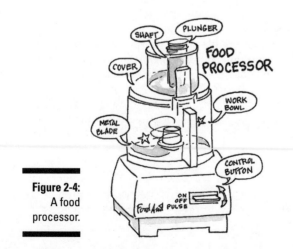

Figure 2-4:
A food
processor.

Food mill

A food mill (see Figure 2-5) purées fruits and vegetables as it removes the peel and seeds. You accomplish this by manually cranking the blade, which forces the pulp through the mill. Look for a food mill that rests on the edge of your bowl or pot. This allows you to use one hand to stabilize the mill while you crank the blade with your other hand.

FOOD MILL

Figure 2-5:
Food mill.

Blender

A blender purees fruits and vegetables in a hurry, but you need to remove the peel and seeds first. Be cautious of incorporating too much air into your food.

Food scale

A food scale is essential when your canning recipe lists your fruit or vegetables by weight. The two most common types of food scales are spring and electronic. Examples of these are shown in Figure 2-6.

A food scale with metric quantity markings makes converting recipe ingredients a breeze.

A spring scale (sometimes referred to as a manual scale) allows you to place a bowl on the scale and manually adjust the weight setting to 0 before weighing your food. After placing your food on the scale, read the indicator on the dial to determine the weight.

An electronic scale is battery operated with a digital readout. It's more costly than a spring scale but easier to read. Look for one with a *tare feature*. This allows you to set the scale to 0 if you add a bowl to hold your food.

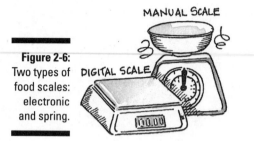

MANUAL SCALE

DIGITAL SCALE

Figure 2-6:
Two types of
food scales:
electronic
and spring.

Vacuum-sealing machines

A vacuum sealer (see Chapter 12) is the most efficient appliance around for removing air from food-storage bags. Use vacuum sealers for packaging dried foods or for storing raw or cooked foods in the freezer. Although it takes up room and can be costly, you'll realize its full value after you own one.

Canning Vessels

The kind of food you'll be canning determines the type of vessel you'll be using: a water-bath canner or a pressure canner. Refer to Chapters 4 and 9, respectively, for detailed information on using each of these vessels.

Water-bath canner

A water-bath canner, also referred to as a boiling-water canner, is illustrated in Figure 4-1. Use this kettle for processing high-acid food (primarily fruits, jams, jellies, condiments, and pickled foods). The canner consists of a large enamelware or stainless-steel pot with a tight-fitting lid and a jar rack. Check out Chapter 4 for instructions on using a water-bath canner.

Pressure canner

A pressure canner, sometimes referred to as a steam-pressure canner (see Figure 9-1), is used for canning low-acid foods (primarily vegetables, meats, fish, and poultry) in an airtight container at a specific pressure. A weighted gauge or a dial gauge measures steam pressure in the canner. This ensures that the high temperature of 240 degrees is attained to safely process your food. Pressure canners and how to use them are described in Chapter 9.

Tools Just for Canning

These are must-haves for water-bath or pressure canning. Safety in the kitchen is number one, and the right tools for handling hot, filled jars and other large canning equipment are indispensable.

Jar lifter

This is the best tool developed for transferring hot canning jars into and out of your canning kettle or pressure canner. This odd-looking, rubberized tong-like item (check out Figure 2-7), grabs the jar around the *neck* (the area just below the threaded portion at the top of the jar) without disturbing the screw band. This is one tool you don't want to be without.

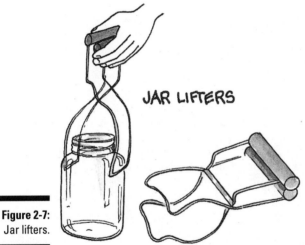

JAR LIFTERS

Figure 2-7:
Jar lifters.

Foam skimmer

A foam skimmer, shown in Figure 2-8, is a slightly curved, not-quite-flat, large disk with small holes in it attached to a long handle. Its angle makes foam removal from the top of hot jelly, jam, or marmalade easy while leaving any pieces of fruit or rind in the hot liquid. (The openings in slotted spoons are too large to achieve quick and efficient foam removal.)

FOAM SKIMMER

Figure 2-8:
A foam
skimmer.

Home-canning jars

Over the years, many types of jars with many varieties of seals have been used for home-canning. The most commonly used jars bear the names of Ball and Kerr and are commonly referred to as Mason jars. They use a two-piece cap to produce a vacuum seal in the jar after heat processing.

To ensure safe home-canning today, use only jars approved for home-canning and made from tempered glass. *Tempering* is a treatment process for glass that allows the jars to withstand the high heat (212 degrees) of a water-bath canner, as well as the high temperature (240 degrees) of a pressure canner, without breaking.

Home-canning jars come in many sizes: 4-ounce, half-pint, 12-ounce, 1-pint, and 1-quart (see Figure 2-9). They offer two widths of openings: regular-mouth (about 2½ inches in diameter) and wide-mouth (about 3⅛ inches in diameter). Regular-mouth jars are used more frequently for jelly, jam, relish, or any other cooked food. Wide-mouth jars are mainly used for canning vegetables and pickles because it's easier to get the large pieces into the wide opening.

CANNING JARS

Figure 2-9:
Varieties of
canning
jars: wide-
mouth,
regular-
mouth, and
jelly jars.

Mason jars

If the most commonly used glass home-canning jars bear the names of Ball and Kerr, why do we call them Mason jars? The Mason jar is named for its creator, James Landis Mason. He designed and patented a unique glass jar that created an airtight seal for food using a screw-top lid. This easy-to-seal jar replaced the large stoneware vessels that were used for food storage.

The tapered jars we use today were introduced after World War II. They use a two-piece cap consisting of a lid and a metal screw band that fits the threaded jar top. Today, all home-canning jars are generically referred to as Mason jars. Thank you, Mr. Mason, for making the task of home-canning easy with the use of screw-top closures.

Two-piece caps

Two-piece caps consist of a lid and a metal screw band (see Figure 2-10). They're made specifically for use with modern-day home-canning jars.

The underside edge of the lid has a rubberlike sealing compound that softens when it's heated. This compound adheres to a clean jar rim and creates a vacuum seal after the heat-processing period. Lids aren't reusable.

The screw band holds the lid in place during the processing period and secures it in place when storing an opened jar in the refrigerator. After verifying that your cooled jars have successfully sealed (see Figure 4-2), remove the screw band for storage. They may be used many times as long as there are no signs of corrosion or rust and they aren't out of round or dented.

Figure 2-10:
Two-piece caps: lids and screw bands.

TWO-PIECE CAPS
FOR CANNING JARS

(INSIDE LID)

SCREW BAND   LID

Lid wand

A lid wand (see Figure 2-11) has a magnet on one end of a heat-resistant stick. This allows you to take a lid from the hot water and place it on the filled-jar rim without touching the lid or disturbing the sealing compound.

Place your lids top to top and underside to underside to prevent them from sticking together in your pan of hot water. If they do stick together, dip them into a bowl of cold water to release the suction. Reheat them in the hot water for a few seconds before using them.

LID WAND

Figure 2-11:
A lid wand.

Thin plastic spatula

A thin, flexible plastic spatula is the right tool for releasing air bubbles between pieces of food in your filled jars (check out Figures 2-12 and 8-1).

Using a metal item or a larger object for this job may damage your food and crack or break your hot jar.

Figure 2-12:
A thin plastic spatula for releasing air bubbles.

THIN PLASTIC SPATULA
FOR RELEASING AIR BUBBLES

Wide-mouth canning funnel

This funnel (see Figure 2-13) fits into the inside edge of a regular-mouth or a wide-mouth canning jar. Use this for quickly and neatly filling your jars.

Figure 2-13:
A wide-mouth canning funnel.

Jelly bag or strainer

A jelly bag is made for extracting juice from cooked fruit for making jelly. They're not expensive, but if you'd rather not purchase one, make your own using a metal strainer lined with cheesecloth. Use a strainer that hangs on the edge of your pot or mixing bowl and doesn't touch the liquid. Both items are illustrated in Figure 6-3.

Stoneware crocks

Stoneware crocks are available in sizes from 1 gallon to 5 gallons, usually without lids. They're nonreactive and are used for making pickles and olives.

Use crocks that are glazed on the interior and certified free of lead and *cadmium,* a form of zinc ore used in pigments or dyes.

Tools and Equipment for Freezing Food

Some of the items required for this simple form of food preservation are already in your kitchen. For a more detailed list, check out Chapter 12.

- ✔ **A freezer:** Usually, the freezer attached to your refrigerator is large enough for freezing food. But if you're serious about freezing lots of food, you may want to invest in a separate freezer unit.

- ✔ **Rigid containers:** These can be made of plastic or glass. Use only containers approved for the cold temperatures of a freezer. Plastic containers should be nonporous and thick enough to keep out odors and dry air in the freezer. Glass containers need to be treated to endure the low temperature of a freezer and strong enough to resist cracking under the pressure of expanding food during the freezing process.

✔ **Freezer bags:** Use bags made for freezing in sizes compatible with the amount of your food.

✔ **Freezer paper and wraps:** This laminated paper protects your food from freezer burn, which results when air comes in contact with your food while it's in the freezer. Tape this paper to keep the wrap tightly sealed. Heavy-duty aluminum foil is another great freezer wrap and requires no taping.

Tools and Equipment for Drying Food

Dehydrating food is a long, slow process of removing moisture from your food while exposing it to low heat. Here are some items you'll want to have for this process, which is explained in Chapter 15:

✔ **An electric dehydrator:** This machine dries your food in an enclosed chamber while it circulates warm air around your food.

✔ **A conventional oven:** If your oven maintains a low temperature and you can stand to be without it for up to 24 hours, use it for drying before making the investment in an electric food dehydrator.

✔ **Oven thermometer:** An oven thermometer tells you if your oven temperature is low enough to dry your food without cooking it (see Chapter 15 for detailed instructions for checking your oven's temperature).

✔ **Trays and racks:** These are used for holding your food while it's drying. They're included with an electric dehydrator. For oven drying, use mesh-covered frames or baking sheets.

The All-Important Headspace

Headspace is the air space between the inside of the lid and the top of your food or liquid in your jar or container (see Figure 2-14). Proper headspace is important to the safety of your preserved food because of the expansion that occurs as your jars are processed or your food freezes.

If you don't trust yourself to eyeball the headspace, use a small plastic ruler (about 6 inches long) to measure the correct headspace in the jar.

Always use the headspace stated in your recipe. If your recipe doesn't give you a headspace allowance, use these guidelines:

✔ For juice, jam, jelly, pickles, relish, chutney, sauces, and condiments, leave headspace of ¼ inch.

✔ For high-acid foods (fruits and tomatoes), leave headspace of ½ inch.

✔ For low-acid foods (vegetables, meats, fish, and poultry), leave headspace of 1 inch.

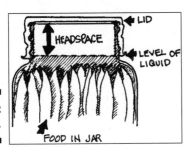

Figure 2-14:
Headspace.

Too little headspace in your canning jars restricts your food from expanding as it boils. Inadequate space for the expanding food may force some of it out of the jar and under the lid, leaving particles of food between the seal and the jar rim. If this occurs, your jar won't produce a vacuum seal.

Leaving too much headspace may cause discoloration in the top portion of your food. Excess headspace can keep your jar from producing a vacuum seal if the processing time isn't long enough to exhaust the excess air in the jar.

Frozen food expands during the freezing process. If you fail to leave the proper headspace in your freezer container, the lid may be forced off the container, or the container may crack or break. When your frozen food comes in direct contact with the air in your freezer, the quality of your food deteriorates and the food develops freezer burn (see Chapter 12).

On the other hand, too much air space allows excess air in your container. Even though your food doesn't come in direct contact with the air in the freezer, the excess space in the top of the container develops ice crystals. When your food thaws, the excess liquid reduces the food's quality

Chapter 3

On Your Mark, Get Set, Whoa!: The Road to Safe Canning and Preserving

- -

In This Chapter

▶ Putting your fears of home-canned food to rest

▶ Determining your processing method by your food's acidity

▶ Making the acquaintance of food-spoiling microorganisms and enzymes

▶ Regulating your processing time in higher elevations

▶ Recognizing the signs of food spoilage

- -

*T*he desire and determination to produce a delicious, safe-to-eat product without the risk of food poisoning is one thing longtime canners and people new to canning have in common. The canning and preserving techniques used today provide you with these results as long as you follow the proper steps and procedures for preparing, processing, and storing your food.

Before you begin your canning and preserving journey, take a stroll through this chapter. Here I introduce you to microorganisms, enzymes, and other potentially dangerous situations that cause food spoilage. I also tell you how to prevent and identify food spoilage. The technical portion of this chapter shouldn't deter you from canning. Rest assured, after reading this information you'll have no fear about preparing and serving your home-canned and -preserved food.

Dispelling Your Fears of Home-Canned and Preserved Food

Preventing food spoilage is the key to safe canning. Over the years, home-canning has become safer and better. Scientists have standardized processing methods, and home-canners know more about using these methods. When you follow up-to-date guidelines exactly, you'll experience little concern about the quality and safety of your home-canned and -preserved foods.

Here are some tips for handling, preparing, and processing your food:

✔ Wash and prepare your food well to remove any dirt and bacteria (refer to Figure 3-1).

Figure 3-1:
How to wash fruit and vegetables well.

✔ Always use the correct processing method for your food. Process all high-acid and pickled food in a water-bath canner. Process all low-acid food in a pressure canner.

✔ Process your filled jars for the correct amount of time and, if you're using a pressure canner, at the correct pressure.

✔ If your elevation is higher than 1,000 feet above sea level, make the proper adjustments in processing time and pressure for your altitude.

✔ Allow your pressure canner to depressurize to 0 naturally.

✔ Allow your processed jars to cool undisturbed at room temperature.

Knowing the Acidity Level of Your Food

Knowing the acidity level of the food you're processing is important because the *pH,* the measure of acidity, determines which method you'll use: water-bath or pressure canning. For canning purposes, food is divided into two categories based on the amount of acid the food registers.

High-acid foods include fruits, tomatoes, and pickled foods. (For detailed information on identifying and processing high-acid food, refer to Chapter 4.) Foods in this group have a pH of 4.6 or lower. Processing them in a water-bath canner destroys harmful microorganisms.

Low-acid foods, primarily vegetables, meat, poultry, and fish, contain little natural acid. Their pH level is higher than 4.6. (Check out Chapter 9 for detailed information on identifying and processing low-acid food.) Process these foods in a pressure canner; this superheats your food and destroys the more heat-resistant bacteria, like botulism.

The *pH,* or potential of hydrogen, is the measure of acidity or alkalinity in food. The values range from 1 to 14. Neutral is 7. Lower values are more acidic, while higher values are more alkaline. The lower the pH value in your food, the more acidic it is.

Meeting the Spoilers

Food spoilage is the unwanted deterioration in canned or preserved food that makes your food unsafe for eating. Ingesting spoiled food causes a wide range of ailments, depending on the type of spoilage and the amount of food consumed. Symptoms vary from mild, flulike aches and pains to more-serious illnesses or even death.

But having said that, the potential for spoiled food shouldn't stop you from canning. When you understand the workings of these microscopic organisms and enzymes, you'll know why using the correct processing method for the correct amount of time destroys these potentially dangerous food spoilers. And you'll have nothing to worry about.

Living microorganisms, independent organisms of microscopic size, are all around — in your home, in the soil, and even in the air you breath. Some of them create spoilage that can't be seen with the naked eye (like botulism), while others (like mold) make their presence known visually.

Testing acidity levels with litmus paper

Litmus paper, also referred to as pH paper, is an acid-sensitive paper that measures the acid in food. When this unique strip of paper is inserted into your prepared food, it changes color. The wet strip is then compared to the pH chart of colors that accompanies the litmus paper to determine if it's a high-acid food (4.6 or lower) or a low-acid food (higher than 4.6). This lets you know which heat-processing method — water-bath or pressure canning — is right for your food.

If you want to feel like you're back in science class all over again, you can buy your own litmus paper at teacher- or scientific-supply stores and test your food yourself.

Meet the four spoilers: mold, yeast, bacteria, and enzymes. *Microorganisms* (mold, yeast, and bacteria) are independent organisms of microscopic size. *Enzymes* are proteins that exist in plants and animals. When any one or more of the spoilers have a suitable environment, they grow rapidly and divide or reproduce every 10 to 30 minutes! With this high-speed development, it's obvious how quickly food can spoil.

Not all microorganisms are bad, just the ones that cause disease and food spoilage. Sometimes microorganisms are added to food to achieve a fermented product, like beer or bread (for leavening). They're also important for making antibiotics.

Mold

Mold is a fungus with dry spores. Poorly sealed jars of high-acid or pickled foods are perfect locations for these spores to set up housekeeping. After the spores float through the air and settle on one of their favorite foods, they start growing. At first you see what looks like silken threads, then streaks of color, and finally fuzz, which covers the food. Processing high-acid and pickled food in a water-bath canner destroys mold spores.

Don't eat food that's had fuzz scraped off of it. This was thought safe at one time but not anymore. Mold contains carcinogens that filter into the remaining food. Although the food appears to be noninfected, ingesting this food can cause illness.

Yeast

Yeast spores grow on food like mold spores. They're particularly fond of high-acid food that contains lots of sugar, like jam or jelly. They grow as a dry film on the surface of your food. Prevent yeast spores from fermenting in your food by destroying them in a water-bath canner.

Bacteria

Bacteria are a large group of single-celled microorganisms. Common bacteria are staphylococcus and salmonella. Botulism is the one to be most concerned with in canning. This is the most dangerous form of bacteria and can be deadly. It's almost undetectable because it's odorless and colorless. Botulism spores are stubborn and difficult to destroy. The only way to destroy them in low-acid food is by pressure canning.

Symptoms from ingesting botulism-infected food occur within 12 to 36 hours after eating it. Symptoms include double vision and difficulty swallowing, breathing, and speaking. Seek medical attention immediately if you believe you've eaten infected food. Antitoxins are available to treat this poisoning, but the sooner, the better.

Botulism spores hate high-acid and pickled foods, but they love low-acid foods. When you provide these spores with an airless environment containing low-acid food, like a jar of green beans, the spores produce a toxin in the food that can kill anyone who eats it.

For safety's sake, boil all home-canned, low-acid food for 10 minutes from the point of boiling at an altitude of 1,000 feet or lower. For altitudes above 1,000 feet, add 1 additional minute for each 1,000 feet of elevation. This process destroys the botulism poison when it's present.

Enzymes

Enzymes are proteins that occur naturally in plants and animals. They encourage growth and ripening in food, which affects the flavor, color, texture, and nutritional value. Enzymes are more active in temperatures of 85 to 120 degrees than they are at colder temperatures. They're not harmful, but they can make your food overripe and unattractive while opening the door for other microorganisms or bacteria.

An example of enzymes in action occurs when you cut or peel an apple. After a few minutes, the apple starts to brown. Stop this browning by treating the cut apple with an antioxidant solution (see Chapter 5). Other methods for halting the enzymatic action in your food are blanching and hot packing.

Adjusting Your Altitude

Properly processing your home-canned foods destroys microorganisms. Knowing your altitude is important because the boiling point of water and pressure in a pressure canner changes at altitudes over 1,000 feet above sea level. This occurs because the air is thinner at higher elevations. With less air resistance, water boils at a temperature below 212 degrees.

Produce food free from microorganisms at higher elevations by adjusting your processing time and pressure to compensate for your altitude. Use the altitude adjustment charts in Chapter 4 (for water-bath canning) and in Chapter 9 (for pressure canning). These adjustments ensure that your food is heated to the correct temperature for destroying microorganisms.

If you don't know the elevation of your city, check with your city offices, your public library, or your state or county Cooperative Extension Service listed in your local telephone directory. Or check out www.mit.edu:8001/geo on the Internet. Just enter your city and state in the box at the bottom of the page, click Submit, and scroll down to find the elevation of your city.

Detecting Spoiled Foods

I can't promise you that your home-canned foods will always be free from spoilage, but I can promise that your chances for spoiled food are greatly reduced when you follow the precise guidelines for each preserving method. If you suspect, for any reason, that your food is spoiled or just isn't right, don't taste it. Also, just because your food doesn't look spoiled, doesn't mean that it's not.

The best way to detect food spoilage is by visually examining your jars. Review the following checklist. If you can answer "true" for each of the following statements, your food should be safe for eating:

✔ The food in the jar is covered with liquid, is fully packed, and has maintained the proper headspace (refer to Chapter 2).

✔ The food in the jar is free from moving air bubbles.

✔ The jars have good, tight seals.

✔ The food has maintained a uniform color.

✔ The food isn't broken or mushy.

✔ The liquid in the jar is clear, not cloudy, and free of sediment.

After your food has passed the previous checklist, examine your jars more closely. If you discover any spoilage during any step of this process, don't continue your search, but properly dispose of your product.

1. **Hold the jar at eye level.**

2. **Turn and rotate the jar, looking for any seepage or oozing from under the lid that indicates a broken seal.**

3. **Examine the food surface for any streaks of dried food originating at the top of the jar.**

   The food and liquid should be clear, not cloudy.

4. **Check the contents for any rising air bubbles or unnatural color.**

5. **Open the jar.**

   There shouldn't be any spurting liquid.

6. **Smell the contents of the jar.**

   Take note of any unnatural or unusual odors.

7. **Look for any cottonlike growth, usually white, blue, black, or green, on the top of your food surface or on the underside of the lid.**

Spoiled low-acid food may exhibit little or no visual evidence of spoilage. Treat any jars that are suspect as if they contained botulism toxins. Follow the detailed instructions for responsibly disposing of spoiled, low-acid food in Chapter 9.

In addition to your specific canning procedures, follow these steps to guard against food spoilage:

✔ Don't experiment or take shortcuts. Use only tested, approved methods.

✔ Use fresh, firm (not overripe) food. Wash it thoroughly. Can fruit and vegetables as soon as possible after they're picked.

- ✔ Use jars and two-piece caps made for home-canning. Discard any jars that are cracked or nicked.

- ✔ Don't overpack foods. Trying to cram too much food into a jar may result in underprocessing because the heat can't evenly penetrate the food.

- ✔ Never use sealing lids a second time. Always use new lids. The sealant on the underside of the lid is good for only one processing.

- ✔ Test your pressure canner before you use it. Have your dial gauge tested annually to verify its accuracy. (Weighted gauges don't require testing.)

- ✔ Process your food for the full amount of time stated in your recipe. Make adjustments to your processing time and pressure for altitudes over 1,000 feet above sea level.

- ✔ Test each jar's seal and remove the screw band before storing your food.

- ✔ Never use or taste any canned food that exhibits signs of spoilage.

Removing the screw bands from your cooled, sealed jars before storing them allows you to easily detect any broken seals or food oozing out from under the lid that indicates spoilage.

Part II
Water-Bath Canning

The 5th Wave   By Rich Tennant

"The kids mixed up the canning labels with the photo album labels. Just hand me a jar of Aunt Thelma so I can finish this pie before Peaches and Pickles get here."

In this part . . .

This part tells you all you need to know about the most popular method of canning: water-bath canning. Some of the products, like jam, jelly, marmalade, relish, and salsa, may be familiar to you, while others, like chutney, conserves, and pickled vegetables, may be new. In addition to taking you step-by-step through this easy and rewarding process, I show you new and different food combinations using some of your favorite products with new serving ideas. What are you waiting for? Dive right in!

Chapter 4

Come On In, the Water's Fine!: Water-Bath Canning

*J*ams, jellies, marmalades, chutneys, relishes, pickled vegetables, and other condiments are some of my favorite items to can and give for gifts. I'm frequently asked, "Is water-bath canning safe for canning food at home?" and "How can I be sure it's safe?"

In this chapter, you'll discover which foods are safely processed in a water-bath canner; what pectin is and why it's used; how the pickling process changes the pH level of low-acid food, converting low-acid food to high-acid food; and step-by-step instructions for completing the canning process. In no time, you'll be turning out sparkling jars full of homemade delicacies to dazzle and satisfy your family and friends.

Defining Water-Bath Canning

Water-bath canning, sometimes referred to as the *boiling-water method,* is the simplest and easiest method for preserving high-acid food, primarily fruit, tomatoes, and pickled vegetables. It's one of the two recommended methods for safely home-canning food (the other method is pressure canning, covered in Chapter 9). Although each processing method uses different equipment and techniques, the goal is the same: to destroy any active bacteria and microorganisms in your food, making it safe for consumption at a later time. This is accomplished by raising the temperature of the food in the jars and creating a vacuum seal.

The water-bath canner consists of a large kettle, usually made of porcelain-coated steel or aluminum. It holds a maximum of 21 to 22 quarts of water, has a fitted lid, and uses a rack to hold the jars (see Figure 4-1).

WATER BATH CANNING KETTLE

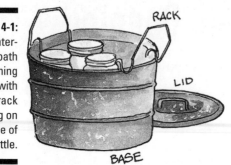

Figure 4-1:
A water-bath canning kettle with the rack hanging on the edge of the kettle.

RACK

LID

BASE

Although the size of your kettle seems large, don't be tempted to process more than seven jars at a time. Seven is the maximum number of jars you may safely process at once, always in a single layer in the jar rack. The jar rack prevents your jars from touching each other and the inside of the kettle, preventing them from breaking and keeping them upright.

After you submerge the jars in your water-filled kettle and the water reaches its boiling point, 212 degrees for an altitude of 1,000 feet above sea level or lower (check out "Adjusting your processing times at high altitudes" later in this chapter), the food in your jars is heated.

Keeping the water boiling in your jar-filled kettle throughout the processing period maintains a water temperature of 212 degrees. This constant temperature is critical for destroying mold, yeast, enzymes, and bacteria that occur in high-acid foods (see "Identifying High-Acid Foods" in this chapter).

Water-bath canning and pressure-canning methods aren't interchangeable because the temperature of a water bath only reaches 212 degrees, while the temperature of a pressure canner reaches 240 degrees.

Identifying High-Acid Foods

High-acid foods are naturally high in acid, with a *pH factor* — the measure of acidity in food — of 4.6 or lower. These foods include fruits, tomatoes, and *pickled vegetables* (low-acid foods with acid added to them, converting them to a high-acid food and making them safe for water-bath canning).

You may change the acid level in low-acid foods by adding an acid, such as vinegar, lemon juice, or *citric acid* — a white powder extracted from the juice of acidic fruits such as lemons, limes, or pineapples. Some examples of altered low-acid foods are pickles made from cucumbers, relish made from zucchini or summer squash, and green beans flavored with dill. (Check out Chapter 8 for information on converting low-acid food to high-acid food.)

If your recipe doesn't tell you which processing method (water-bath canning or pressure canning) is appropriate for your food, don't guess. Instead, use litmus paper to test the pH level of your food (see Chapter 3). If your food has a pH of 4.6 or lower, use the water-bath canning method; if it has a pH of 4.7 or higher, use the pressure-canning method.

Lining Up Your Equipment

Just as you wouldn't alter the ingredients in a recipe or skip a step in the canning process, you don't want to use the wrong equipment when you're home-canning. This equipment allows you to handle and process your filled jars safely.

The equipment for water-bath canning is less expensive than the equipment for pressure canning (check out Chapter 9 to see what equipment pressure canning requires). Water-bath canning kettles cost anywhere from $25 to $45. In some instances, you may purchase a "starter kit" that includes the canning kettle, the jar rack, a jar lifter, a wide-mouth funnel, and jars for about $50 to $60. (If you don't have a supplier near you, check out Chapter 18.)

Equipment you can't do without

Use the following equipment, no exceptions or substitutions, for safe and successful water-bath canning.

A water-bath canner

The water-bath canner (refer to Figure 4-1) is a large kettle that holds a maximum of 21 to 22 quarts of water. It's usually made of porcelain-coated steel or aluminum and includes a cover for the kettle.

Although aluminum is a *reactive metal* (a metal that transfers flavor to food coming in direct contact with it), it's permitted for a water-bath canner because your sealed jar protects the food from directly touching the aluminum.

A jar rack

The jar rack for a water-bath canner is usually made of stainless steel and rests on the bottom of your canning kettle. It keeps your jars from touching the bottom of the kettle, or each other, while holding the filled jars upright during the water-bath processing period. The rack has lifting handles for hanging it on the inside edge of your canning kettle (refer to Figure 4-1), allowing you to safely transfer your filled jars into and out of your kettle.

Canning jars

Canning jars (refer to Figure 2-9) are the only jars recommended for home-canning. Use the jar size recommended in your recipe.

Two-piece caps (lids and screw bands)

These lids and screw bands (refer to Figure 2-10) create a vacuum seal after the water-bath processing period, preserving the contents of the jar for use at a later time. This seal protects your food from the reentry of microorganisms.

Additional equipment you may want

These items aren't critical to the outcome of your product, but you'll discover a more streamlined, efficient level of work if you use them:

- **A teakettle or saucepan:** Keep this filled with boiling water as a reserve for adding extra water to your canning kettle.

- **A food scale:** Use this for weighing your food.

- **Measuring cups and spoons:** Be sure to use heatproof ones.

- **A ladle:** Use this to easily transfer your hot food and liquid to the jars.

- **A wide-mouth funnel:** This fits inside your jars rims, making it easier to quickly fill your jars with a minimum of spillage.

- **A lid wand:** Use a lid wand to transfer your lids from the hot water to the jars without touching them.

- **A jar lifter:** This plastic-coated tool is specially made for lifting canning jars in and out of your canning kettle.

- **A thin plastic spatula:** Use this for releasing air bubbles in the jar.

- **Cooking timer:** A timer keeps accurate time for cooking and processing.

- **Dishtowels or paper towels:** Use these for cleaning your jar rims and as a resting place for cooling your processed jars.

The Road to Your Finished Product

Every aspect of the canning procedure is important, so don't skip anything, no matter how trivial it seems. When your food and canning techniques are in perfect harmony and balance, you'll have a safely processed product for use at a later time.

Readying your food

Always use food of the highest quality when you're canning. If you settle for less than the best, your final product won't have the quality you're looking for. Carefully sort through your food, discarding any bruised pieces or pieces you wouldn't eat in the raw state. Follow the instructions in your recipe for preparing your food, like removing the skin or peel or cutting it into pieces. If your recipe states something specifically, it's there for a reason. If you don't follow the recipe instructions to the letter, your final results won't be what the recipe intended.

Preparing your jars, lids, and screw bands

Always review the manufacturer's instructions for readying your jars, lids, and screw bands. Then proceed as follows:

1. **Inspect your jars, lids, and screw bands for any defects:**

   - Jars: Check the jar edges for any nicks, chips, or cracks in the glass, discarding any jars with these defects. If you're reusing jars, clean any stains or food residue from them.

   - Screw bands: You may use these over and over if they're not warped, corroded, or rusted. Test the roundness of the band by screwing it onto a jar. If it tightens down smoothly without resistance, it's useable. Discard any bands that are defective or *out of round* (bent or not completely round).

   - Lids: All lids must be new. Lids aren't reusable. Check the sealant on the underside of each lid for evenness. Don't use scratched or dented lids. Defective lids won't produce a vacuum seal.

2. **Wash the jars, lids, and screw bands in hot, soapy water.**

3. **Rinse all the washed items well, removing all soapy residue.**

4. While you're waiting to fill your jars, treat them as follows:

- Jars: Submerge them in hot water in your kettle for a minimum of 10 minutes, until you're ready to fill them.

- Lids: Submerge them in hot, not boiling, water in a saucepan. Keeping them separate from your jars protects the lid sealant.

- Screw bands: These don't need to be kept hot, but they do need to be clean. Place them where you'll be filling your jars.

Filling your jars

Add your prepared food (cooked or raw) and hot liquid to your prepared jars as soon as they're ready. Release any air bubbles in the jars (refer to Figure 8-1) before applying the two-piece caps. Always leave the headspace specified in your recipe (refer to Figure 2-14). These steps are critical for creating a vacuum seal and preserving your food.

Use a wide-mouth funnel (refer to Figure 2-13) and a ladle for quickly filling your jars. You'll eliminate a lot of spilling and have less to clean from your jar rims. After filling your jars and allowing the headspace stated in your recipe, wipe the jar rims with a damp cloth or paper towel. If there's one speck of food on the jar rim, the sealant on the lid edge won't make contact with the jar rim and your jar won't seal.

Processing your filled jars

Hang your jar rack on the inside edge of your kettle filled with hot water and place your filled jars in the rack. Lower the rack into the kettle. Cover the kettle with the lid and bring the water to a boil. Begin your processing time after the water comes to a full rolling boil.

Cover the tops of the submerged jars with 1 to 2 inches of hot water. Add additional water from your reserve teakettle or saucepan to achieve this level.

Never process half-pint or pint jars with quart jars because the larger amount of food in quart jars requires a longer processing time to kill any bacteria and microorganisms. If your recipe calls for the same processing times for half-pint and pint jars, you may process those two sizes together.

After you complete the processing time, immediately remove your jars from the boiling water and place them on clean, dry, kitchen or paper towels away from drafts. You may test your seals after your jars have completely cooled (see Figure 4-2).

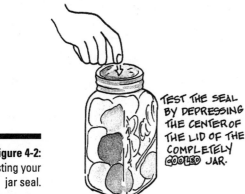

TEST THE SEAL BY DEPRESSING THE CENTER OF THE LID OF THE COMPLETELY COOLED JAR.

Figure 4-2:
Testing your
jar seal.

Adjusting your processing times at high altitudes

When you're canning at an altitude higher than 1,000 feet above sea level, you need to adjust your processing time (see Table 4-1). Because the air is thinner at higher altitudes, water boils below 212 degrees. As a result, you need to process your food for a longer period of time to kill any microorganisms that can make your food unsafe.

If you don't know your altitude level, you can get this information from many sources. Try contacting your public library, a local college, or the Cooperative Extension Service in your county or state. Check your local phone books for contact numbers. Or check out www.mit.edu:8001/geo on the Internet. Just enter your city and state in the box at the bottom of the page, click Submit, and scroll down to find the elevation of your city.

Table 4-1	High-Altitude Processing Times
Altitude (in feet)	*Increase in Your Processing Time*
1,001 to 3,000	5 minutes
3,001 to 6,000	10 minutes
6,001 to 8,000	15 minutes
8,001 to 10,000	20 minutes

Reprocessing unsealed jars

Jars may not seal for several reasons: You may have miscalculated the processing time, pieces of food may not have been cleaned from the jar rim, you may have left an improper amount of headspace, or the sealant on the lids may have been defective. The safest and easiest method for treating processed jars that didn't seal is to refrigerate the jar immediately and use the product within two weeks.

If you want to reprocess jars that didn't seal, you can do that. But keep in mind that reprocessing your food takes almost as much time as making the recipe from the beginning. The only time I consider reprocessing jars is if every jar in the kettle doesn't seal.

To reprocess unsealed jars, follow these steps:

1. **Remove the lid and discard it.**

2. **Check the edge of the jar for damage.**

   If the jar is damaged, discard the food in case a broken piece of glass fell into the food.

3. **Discard any damaged jars.**

4. **Reheat the food.**

5. **Follow the step-by-step instructions in this chapter for filling your jars, releasing air bubbles, and processing your filled jars.**

6. **Reprocess the filled jars for the recommended time for your recipe.**

7. **Check the seal after your jars have completely cooled.**

Following step-by-step instructions for canning high-acid foods

In this section, I guide you through the step-by-step process for creating delicious, high-quality, homemade treats for your family and friends.

Always practice proper kitchen sanitation and cleanliness, carefully handle your food, and follow your recipe to the letter. Don't alter your recipes or skip any processing step.

1. **Assemble your prechecked equipment and utensils.**

   After examining the jars for nicks or chips, the screw bands for proper fit and corrosion, and the new lids for imperfections and scratches, wash everything in warm, soapy water, rinsing the items well and removing any soap residue. Discard any damaged or imperfect items.

2. **Fill your canning kettle one-half to two-thirds full of water and begin heating the water.**

   Heat extra water in a teakettle or saucepan as a reserve (see Step 11).

3. **Submerge your clean jars and lids in hot, not boiling, water.**

   Use your canning kettle for the jars and a saucepan for the lids.

4. **Prepare your food exactly as instructed in your recipe.**

   Don't make any adjustments in ingredients or quantities of ingredients. Any alteration may change the acidity of the product, requiring pressure canning (see Chapter 9) instead of water-bath canning to kill microorganisms.

5. **Transfer your prepared food into the hot jars, adding hot liquid or syrup if your recipe calls for it.**

   Leave the proper headspace stated in your recipe.

6. **Release any air bubbles with a nonmetallic spatula or a tool to free air bubbles (refer to Figure 2-12 and Figure 8-1).**

   Add more prepared food or liquid to the jar after releasing the air bubbles to maintain the recommended headspace.

7. **Wipe the jar rims with a clean, damp cloth.**

8. **Place a hot lid onto each jar rim, sealant side touching the jar rim, and hand-tighten the screw band.**

9. **Place the jar rack in your canning kettle, suspending it with the handles on the inside edge of the kettle.**

10. **Place the filled jars in the jar rack, making sure they're standing upright and not touching each other.**

11. **Unhook the jar rack from the edge of the kettle, carefully lowering it into the hot water.**

    Air bubbles coming from the jars are normal. If your jars aren't covered by at least 1 inch of water, add boiling water from your reserve.

12. **Cover the kettle and heat the water to a full rolling boil, reducing the heat and maintaining a gentle rolling boil.**

    Start your processing time after the water boils. Maintain a boil for the entire processing period.

13. **Upon completion of the processing time, remove your jars from the kettle with a jar lifter, placing them on a clean towel or paper towels away from drafts with 1 or 2 inches of space around them.**

    Don't attempt to adjust the bands or check the seals.

14. **Completely cool the jars.**

    The cooling period may take 12 to 24 hours.

15. **Test the seals on the cooled jars by pushing on the center of the lid (see Figure 4-2).**

    If the lid feels solid and doesn't indent, you have a successful vacuum seal. If the lid depresses in the center and makes a popping noise when you apply pressure, the jar isn't sealed. Immediately refrigerate unsealed jars, using the contents within two weeks or as stated in your recipe.

16. **Remove the screw bands from your sealed jars.**

17. **Wash the sealed jars and the screw bands in hot, soapy water.**

    This removes any residue from the jars and screw bands.

18. **Label your filled jars, including the date processed.**

19. **Store your jars, without the screw bands, in a cool, dark, dry place.**

Chapter 5

Simply Fruit

Canning fresh fruit is a great way to preserve large quantities of ripe fruit in a short period of time. Unlike making jams and jellies, no lengthy cooking time is involved.

In this chapter, I explain the importance of using freshly picked, perfectly ripe fruit and keeping your fruit looking and tasting its best. Just fill your jars with fruit and hot liquid, and give your filled jars a water-bath!

Picking and Preparing Your Fresh Fruit

When selecting your fruit, think fresh, fresh, fresh! Almost all fresh fruits can well with these exceptions: bananas, lemons, limes, melons, persimmons, and strawberries. The sooner you process your picked fruit, the better the texture and flavor of your final product. Your fruit can wait a few hours or overnight before you process it, but be sure to refrigerate it until you're ready.

The best fruit for this canning method is freshly picked, ripe fruit. You're lucky if you grow your own fruit or have a friend who shares hers with you. Some growers offer a "pick your own" option in their growing area for a fee. (Ask growers at farmer's markets or check your local phone directory for locations in your area.) You'll need to bring your own containers for the fruit.

Fruit from your supermarket isn't the best choice for this method because it's often picked underripe. Picking fruit before it's ripe compensates for the time it takes to get the fruit from the field to the store shelf. Don't boycott your supermarket — just be finicky when selecting your fruit for this method.

Identifying the proper degree of ripeness

So, how do you know if your fruit is ripe? *Ripe* fruit is defined as being fully developed, or mature, and ready for eating. If you grow your own fruit, you can check its development and maturity daily.

To check the fruit ripeness before you pick it: Hold a piece of fruit, still attached to the tree, in the palm of your hand and apply gentle pressure with your thumb and fingers. It should be firm to the touch. If there's an impression in the fruit that doesn't bounce back, the fruit is overripe and shouldn't be canned. If the fruit is as hard as a rock, leave it on the tree.

Smell the fruit: Ripe fruit has a rich, full fruit aroma. A peach should smell like a peach; an apple should smell like an apple. The fragrance should be strong enough to entice you to devour the fruit on the spot.

Always use fruit picked directly from the bush or tree. Fruit collected from the ground (referred to as *dropped fruit* or *ground fruit*) is an indication that the fruit is overripe. Don't use it.

Skin on or skin off

Sometimes leaving the skin on your fruit is optional. Other times, the peel must be removed. Always follow your recipe for specific guidelines.

To cut or not to cut your fruit

The fruit you select dictates using it whole or cutting it into pieces. For example, fitting whole apples into a canning jar is difficult, but peeled apples cut into slices easily pack into a jar. Leave small fruit, like berries, whole.

Deter fruit discoloration

There's probably nothing more unattractive than a piece of perfectly ripe cut fruit that's *oxidized or discolored,* dark or brown. Discoloration primarily occurs in apples, apricots, nectarines, peaches, and pears but may occur in other fruits.

Protect your fruit from oxidation by slicing it directly into one of the following *antioxidant solutions,* a liquid to keep your fruit from darkening. Rinse and drain your fruit before packing it into your prepared jars.

✓ **An ascorbic acid or citric solution:** Make a solution with 1 teaspoon of lemon or lime juice in 1 cup of cold water, or use a commercial product, like Ever-Fresh or Fruit-Fresh, available in most supermarkets. When using one of these products, follow the instructions on the container.

Ascorbic acid or citric acid is simply vitamin C and doesn't change the fruit flavor. It's sold in powder form and is usually found in drugstores.

✓ **Vinegar, salt, and water:** Make this solution with 2 tablespoons of vinegar (5 percent acidity), 2 tablespoons of salt (pickling or kosher), and 1 gallon of cold water. Don't leave your fruit in this solution longer than 20 minutes because the solution extracts nutrients from your fruit and changes its flavor.

Raw pack and hot pack

With a few exceptions, most fresh fruits may be packed raw or hot. Always start with clean, ripe fruit and follow your recipe instructions.

Raw pack

A raw pack is the preferred method for fruits that become delicate after cooking, such as peaches and nectarines. This method is what it says: packing raw fruit into hot jars.

Hot pack

Hot packing heats your fruit in a hot liquid before packing it into your prepared jars. The advantages over raw packing include fitting more fruit into the jars because the fruit's softer and more pliable, using fewer jars because you can fit more fruit into the jars, and spending less time waiting for the water in your kettle to boil because the filled jars are hot in the middle.

Lining Your Jars with Liquid

You always add liquid when canning fresh fruit. Your options are boiling water, sugar syrup, or fruit juice. Determining which liquid you use is up to you, but consider the final use for your canned fruit. For instance, if you're using your canned berries in a fruit cobbler, boiling water may be the better choice because you'll add sugar to the cobbler. If you'll be eating your canned fruit out of the jar, use a sugar syrup or fruit juice.

After adding the hot liquid to your filled jars, release any trapped air bubbles in the jar (refer to Figure 8-1). If the headspace drops after releasing the air bubbles, add more liquid to maintain the proper headspace (refer to Figure 2-14). If the fruit level drops, you'll need to add fruit.

Using sugar syrup

Sugar syrup is simply a mixture of sugar and water. It adds flavor to your canned fruit, preserves its color, and produces a smooth, firm texture. Other sweeteners, such as honey, may be added in addition to or without the sugar.

Use these guidelines for making your sugar-syrup choice:

- **Super-light syrup:** This syrup adds the least amount of calories. The sweetness level is the closest to the natural sugar level in most fruits.

- **Extra-light syrup:** Use this syrup for a sweet fruit, such as figs.

- **Light syrup:** This is best with sweet apples and berries.

- **Medium syrup:** This syrup complements tart apples, apricots, nectarines, peaches, and pears.

- **Heavy syrup:** Use this with sour fruit, such as grapefruit.

Table 5-1 offers you five concentrations of sugar syrup. Allow ½ to ¾ cup of liquid for each filled pint jar and 1½ cups of liquid for each filled quart jar of fruit. Bring your syrup ingredients to a boil in a saucepan over high heat; stir to dissolve the sugar.

Table 5-1	Sugar Syrup Concentrations		
Syrup Strength	*Granulated Sugar*	*Water*	*Approximate Yield*
Super-light	¼ cup	5¾ cups	6 cups
Extra-light	1¼ cups	5½ cups	6 cups
Light	2¼ cups	5¼ cups	6½ cups
Medium	3¼ cups	5 cups	7 cups
Heavy	4¼ cups	4¼ cups	7 cups

Always prepare your hot liquid before you prepare your fruit. The liquid should be waiting for you; you shouldn't be waiting for your liquid to boil.

Using water or fruit juice

Packing fresh fruit in boiling water or fruit juice produces fruit with a soft texture. Two good choices for fruit juices are unsweetened pineapple juice or white grape juice. Use water you like to drink, without minerals and not the sparkling variety.

Sugar syrup recipe alternatives

Although syrup of sugar and water is the most common liquid used when canning fresh fruit, you may use honey in place of or in addition to granulated sugar. Use a mild-flavored honey that won't detract from the natural flavor of your fruit. Here are some suggestions:

Type of Syrup	Sugar	Honey	Water	Syrup Yield
Light	1 cup	1 cup	4 cups	5½ cups
Light	None	1 cup	3 cups	4 cups
Medium	2 cups	1 cup	4 cups	6 cups
Medium	None	2 cups	2 cups	4 cups

Combine the syrup ingredients in a saucepan over medium heat, stirring the syrup to dissolve the sugar and/or the honey. After the liquid boils, keep it hot or refrigerate it up to two days. If you refrigerate your syrup, reheat it to a boil before adding it to your filled jars.

REMEMBER

Always use the hot-pack method (see the "Hot pack" section earlier in this chapter) when using water or unsweetened fruit juice for your canning liquid.

Fresh Fruit Canning Guidelines

In the following section, I list fruits that are commonly grown in home gardens. The quantity guide for each fruit fills a one-quart jar. If you're using pint jars, cut the quantity in half. (For detailed instructions on water-bath canning, filling and processing your jars, and releasing air bubbles, refer to the step-by-step guidelines in Chapter 4.) For a more extensive list of fruits, refer to the *Complete Guide to Home Canning and Preserving*, Second Revised Edition, by the United States Department of Agriculture.

Apples

Choose apples suitable for eating or making pies. Peel the skin and remove the core from your apples with a vegetable peeler. Cut the apple into slices or quarters. Treat the fruit with an antioxidant to prevent discoloring (refer to the "Deter fruit discoloration" section of this chapter).

- ✔ **Quantity guide:** 2½ to 3 pounds for a 1-quart jar.

- ✔ **Hot pack preferred:** Add your rinsed fruit to your hot syrup or other hot liquid and cook for 3 to 5 minutes. Transfer the fruit to your prepared jars and fill the jars with the hot liquid. Allow headspace of ½ inch.

- ✔ **Processing time:** Pints and quarts (20 minutes).

Apricots, nectarines, and peaches

Peel the fruit (see Figure 5-1); cut in half and remove the pits. Treat the fruit with an antioxidant to prevent discoloring (refer to the "Deter fruit discoloration" section of this chapter).

- ✔ **Quantity guide:** 2 to 2½ pounds for a 1-quart jar.

- ✔ **Raw pack:** Pack your fruit into your prepared jars, cut side down. Add your hot liquid. Allow headspace of ½ inch.

- ✔ **Hot pack:** Add your fruit to your hot syrup or other hot liquid and bring the liquid to a boil. Pack the fruit into your prepared jars, cut side down. Fill the jars with the hot liquid. Allow headspace of ½ inch.

- ✔ **Processing time:** Raw pack: pints, 25 minutes; quarts, 30 minutes. Hot pack: pints, 20 minutes; quarts, 25 minutes.

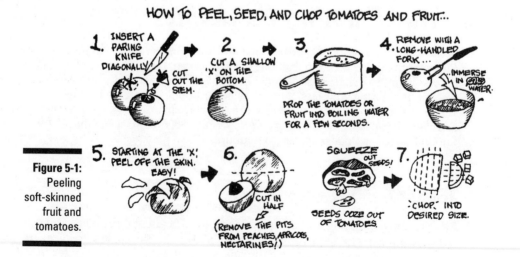

Figure 5-1: Peeling soft-skinned fruit and tomatoes.

Berries (except strawberries)

Select perfect, not soft or mushy, berries. Leave them whole. Wash and drain the berries (handling them as little as possible); remove any stems or hulls.

- **Quantity guide:** 1½ to 3 pounds for a 1-quart jar.

- **Raw pack:** This is the best method for soft berries, like blackberries, boysenberries, and raspberries. Fill the prepared jars with the berries, gently shaking the jar to compact the fruit. Fill the jars with the hot liquid. Allow headspace of ½ inch.

- **Hot pack:** Use this method for firmer berries, such as blueberries, cranberries, and huckleberries. Measure the berries into a saucepan adding ½ cup of sugar for each quart of berries. Bring the mixture to a boil over medium-high heat; stir to prevent sticking. Ladle the hot berries and liquid into your prepared jars, adding boiling water if there isn't adequate liquid to fill the jars. Allow headspace of ½ inch.

- **Processing time:** Raw pack: pints, 15 minutes; quarts, 20 minutes. Hot pack: pints and quarts, 15 minutes.

Figs

Ripe figs have a short shelf life — about two or three days. Pick fruit that's firm to the touch. Use canned figs as an ice-cream topper or a sweet-roll filling.

- **Quantity guide:** 2½ pounds for a 1-quart jar.

- **Hot pack preferred:** Cover washed, whole figs with water. Bring to a boil and cook for 2 minutes; drain. Place the figs in a boiling syrup and cook for 5 minutes longer. Add bottled lemon juice to your prepared jars, 1 tablespoon per 1-pint jar, and 2 tablespoons per 1-quart jar. Fill the jars with the hot figs and the hot syrup. Allow headspace of ½ inch.

- **Processing time:** Pints, 45 minutes; quarts, 50 minutes.

Grapefruit and oranges

Mix grapefruit and oranges for a sweet and tart flavor. Use white grape juice for your filling liquid in place of a sugar syrup.

- ✔ **Quantity guide:** 2 to 2½ pounds for a 1-quart jar.
- ✔ **Raw pack preferred:** Remove the peel from the fruit. Use a paring knife and carefully remove each fruit section from the membrane. Fill the jars with your fruit and add the hot liquid. Allow headspace of ½ inch.
- ✔ **Processing time:** Pints and quarts, 10 minutes.

Pears

All varieties of pears can well, so use your favorite variety. After cutting and peeling the pears, treat your fruit with an antioxidant to prevent discoloring (refer to the "Deter fruit discoloration" section of this chapter).

- ✔ **Quantity guide:** 2 to 3 pounds for a 1-quart jar.
- ✔ **Hot pack preferred:** Cut the peeled and cored pears into halves or slices. Cook them in boiling syrup for 5 to 6 minutes or until the pears are hot. Transfer the fruit and the hot syrup to the prepared jars. Allow headspace of ½ inch.
- ✔ **Processing time:** Pints, 20 minutes; quarts, 25 minutes.

Rhubarb

Rhubarb looks like red celery but isn't related to celery. It's usually mixed with strawberries for a pie filling but is delectable when combined with tart apples. Although rhubarb is a vegetable, it's treated as a fruit because its acid level makes the rhubarb safe for water-bath canning.

Rhubarb leaves are toxic. Always remove and discard any leaves from the stalks before preparing your rhubarb.

- ✔ **Quantity guide:** 1½ to 2 pounds for a 1-quart jar.
- ✔ **Hot pack preferred:** Remove and discard any leaves. Wash the rhubarb. Cut the stalks into 1-inch pieces and measure them into a bowl, adding ½ cup of granulated sugar for each quart of rhubarb. Stir to coat the pieces with the sugar. Let the mixture stand in a cool place until juice appears, about 3 to 4 hours. Transfer the rhubarb and the juice to a saucepan; bring the mixture to a boil over low heat. Stir once and fill the prepared jars with rhubarb and liquid. Allow headspace of ½ inch.
- ✔ **Processing time:** Pints and quarts, 15 minutes.

Transforming Your Fresh Fruit into Side Dishes

Side dishes are an important part of every meal. They round out the meal and complement the flavors of your food. The recipes I include in this section go well with almost any main dish, from soup to stew to roast meat or chicken.

Cranberry Sauce

Although cranberries aren't grown at home, they make a wonderful addition to a pantry of side dishes. Cranberries are seasonal, appearing in stores beginning as early as October and available until they're gone, usually before December.

Preparation time: *10 minutes*

Cooking time: *20 minutes*

Processing time: *10 minutes*

Yield: *About 6 pints*

8 cups fresh cranberries, rinsed, drained, and picked over for bruised berries

4 cups granulated sugar

4 cups water

1 Prepare your canning jars and two-piece caps (lids and screw bands) according to the manufacturer's instructions. Keep the jars and lids hot. (For information on water-bath canning and detailed instructions on preparing and filling your jars, releasing air bubbles, and testing the seals, see Chapter 4.)

2 Combine the sugar and water in a 5- to 6-quart pot. Bring the mixture to a boil over high heat. Boil the liquid for 5 minutes, stirring to dissolve the sugar. Add the cranberries and return the liquid to a boil. Cook the cranberries until the skins burst, about 10 to 15 minutes.

3 Ladle the hot sauce into the prepared jars, leaving headspace of ¼ inch. Release any air bubbles with a nonreactive tool. Wipe the jar rims; seal the jars with the two-piece caps, hand-tightening the bands. Process the pint jars for 10 minutes from the point of boiling in a water-bath canner.

4 Remove the hot jars from the kettle with a jar lifter. Place them on a clean kitchen towel or paper towels, away from drafts. After the jars cool completely, test the seals. (If you find jars that haven't sealed, refrigerate them and use them within two weeks.)

Smooth Applesauce

The yield of this recipe is determined by the amount of apples you process. Don't remove the apple peel and cores before cooking; you'll accomplish this after cooking.

Preparation time: *15 minutes for 2½ to 3½ pounds of apples (enough for a 1-quart jar)*

Cooking time: *20 minutes*

Processing time: *Pints and quarts, 20 minutes*

Yield: *Determine this based on the amount of apples you want to handle, but make no more than 7 pints or 7 quarts at one time (this is the maximum number of jars for one full kettle)*

2½ to 3½ pounds of apples for each quart

Water

Granulated sugar, ¼ cup for each quart of apples, or to taste

Ground cinnamon, ground nutmeg, ground cloves, ground allspice, all to taste (optional, use one or more)

1 Wash the apples. Cut each apple into quarters and remove the stems and the fuzzy part opposite the stem. Place the apples in a 6- to 8-quart pot. Add enough water to cover the bottom of the pot, about ½-inch deep, to prevent the apples from sticking. (Apples produce liquid as they cook.)

2 Cook the apples, covered, over medium to medium-low heat, simmering the liquid until the apples are soft and tender and pierce easily with a fork. For 2½ to 3½ pounds of apples, this may take 10 to 20 minutes. (Time may vary with more apples.)

3 Press the soft apples and any liquid left in the pot through a sieve or a food mill (refer to Figure 2-5), capturing the strained fruit and juice in a large mixing bowl. (This procedure removes the apple peel and seeds.) Transfer the contents of the bowl back into a clean pot. Add the sugar and bring the applesauce to a boil; stir to prevent any sticking. Reduce the heat to low and boil for 5 minutes, stirring constantly. Remove the applesauce from the heat and add your spices, if desired.

4 While the apples are cooking, prepare your canning jars and two-piece caps (lids and screw bands) according to the manufacturer's instructions. Keep the jars and lids hot. (For information on water-bath canning and detailed instructions on preparing and filling your jars, releasing air bubbles, and testing the seals, see Chapter 4.)

5 Ladle the hot applesauce into the prepared jars, leaving headspace of ½ inch. Release any air bubbles with a nonreactive tool. Wipe the jar rims; seal the jars with the two-piece caps, hand-tightening the bands. Process your jars (pints or quarts), for 20 minutes from the point of boiling in a water-bath canner.

6 Remove the hot jars from the kettle with a jar lifter. Place them on a clean kitchen towel or paper towels away from drafts. After the jars cool completely, test the seals. (If you find jars that haven't sealed, refrigerate them and use them within two weeks.)

Mixed Fruit Cocktail

This is a flexible recipe that lets you choose the combination of fruit you like for your fruit cocktail. You can also choose the size of your fruit pieces.

Preparation time: *20 minutes, for enough fruit to fill a 1-quart jar*

Cooking time: *10 minutes*

Processing time: *Pints, 20 minutes; quarts, 25 minutes*

Yield: *Determined by the amount of fruit you prepare (see note at the end of this recipe)*

Apricots, grapefruit, nectarines, peaches, pears, or grapes

Maraschino cherries, drained (optional)

Light sugar syrup

1 Prepare your canning jars and two-piece caps (lids and screw bands) according to the manufacturer's instructions. Keep the jars and lids hot. (For information on water-bath canning and detailed instructions on preparing and filling your jars, releasing air bubbles, and testing the seals, see Chapter 4.)

2 Prepare each fruit as directed in the "Fresh Fruit Canning Guidelines" section in this chapter. Grapes should be underripe with the stems removed. Measure the quantity of your fruit to determine the amount of jars and syrup you'll need (check out approximate quantities of syrup in Table 5-1).

3 Heat the syrup to a boil over high heat. Add the fruit to the syrup and simmer until the fruit pieces are hot throughout.

4 Pack the hot fruit into the prepared jars, leaving headspace of ½ inch. Ladle the hot syrup over the fruit, leaving headspace of ½ inch. Release any air bubbles with a nonreactive tool. Wipe the jar rims; seal the jars with the two-piece caps, hand-tightening the bands. Process the jars, pints for 20 minutes, quarts for 25 minutes, from the point of boiling in a water-bath canner.

5 Remove the hot jars from the kettle with a jar lifter. Place them on a clean kitchen towel or paper towels away from drafts. After the jars cool completely, test the seals. (If you find jars that haven't sealed, refrigerate them and use them within two weeks.)

Note: *You'll need approximately 2 to 2½ cups of fruit and ½ to ¾ cup of liquid to fill a 1-pint jar. Double this for a 1-quart jar.*

Tackling Tomatoes

Tomatoes are misunderstood. Are they a fruit or a vegetable? By definition, a *fruit* is a sweet, edible plant structure containing seeds inside a juicy pulp. And this defines tomatoes perfectly.

A ripe tomato is red all the way to the stem with no soft spots and a strong tomatoey aroma. Each tomato variety has its own flavor and texture. Ensure the proper acidity level for water-bath canning your variety (4.6 or lower) by adding an acid, like bottled lemon juice or powdered citric acid.

- **Quantity guide:** 2½ to 3½ pounds for a 1-quart jar.

- **Hot pack preferred:** Peel your tomatoes as shown in Figure 5-1. Leave whole or cut into halves or quarters. Place them in a 5- to 8-quart pot and cover them with water. Bring to a boil; gently boil for 5 minutes.

 Add 2 tablespoons of bottled lemon juice to each quart jar, or 1 tablespoon to each pint jar. (**Note:** For citric acid, add ½ teaspoon to each quart jar, and ¼ teaspoon to each pint jar.) Add your hot tomatoes and the hot cooking liquid to the jars; release any air bubbles, adjusting the liquid level to maintain headspace of ½ inch.

- **Processing time:** Pints, 40 minutes; quarts, 45 minutes.

Tomato Paste

This recipe uses lots of ripe tomatoes in a short period of time and produces a thick, chunky, rich paste. I like the flavor from Roma tomatoes, but any variety may be used.

Preparation time: 30 minutes

Cooking time: 4 to 5 hours

Processing time: 30 minutes

Yield: 5 pints

15 pounds ripe tomatoes, stems and cores removed (about 8 quarts)

4 bell peppers (2 red and 2 green), seeds removed and chopped

3 medium onions, peeled and chopped

4 carrots, chopped

3 to 5 cloves of garlic, chopped

1 Process the tomatoes, peppers, onions, carrots, and garlic in small batches in a food processor fitted with a metal blade until the food is smooth. Press the food through a mesh strainer or a sieve to remove any pulp and seeds.

2 Place the tomato puree in an 8-quart pot and bring the mixture to a boil over medium-high heat. Gently boil the puree, uncovered, reducing the liquid and thickening the puree, about 4 to 5 hours. Stir the mixture occasionally, and then more often as it thickens. Partially cover the pot; reduce the heat as the puree thickens. The paste is done if a generous spoonful of puree stays in a mound on the spoon. If it runs off the spoon, cook it longer and repeat the test.

3 While the puree is cooking, prepare your canning jars and two-piece caps (lids and screw bands) according to the manufacturer's instructions. Keep the jars and lids hot. (For information on water-bath canning and detailed instructions on preparing and filling your jars, releasing air bubbles, and testing the seals, see Chapter 4.)

4 Ladle the hot puree into the prepared jars, leaving headspace of ¼ inch. Release any air bubbles with a nonreactive tool. Wipe the jar rims; seal the jars with the two-piece caps, hand-tightening the bands. Process your pints for 30 minutes from the point of boiling in a water-bath canner.

5 Remove the hot jars from the kettle with a jar lifter. Place them on a clean kitchen towel or paper towels, away from drafts. After the jars cool completely, test the seals. (If you find jars that haven't sealed, refrigerate them and use them within two weeks.)

Chile Sauce

Try this sauce on hamburgers, veggie burgers, meatloaf, or pot roast. You'll never ask for bottled ketchup again!

Preparation time: *30 minutes*

Cooking time: *2 hours*

Processing time: *15 minutes*

Yield: *About 2 pints*

4 to 5 pounds ripe tomatoes

1 large onion, peeled and chopped

¾ cup granulated sugar

1¼ cups apple cider vinegar

1 teaspoon dried, crushed red pepper

1 teaspoon mustard seeds

1 teaspoon pickling or kosher salt

½ teaspoon ground ginger

½ teaspoon ground nutmeg (use fresh nutmeg, if you have it)

¼ teaspoon curry powder

1 Peel (refer to Figure 5-1), core, and coarsely chop your tomatoes to measure 8 cups. Combine the tomatoes, onion, sugar, vinegar, red pepper, mustard seed, salt, ginger, nutmeg, and curry powder in a 5- to 6-quart pot. Bring the contents to a boil over medium-high heat; reduce the heat and simmer, uncovered, until the mixture thickens and the sauce reduces to about 2 pints. This can take as long as 2 hours.

2 While the sauce is cooking, prepare your canning jars and two-piece caps (lids and screw bands) according to the manufacturer's instructions. Keep the jars and lids hot. (For information on water-bath canning and detailed instructions on preparing and filling your jars and testing the seals, see Chapter 4.)

3 Ladle the hot sauce into the prepared jars, leaving headspace of ¼ inch. Wipe the jar rims; seal the jars with the two-piece caps, hand-tightening the bands. Process the pints for 15 minutes from the point of boiling in a water-bath canner.

4 Remove the hot jars from the kettle with a jar lifter. Place them on a clean kitchen towel or paper towels, away from drafts. After the jars cool completely, test the seals. (If you find jars that haven't sealed, refrigerate them and use them within two weeks.)

Chapter 6

Sweet Spreads: Jams, Jellies, Marmalades, and More

Sweet spreads are my most favorite items to can. You can make combinations of ingredients that aren't commercially available. In this chapter, I include a variety of my favorite recipes with unique flavor combinations. The recipes utilize a variety of preparation techniques that will take you step by step through each process. In addition to fresh fruit, some recipes use frozen fruit and fruit juice.

Think outside of the box for ways to serve your homemade creations. For some of my favorite serving ideas, check out the introductory notes in the recipes. I hope you'll come up with even more ideas. *Remember:* Sweet spreads aren't just for toast anymore!

Understanding Your Sweet Spreads

Making sweet spreads is basic chemistry, using exact proportions of fruit and sugar, cooking the two, and sometimes adding acid or pectin. Don't worry if chemistry wasn't your strong suit in school. Good recipes do the homework for you. Your responsibility is to follow the recipe exactly, using the correct ingredients and measuring them accurately.

Never double a sweet spread recipe or adjust the sugar amount. Recipes are balanced to achieve a specific consistency and texture. Any alteration or adjustment to the recipe upsets the perfect chemical balance and adversely affects your spread by producing inferior results. If you want more of the same recipe, make it twice.

Sweet spreads, generically referred to as *preserves,* come in many forms and textures. The various types of sweet spreads are:

- **Jam:** Jam is a combination of fruit (crushed or chopped), sugar, and sometimes pectin and acid, cooked until the pieces of fruit are soft and almost lose their shape. Common uses for jam include bread spreads, cookie and pastry fillings, and a topping for cheesecake!

- **Jelly:** This mixture combines fruit juice, sugar, and sometimes pectin. It's transparent with a bright color and should be firm, yet jiggly. If you use fresh fruit, you may be instructed to strain it (refer to Figure 6-3). Use this for a bread spread or a filling for cakes and cookies.

- **Marmalade:** These are soft jellies with pieces of fruit rind, usually citrus fruit, suspended in them. In addition to bread spread, use your favorite flavor as a glaze on a baked ham.

- **Preserves:** In addition to representing all sweet spreads, preserves have a definition of their own. They contain cooked fruit, sugar, and some-times pectin and have a jam like consistency, but with whole or large pieces of fruit. The fruit maintains its shape during the cooking process.

- **Butter:** This smooth, thick spread is made from fruit puree and sugar cooked for a long period of time. The results are a thick spread. Butters normally use less sugar than other sweet spreads and may have spices added to enhance the flavor of the fruit.

- **Conserves:** These usually contain two fruits mixed with sugar and nuts and cooked to achieve a consistency similar to jam. Traditionally, con-serves were used as a spread on biscuits and crumpets.

Meeting Your Fruit

Always select the freshest fruit available to you. Everyone has his or her favorite. Know when your favorites are in season for the best selection, the highest quality, and, usually, the most reasonable pricing. (For detailed infor-mation on selecting fresh fruits, check out Chapter 5.)

Local growers are good indicators of the types of fruit grown in your area. Check out your local farmers' markets and ask the sellers about their fruit.

People love to talk about their passion, and who better to learn from than the person who grows the food you're buying? Ask questions about the fruit you see, how they determine ripeness, and how a particular fruit tastes. If they're not passing out samples, they'll probably be happy to cut you a taste.

Carry copies of your favorite recipes when you're visiting local growers or farmers' markets. That way, you'll always buy the right amount of fruit for your favorite recipe.

Getting Up to Speed with Fruit Pectin

Pectin is a natural, water-based substance that's present in ripe fruit. It's essential for thickening jams, jellies, and other types of preserves. Some recipes add commercial fruit pectin. If your recipe does, you'll see the kind of pectin (powdered or liquid) listed in your recipe ingredients.

Never alter the amount of sugar your recipe calls for or use sugar substitutes. Exact amounts of sugar, fruit, and pectin are a must for a good set.

Fruit pectin basics

Commercial pectin is available in most supermarkets or where canning supplies are sold. Pectin may be in short supply in the spring and summer months because these are such popular times of year for canning. So be sure you have enough on hand before you start preparing your recipe.

Inspect the pectin container for water stains, holes, or any other sign that it's come into contact with food (like food stuck to the package). Check to make sure the package is sealed and that it's not past the use-by-date.

Using pectin after the date on the package may affect your final product because the quality of the pectin may have deteriorated. Pectin wasn't always marked with a date. If your pectin container doesn't provide an expiration date, don't use it; it may be a sign that your product is extremely old.

Types of commercial fruit pectin

Pectin is available in two forms: liquid and powdered, or dry. Although both products are made from fruit, they're not interchangeable. Be sure to use the correct type and amount of pectin your recipe calls for.

✔ **Liquid fruit pectin:** Liquid pectin is usually made from apples. Today, a box contains two 3-ounce pouches. The most common brand is Certo.

Liquid fruit pectin was originally sold in 6-ounce bottles. Older recipes may call for "one-half of a bottle." If you read a pouch of liquid pectin today, it states, "1 pouch equals ½ bottle."

When it's time to add the liquid pectin, add it all at the same time, squeezing the pouch with your fingers like you do to get the last bit of toothpaste out of the tube. Prepare your pouch as shown in Figure 6-1.

✔ **Powdered (dry) fruit pectin:** Powdered pectin is made from citrus fruits or apples. It comes in a box similar to a gelatin- or pudding-mix box and contains 1¾ ounces (the most commonly used size) or 2 ounces. Use the size stated in your recipe ingredients.

In addition to different sizes, powdered pectin comes in two varieties: fruit pectin for homemade jams and jellies, and fruit pectin for lower-sugar recipes. Use the variety your recipe calls for; they're not interchangeable.

LIQUID PECTIN AT THE READY!

Figure 6-1: A pouch of liquid pectin at the ready.

Setting Up without Adding Pectin

Not all recipes require the addition of extra pectin. Some recipes cook the fruit mixture for a long period of time, which reduces the liquid in the mixture to achieve a consistency described in your recipe. For this process, you need patience and the knowledge of what to look for when testing your cooked product. You may test your food with the spoon or the plate test (shown in Figure 6-2), or with a candy thermometer.

Use one of the following methods for testing the *gel point,* the cooking point at which jelly is considered done. This temperature is 8 degrees above boiling at an elevation of 1,000 feet or lower above sea level or 220 degrees.

✔ **A candy thermometer:** This is the most accurate method for testing the gel point of your spread. Use a thermometer that's easy to read. One degree over or under the gel point makes a difference in your final product.

If you're at an altitude higher than 1,000 feet above sea level, follow these instructions to determine the temperature of your gel point: Bring a pot of water to a boil over high heat. When the water boils, check the temperature on your thermometer and add 8 degrees. This is the gel point for your altitude.

✔ **The spoon, or sheet, test (refer to Figure 6-2):** Dip a cool metal spoon into your cooked fruit and hold it so the fruit runs off the spoon. When the temperature of the fruit approaches the gel point, it falls off in a couple of drops. When it slides off the spoon in one sheet, the fruit's done. Proceed with your next step.

This test takes a bit of practice to visually master. Until you master it, use a candy thermometer in conjunction with this test. When the temperature of the fruit climbs toward the gel point, you'll be able to see the changes in the liquid and compare it to the sheeting from the spoon.

✔ **The plate test (refer to Figure 6-2):** Place about 1 tablespoon of cooked fruit onto a chilled plate. Put the plate in the freezer and cool the spread to room temperature. If the fruit is set and doesn't roll around on the plate, the mixture is done. Proceed to your next step.

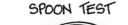

SPOON TEST

WHEN THE JUICE HAS ALMOST REACHED THE GEL POINT, IT WILL SLOWLY COME TOGETHER AND FALL OFF THE SPOON IN 2 DROPS. WHEN IT SLIDES OFF THE SPOON IN A SHEET, THE JELLY IS READY!

Figure 6-2:
Gel testing your food without adding pectin: the spoon test and the plate test.

PLATE TEST

PLACE A SMALL AMOUNT OF SPREAD ON A CHILLED PLATE. SET THE PLATE IN THE FREEZER UNTIL IT COOLS TO ROOM TEMPERATURE. IF THE MIXTURE IS SET, IT IS READY TO CAN.

The Road to Sweet Canning Success

The only method for safely processing your sweet spreads, as approved by the United States Department of Agriculture (USDA), is water-bath canning. The harmful bacteria and microorganisms living in high-acid foods are destroyed at the temperature of boiling water (212 degrees at 1,000 feet or lower above sea level) by sterilizing the food and vacuum sealing the jar.

Tested recipes are always the best. If I know a recipe works each time I make it, I stick with it. Don't experiment with different quantities of ingredients in any canning method. Quantity adjustments to your fruit or your sugar can seriously change the acid (pH level) in your food. And if the acidity changes, you may not use the correct home-canning method to produce a safe product, free from microorganisms.

Always practice safe food-handling procedures. Complete each recipe, start to finish, without interruption. Any break between cooking your fruit to filling the jars and processing them may produce a product of inferior quality, one that may be unsafe for eating.

Jamming and Canning

Jam is fun to make. It takes me back to my childhood days when I created my own daily specials from crushed leaves, flowers, dirt, rocks, and water. I've grown up, but I still love playing with food. My husband is pleased to report that I now use real food instead of dirt and rocks!

Strawberry-Pineapple Jam

Strawberry jam is one of the most popular flavors. This recipe mixes the sweetness of fresh strawberries with the sweet tartness of pineapple.

Preparation time: *10 minutes*

Cooking time: *25 minutes*

Processing time: *10 minutes*

Yield: *8 half-pints*

1 small orange, quartered, seeds removed

1 small lemon, quartered, seeds removed

3 pints strawberries, washed, hulled, and coarsely chopped, reserving any juice

2 8-ounce cans crushed pineapple, drained

1 cup golden raisins

8 cups granulated sugar

1 Coarsely chop the orange and lemon in a food processor fitted with a metal blade.

2 Transfer the orange, lemon, and strawberries to a 5- to 6-quart pot. Stir in the pineapple, raisins, and sugar. Bring the mixture to a simmer over medium-high heat, stirring frequently. Reduce the heat and simmer until the liquid sheets when dropped from the side of a spoon (refer to Figure 6-2) or registers 220 degrees on a candy thermometer, about 20 to 25 minutes. Remove the jam from the heat. Remove any foam from the surface with a foam skimmer.

3 While the jam is cooking, prepare your canning jars and two-piece caps (lids and screw bands) according to the manufacturer's instructions. Keep the jars and lids hot. (For information on water-bath canning and detailed instructions on preparing and filling your jars and testing the seals, see Chapter 4.)

4 Ladle your hot jam into the prepared jars, leaving headspace of ¼ inch. Wipe the jar rims; seal the jars with the two-piece caps, hand-tightening the bands. Process the filled jars in a water bath for 10 minutes from the point of boiling. Remove the jars from the boiling water with a jar lifter. Place them on a clean kitchen towel or paper towels away from drafts. After the jars cool completely, test the seals. If you find jars that haven't sealed, refrigerate them and use them within two months.

Cranberry-Pineapple Jam

This is my favorite sweet spread in a peanut butter and jelly sandwich. Purchase an extra bag or two of cranberries and freeze them for making this jam any time of the year.

Preparation time: *15 minutes*

Cooking time: *10 minutes*

Processing time: *15 minutes*

Yield: *6 to 7 12-ounce jars*

4 cups (about 1 pound) cranberries, washed and picked over to remove any stems or bruised fruit

1½ cups water

20-ounce can crushed pineapple including the juice

8 cups granulated sugar

½ cup fresh lemon juice (about 2 to 3 lemons)

1 tablespoon orange zest

¼ teaspoon unsalted butter

3-ounce pouch liquid fruit pectin

1 Prepare your canning jars and two-piece caps (lids and screw bands) according to the manufacturer's instructions. Keep the jars and lids hot. (For information on water-bath canning and detailed instructions on preparing and filling your jars and testing the seals, see Chapter 4.)

2 Finely chop the cranberries, in two batches, in a food processor fitted with a metal blade.

3 Place the cranberries and water in a 5-quart pot. Bring the mixture to a boil over high heat; reduce the heat to medium and simmer, uncovered, for 5 minutes. Add the pineapple and sugar. Bring the mixture to a hard rolling boil, a boil that can't be stirred down. Boil, uncovered, for 2 minutes, stirring constantly.

4 Remove the pot from the heat. Add the lemon juice, orange zest, butter, and pectin; stir to combine. Let the jam stand for 3 minutes. Remove any foam from the surface of the jam with a foam skimmer.

5 Ladle your hot jam into the prepared jars, leaving headspace of ¼ inch. Wipe the jar rims; seal the jars with the two-piece caps, hand-tightening the bands. Process the filled jars in a water bath for 15 minutes from the point of boiling. Remove the jars from the boiling water with a jar lifter. Place them on a clean kitchen towel or paper towels away from drafts. After the jars cool completely, test the seals. If you find jars that haven't sealed, refrigerate them and use them within two months.

Spiced Pear Jam

Although this is a jam, I like to serve it with a juicy pork roast or grilled pork chops. The flavor and texture of this jam are almost like applesauce.

Preparation time: *35 minutes*

Cooking time: *6 minutes*

Processing time: *10 minutes*

Yield: *6 half-pints*

3¼ pounds fully ripe, but not overly ripe, pears, peeled, cored, and mashed to measure 4 cups

3 tablespoons fresh lemon juice

¾ teaspoon ground cinnamon

½ teaspoon ground allspice

1 package (1¾ ounce) powdered fruit pectin

½ cup golden raisins brought to a boil in ⅓ cup red wine and left to stand for 15 minutes, drained

5 cups granulated sugar

⅛ teaspoon unsalted butter

6 3-inch cinnamon sticks (one for each jar)

1 Prepare your canning jars and two-piece caps (lids and screw bands) according to the manufacturer's instructions. Keep the jars and lids hot. (For information on water-bath canning and detailed instructions on preparing and filling your jars and testing the seals, see Chapter 4.)

2 Place your mashed pears into a 5- to 6-quart pot. Add the lemon juice, cinnamon, all-spice, pectin, and drained raisins; stir to combine. Bring the mixture to a full rolling boil, one that can't be stirred down. Add the sugar. Return the mixture to a full rolling boil; stir constantly and boil hard for 1 minute. Remove the pot from the heat and stir in the butter; let the jam stand for 3 minutes. Remove any foam from the surface with a foam skimmer.

3 Ladle your hot jam into the prepared jars, leaving headspace of ¼ inch. Wipe the jar rims; seal the jars with the two-piece caps, hand-tightening the bands. Process the filled jars in a water bath for 10 minutes from the point of boiling. Remove the jars from the boiling water with a jar lifter. Place them on a clean kitchen towel or paper towels away from drafts. After the jars cool completely, test the seals. If you find jars that haven't sealed, refrigerate them and use them within two months.

Pear-Raspberry Jam

The first time I made this recipe, I was shocked by the glorious color the pears took on from the raspberries. This is one of my core recipes, one that I make each year.

Preparation time: *20 minutes*

Cooking time: *5 minutes*

Processing time: *15 minutes*

Yield: *6 to 7 half-pints*

2 pounds (about 6) pears, peeled and cored

10 ounces (about 1½ cups) fresh red raspberries

6 cups granulated sugar

2 tablespoons fresh lemon juice

2 teaspoons grated orange zest

3-ounce pouch liquid fruit pectin

1 Prepare your canning jars and two-piece caps (lids and screw bands) according to the manufacturer's instructions. Keep the jars and lids hot. (For information on water-bath canning and detailed instructions on preparing and filling your jars and testing the seals, see Chapter 4.)

2 Coarsely chop the pears and add them to the raspberries to measure 4 cups. Combine the pears, raspberries, sugar, lemon juice, and orange zest in a 4- to 5-quart pot. Bring the fruit to a full rolling boil (a boil that can't be stirred down), uncovered and stir constantly. Boil hard for 1 minute, stirring constantly. Remove the pot from the heat and add the pectin all at the same time; stir to combine. Remove any foam from the surface with a foam skimmer.

3 Ladle your hot jam into the prepared jars, leaving headspace of ¼ inch. Wipe the jar rims; seal the jars with the two-piece caps, hand-tightening the bands. Process the filled jars in a water bath for 15 minutes from the point of boiling. Remove the jars from the boiling water with a jar lifter. Place them on a clean kitchen towel or paper towels away from drafts. After the jars cool completely, test the seals. If you find jars that haven't sealed, refrigerate them and use them within two months.

Note: Frozen raspberries may be used in place of fresh raspberries. Thaw them in their container and add all the juice from the berries.

Mango-Jalapeño Jam

I believe that mangoes are fruit of the gods; nothing else comes close to their flavor. Combining sweet mangoes and spicy jalapeño chiles will wake up your taste buds.

Preparation time: *25 minutes*

Cooking time: *5 minutes*

Processing time: *10 minutes*

Yield: *4 to 5 half-pints*

6 to 9 ounces jalapeño chilies (6 to 10 chilies, depending on your taste buds)

6 cups ripe mangoes (about 8), peeled and coarsely diced

¾ cup fresh lemon juice

1¾-ounce package powdered fruit pectin for lower-sugar recipes

4 cups granulated sugar

1 Preheat your oven broiler. Place the chilies on a baking sheet 3 to 4 inches from the heat. Broil the chilies until the skins are charred and blistered, about 10 to 12 minutes, turning them every few minutes. Cool them on the baking sheet.

2 Prepare your canning jars and two-piece caps (lids and screw bands) according to the manufacturer's instructions. Keep the jars and lids hot. (For information on water-bath canning and detailed instructions on preparing and filling your jars and testing the seals, see Chapter 4.)

3 Remove and discard the skins, seeds, and stems from the cooled chilies. (Wear rubber gloves when handling chilies. This protects your skin from the oils in the chilies that may produce a burning sensation on your bare skin.) Coarsely chop the flesh and place it in a 6- to 8-quart pot. Add the mangoes and the lemon juice; stir to combine.

4 Combine the dry pectin with ¼ cup of the sugar in a small bowl; then add it to the prepared fruit. Bring the mixture to a full rolling boil, a boil that can't be stirred down, over high heat, stirring occasionally. Add the remaining 3¾ cups of sugar to the fruit. Return the mixture to a full rolling boil and boil 1 minute longer, stirring constantly. Remove the pot from the heat. Remove any foam from the surface with a foam skimmer.

5 Ladle your hot jam into the prepared jars, leaving headspace of ¼ inch. Wipe the jar rims; seal the jars with the two-piece caps, hand-tightening the bands. Process the filled jars in a water bath for 10 minutes from the point of boiling. Remove the jars from the boiling water with a jar lifter. Place them on a clean kitchen towel or paper towels away from drafts. After the jars cool completely, test the seals. If you find jars that haven't sealed, refrigerate them and use them within two months.

If you have a small amount of jam that doesn't completely fill a canning jar, use it to make fruit leather (see Chapter 16).

Jiggling with Jelly

Jelly always has such a bright, cheerful look. It's a great last-minute appetizer that doesn't taste last-minute. Spoon jelly over a block of cream cheese, allowing it to cascade over the sides. Serve it with rich, buttery crackers.

But in order to achieve a bright, crystal-clear jelly, you need to properly strain your fruit. You may use a commercially manufactured stand and a jelly bag, or make your own using a mesh strainer lined with several layers of cheesecloth (see Figure 6-3).

Dry fabric absorbs flavor from your fruit, weakening the flavor of your final product. Moisten your jelly bag (or cheesecloth) with cold water, wringing out any excess moisture before straining your liquid through it.

STRAINING JELLY

Figure 6-3:
Straining jelly using a jelly bag and stand or through a cheesecloth-lined strainer.

THROUGH CHEESECLOTH IN A MESH OR METAL STRAINER
OR
IN A JELLY BAG WITH STAND

Apple and Herb Jelly

You can whip this recipe up in no time when your herbs are plentiful and full of flavor. Always pick your fresh herbs in the morning for optimum flavor.

Preparation time: *10 minutes (not including the herb infusion time)*

Cooking time: *5 minutes*

Processing time: *10 minutes*

Yield: *4 half-pints*

2 cups filtered (clear) apple juice

1 cup fresh mint

3 tablespoons fresh lemon juice

⅛ teaspoon unsalted butter

3½ cups granulated sugar

Green or yellow food coloring (optional)

3-ounce pouch liquid fruit pectin

1 Heat the apple juice to a boil in a 3- to 4-quart saucepan over high heat. Remove the pan from the heat and add the herbs. Cover the pot and let the herbs transfer (infuse) their flavor into the apple juice for 30 minutes.

2 While your herbs are infusing, prepare your canning jars and two-piece caps (lids and screw bands) according to the manufacturer's instructions. Keep the jars and lids hot. (For information on water-bath canning and detailed instructions on preparing and filling your jars and testing the seals, see Chapter 4.)

3 Pour the infused mixture through a cheesecloth-lined strainer or a jelly bag placed over a bowl. After straining the liquid, discard the herbs.

4 Transfer the liquid to a clean 4- to 5-quart pot. Add the lemon juice, butter, sugar, and your food coloring. Place the mixture over medium-low heat to dissolve the sugar. Increase the heat to high and bring the mixture to a boil, stirring constantly. Add the pectin all at the same time and return the mixture to a full rolling boil, one that can't be stirred down. Boil for 1 minute, stirring constantly. Remove the pot from the heat and let it stand for 1 minute. Remove any foam from the surface with a foam skimmer.

5 Ladle your hot jelly into the prepared jars, leaving headspace of ⅛ inch. Wipe the jar rims; seal the jars with the two-piece caps, hand-tightening the bands. Process the filled jars in a water bath for 10 minutes from the point of boiling. Remove the jars from the boiling water with a jar lifter. Place them on a clean kitchen towel or paper towels away from drafts. After the jars cool completely, test the seals. If you find jars that haven't sealed, refrigerate them and use them within two months.

Cranberry-Pepper Jelly

After tasting this jelly, you won't believe it's made with cranberry juice, not fresh cranberries. Don't be surprised if this jelly takes a few days to set-up.

Preparation time: *5 minutes*

Cooking time: *15 minutes*

Processing time: *10 minutes*

Yield: *5 half-pints*

2 to 4 jalapeño chilies, halved and seeded	*5 cups granulated sugar*
1½ cups bottled cranberry juice	*3-ounce pouch liquid fruit pectin*
1 cup apple cider vinegar	

1 Prepare your canning jars and two-piece caps (lids and screw bands) according to the manufacturer's instructions. Keep the jars and lids hot. (For information on water-bath canning and detailed instructions on preparing and filling your jars and testing the seals, see Chapter 4.)

2 Combine the jalapeños, cranberry juice, and vinegar in a 3- to 4-quart saucepan. Bring the mixture to a boil over high heat; reduce the heat and simmer, covered, for 10 minutes. Pour the mixture through a mesh strainer resting on the edges of a 4-cup heat-proof measuring cup. Press the jalapeños against the strainer with the back of a spoon to extract all the liquid and flavor to measure 2 cups. (Refrigerate any additional liquid and serve it as a beverage. Mix one part juice and one part sparkling water; add an orange slice.) Discard the pulp. For crystal-clear jelly, strain the liquid through a jelly bag or a cheesecloth-lined mesh strainer (refer to Figure 6-3).

3 Combine the two cups of liquid with the sugar in a 3- to 4-quart saucepan. Turn the heat to high and bring the mixture to a full rolling boil, one that can't be stirred down, stirring constantly. Add the pectin and return the mixture to a rolling boil. Boil for one minute, stirring constantly. Remove the pan from the heat. Remove any foam from the surface with a foam skimmer.

4 Ladle your hot jelly into the prepared jars, leaving headspace of ¼ inch. Wipe the jar rims; seal the jars with the two-piece caps, hand-tightening the bands. Process the filled jars in a water bath for 10 minutes from the point of boiling. Remove the jars from the boiling water with a jar lifter. Place them on a clean kitchen towel or paper towels away from drafts. After the jars cool completely, test the seals. If you find jars that haven't sealed, refrigerate them and use them within two months. The jelly may take a few days to set up.

Vary It! *Try this with cranberry-apple, cranberry-grape, or cranberry-mango juice blends.*

Mastering Marmalade, Butters, and More

Introduce your family and friends to the spreads that were once more common than jams and jellies. Add variety to your canning pantry while you share the wonderful flavors and textures with those lucky enough to be around when you open a jar. After all, there's more to marmalade than oranges.

Mango Butter

Here's a new way to savor that great mango flavor.

Preparation time: *15 minutes*

Cooking time: *1 hour, 15 minutes*

Processing time: *15 minutes*

Yield: *4 half-pints*

4½ pounds ripe mangoes (about 4 to 6 mangoes), peeled and cut into chunks

1 cup fresh lime juice (about 5 to 6 limes)

1 cup granulated sugar

2 cinnamon sticks

1 Puree the mangos and the lime juice in two batches in a food processor fitted with a metal blade. Strain the puree through a mesh strainer into a 5- to 6-quart pot. Add the sugar and the cinnamon sticks.

2 Bring the mixture to a simmer over medium heat, stirring to dissolve the sugar. Reduce the heat to low and simmer for 60 to 75 minutes, until it's very thick. (The consistency should hold its shape when mounded on a spoon.) Stir the fruit every 10 to 15 minutes to prevent any sticking.

3 While the fruit cooks, prepare your canning jars and two-piece caps (lids and screw bands) according to the manufacturer's instructions. Keep the jars and lids hot. (For information on water-bath canning and detailed instructions on preparing and filling your jars, releasing air bubbles, and testing the seals, see Chapter 4.)

4 Ladle your hot fruit butter into the prepared jars, leaving headspace of ¼ inch. Release any air bubbles with a nonreactive tool. Wipe the jar rims; seal the jars with the two-piece caps, hand-tightening the bands. Process the filled jars in a water bath for 15 minutes from the point of boiling. Remove the jars from the boiling water with a jar lifter. Place them on a clean kitchen towel or paper towels away from drafts. After the jars cool completely, test the seals. If you find jars that haven't sealed, refrigerate them and use them within two months.

Kumquat Marmalade

I'm not a fan of orange marmalade, but when a neighbor handed me a bag of these small orange fruits and said, "Figure out what to do with these!" I discovered a new love for marmalade. Kumquats have a thin, sweet skin and a very sour flesh. Eat a kumquat by popping the whole thing into your mouth and chew (watch out for the seeds). Slicing the fruit must be done by hand, but it's worth the effort when you taste the fabulous flavor.

Preparation time: *30 minutes*

Cooking time: *30 minutes*

Processing time: *10 minutes*

Yield: *7 half-pints or 5 12-ounce jars*

2 pounds kumquats, unpeeled	½ cup fresh lemon juice (about 2 to 3 lemons)
1½ cups water	5 cups granulated sugar
⅛ teaspoon baking soda	3-ounce pouch liquid fruit pectin

1 Slice the kumquats in half lengthwise, then slice each half into fourths lengthwise. Discard the bitter seeds. Place the kumquats into a 6- to 8-quart pan. Add the water and the baking soda. Bring the mixture to a boil over medium-high heat. Reduce the heat and simmer, covered, for 20 minutes, stirring occasionally. Add the lemon juice and simmer, covered, for 10 minutes longer, stirring occasionally.

2 While the kumquats are cooking, prepare your canning jars and two-piece caps (lids and screw bands) according to the manufacturer's instructions. Keep the jars and lids hot. (For information on water-bath canning and detailed instructions on preparing and filling your jars and testing the seals, see Chapter 4.)

3 Stir the sugar into your cooked fruit. Bring the mixture to a full rolling boil, a boil that can't be stirred down, over high heat. Boil hard for 1 minute, stirring constantly. Remove the pot from the heat. Add the pectin, stirring to combine. Remove any foam from the surface with a foam skimmer.

4 Ladle your hot marmalade into the prepared jars, leaving headspace of ¼ inch. Wipe the jar rims; seal the jars with the two-piece caps, hand-tightening the bands. Process the filled jars in a water bath for 10 minutes from the point of boiling. Remove the jars from the boiling water with a jar lifter. Place them on a clean kitchen towel or paper towels away from drafts. After the jars cool completely, test the seals. If you find jars that haven't sealed, refrigerate them and use them within two months.

Lime-Ginger Marmalade

This is a combination of flavors that I was introduced to in Hawaii. It's close to the last combination I thought would become one of my many favorites.

Preparation time: *20 minutes*

Cooking time: *1 hour*

Processing time: *10 minutes*

Yield: *4 half-pints*

3 to 4 limes, cut in half lengthwise and sliced crosswise (about ⅛-inch thick), to measure 1½ cups of fruit

½ cup grated lemon zest (about 2 to 4 lemons)

5 cups water

¼ cup finely shredded fresh ginger (about a 5- to 6-inch piece)

4¼ cups granulated sugar

1 Place the lime slices, lemon zest, water, and ginger in a 5- to 6-quart pot. Bring the mixture to a boil over medium-high heat and boil rapidly until the fruit is tender, about 30 minutes. Remove the pot from the heat.

2 While your fruit is cooking, prepare your canning jars and two-piece caps (lids and screw bands) according to the manufacturer's instructions. Keep the jars and lids hot. (For information on water-bath canning and detailed instructions on preparing and filling your jars and testing the seals, see Chapter 4.)

3 Measure the hot mixture into a heatproof measuring cup and return it to the pot. For each cup of fruit, add 1 cup of sugar to the hot mixture. Return the pot to the stove and bring the mixture to a boil over high heat, stirring often to dissolve the sugar. Cook the marmalade about 30 minutes until it sheets off of a spoon (shown in Figure 6-2) or registers 220 degrees on a candy thermometer. Remove the pan from the heat and cool the mixture for 5 minutes. Remove any foam from the surface with a foam skimmer.

4 Ladle your hot marmalade into the prepared jars, leaving headspace of ¼ inch. Wipe the jar rims; seal the jars with the two-piece caps, hand-tightening the bands. Process the filled jars in a water bath for 10 minutes from the point of boiling. Remove the jars from the boiling water with a jar lifter. Place them on a clean kitchen towel or paper towels away from drafts. After the jars cool completely, test the seals. If you find jars that haven't sealed, refrigerate them and use them within two months.

Apple Butter

This spread is a cross between a jam and homemade applesauce. The rich flavor almost makes me feel guilty when I slather it on a toasted bagel.

Preparation time: *20 minutes*

Cooking time: *1 hour, 10 minutes*

Processing time: *15 minutes*

Yield: *About 6 half-pints*

3½ cups apple cider	*¼ teaspoon kosher or pickling salt*
8 large apples (about 4 to 4½ pounds), peeled, cored, and sliced	*¾ teaspoon ground cinnamon*
1½ cups granulated sugar	*3-inch cinnamon stick*

1 Place the cider in a 5- to 6-quart pot and bring it to a boil over high heat. Add the apple slices and reduce the heat. Simmer the fruit, uncovered, for 45 minutes. Stir the fruit every 10 to 15 minutes to prevent sticking.

2 Stir in the sugar, salt, and the ground and stick cinnamon. Cook the mixture over medium-low heat, uncovered and stirring occasionally, until the mixture thickens, about 20 to 25 minutes. (The consistency should be like applesauce.) Remove and discard the cinnamon stick.

3 While the fruit cooks, prepare your canning jars and two-piece caps (lids and screw bands) according to the manufacturer's instructions. Keep the jars and lids hot. (For information on water-bath canning and detailed instructions on preparing and filling your jars, releasing air bubbles, and testing the seals, see Chapter 4.)

4 Ladle your hot fruit into the prepared jars, leaving headspace of ¼ inch. Release any air bubbles with a nonreactive tool. Wipe the jar rims; seal the jars with the two-piece caps, hand-tightening the bands. Process the filled jars in a water bath for 15 minutes from the point of boiling. Remove the jars from the boiling water with a jar lifter. Place them on a clean kitchen towel or paper towels away from drafts. After the jars cool completely, test the seals. If you find jars that haven't sealed, refrigerate them and use them within two months.

Any-Time-of-the-Year Strawberry Preserves

Make this recipe when you crave strawberries but their season isn't within sight. It'll lift your spirits until it's fresh berry time!

Preparation time: *10 minutes*

Cooking time: *5 minutes*

Processing time: *10 minutes*

Yield: *6 half-pints*

3 10-ounce packages of frozen, sliced strawberries, thawed

¼ cup water

1¾-ounce package powdered fruit pectin

6 cups granulated sugar

⅓ cup orange liqueur

3 tablespoons fresh lemon juice

1 Prepare your canning jars and two-piece caps (lids and screw bands) according to the manufacturer's instructions. Keep the jars and lids hot. (For information on water-bath canning and detailed instructions on preparing and filling your jars and testing the seals, see Chapter 4.)

2 Combine the strawberries with the water and pectin in a 5- to 6-quart pot. Bring the mixture to a boil over high heat, stirring occasionally to dissolve the pectin. Boil hard for 1 minute. Stir in the sugar and return the mixture to a full rolling boil, one that can't be stirred down. Boil hard for 1 minute, stirring constantly. Remove the pan from the heat. Stir in the liqueur and the lemon juice. Cool for 5 minutes, stirring occasionally. Remove any foam from the surface with a foam skimmer.

3 Ladle your hot preserves into the prepared jars, leaving headspace of ¼ inch. Wipe the jar rims; seal the jars with the two-piece caps, hand-tightening the bands. Process the filled jars in a water bath for 10 minutes from the point of boiling. Remove the jars from the boiling water with a jar lifter. Place them on a clean kitchen towel or paper towels away from drafts. After the jars cool completely, test the seals. If you find jars that haven't sealed, refrigerate them and use them within two months.

Peach-Pineapple-Orange Conserve

This combination of flavors is exotic and sweet. Use this for a glaze for your ham or for a side dish for pork.

Preparation time: *20 minutes*

Cooking time: *35 minutes*

Processing time: *15 minutes*

Yield: *6 half-pints*

8 to 10 medium ripe peaches

2 medium oranges

8-ounce can crushed pineapple, undrained, packed in syrup or pineapple juice

6 cups granulated sugar

1 Peel the peaches (refer to Figure 5-1) and remove the pits. Coarsely dice them and process them in a food processor fitted with a metal blade or force them through a food mill, to measure 4 cups of fruit and juice. Cut your oranges into quarters and discard any seeds. Finely chop them in a food processor fitted with a metal blade.

2 Transfer the measured peaches and oranges into a 5- to 6-quart pot. Add the pineapple and the sugar; stir to combine. Bring the mixture to a slow boil over medium-low heat. Cook the mixture, uncovered and stirring occasionally, until it thickens, about 35 minutes.

3 While the fruit cooks, prepare your canning jars and two-piece caps (lids and screw bands) according to the manufacturer's instructions. Keep the jars and lids hot. (For information on water-bath canning and detailed instructions on preparing and filling your jars, releasing air bubbles, and testing the seals, see Chapter 4.)

4 Ladle your hot fruit into the prepared jars, leaving headspace of ¼ inch. Release any air bubbles with a nonreactive tool. Wipe the jar rims; seal the jars with the two-piece caps, hand-tightening the bands. Process the filled jars in a water bath for 15 minutes from the point of boiling. Remove the jars from the boiling water with a jar lifter. Place them on a clean kitchen towel or paper towels away from drafts. After the jars cool completely, test the seals. If you find jars that haven't sealed, refrigerate them and use them within two months.

Chapter 7

Condiments and Accompaniments: Chutneys, Relishes, and Sauces

In This Chapter

▶ Expanding your world of condiments and accompaniments

▶ Celebrating chutney

▶ Relishing your fruits and vegetables

▶ Spicing up your sauces

The first time I heard the word *chutney,* I cringed. I thought, "What an awful name for a food." Then I closed my eyes and took a bite. My taste buds didn't believe the flavors they were sensing — sweet and spicy, no, tart, and a toasted nut? What was going on? From this early food experience, I vowed never to prejudge any food. I gladly welcome all new taste opportunities.

In this chapter, I open the door to flavors and tastes from around the world. Chutneys are common in Asia and Middle Eastern countries, salsas are native to Mexico, and cranberries are well used in North America. Expand your taste experience as you visit the world of fascinating and enticing flavors.

Mastering and Preserving Your Condiments and Other Accompaniments

Condiments and accompaniments are to food what accessories are to clothing. They're not necessary, but they enhance what's there. They cover a wide range of flavors including savory, spicy, salty, sweet, or a combination.

The water-bath canning principles and step-by-step instructions used in Chapters 4, 5, and 6 apply to the recipes in this chapter. ***Remember:*** Always use the freshest fruit and other products you need to make your recipes.

Dried herbs and spices are used extensively in this chapter. Here are some tips for purchasing and using them:

- ✔ **Buy small amounts.** Purchase an amount you'll use within six months to one year. Flavors deteriorate over time.

- ✔ **Buy the amount you need.** Stores that offer herbs and spices in containers where you can scoop out what you need is a great option. Check out the turnover rate, you don't want to buy old products.

- ✔ **Store dried herbs and spices in airtight containers.** Glass or plastic jars are good choices, but make sure you screw the lid all the way back on. If you purchase cans, snap the lid in place to seal in the freshness.

- ✔ **Keep your dried herbs and spices in a cool, dark, dry location.** Sunlight and heat destroys flavor. Store your containers in a cabinet.

- ✔ **Inventory your dried herbs and spices at least once a year.** Write the purchase date on the container. Discard any over one year old.

Complementing Your Chutney

Chutney contains fruit, vinegar, sugar, and spices. It ranges in flavor from sweet to spicy and mild to hot, with a texture ranging from smooth to chunky. It usually accompanies curry dishes, but use sweet chutney, like Pear Chutney, for a bread spread or with a slice of cheddar cheese on a cracker.

Pear Chutney

Juicy ripe pears are one of those fruits I can't get enough of. When pears are ripe, get busy. Try this recipe for a dipping sauce for homemade egg rolls.

Preparation time: 30 minutes

Cooking time: 2 hours to 2 hours and 30 minutes

Processing time: 15 minutes

Yield: 4 pints

3 pounds pears	1 cup golden raisins
2 cups apple cider vinegar	2 teaspoons ground cinnamon
1¼ cups packed brown sugar	1 teaspoon ground cloves
1 onion, finely chopped	1 teaspoon cayenne pepper

1 Peel the pears with a vegetable peeler or a paring knife. Remove and discard the core and stems. Dice the pears into ⅜- to ½-inch pieces.

2 Place the vinegar and brown sugar in a 4- to 5-quart pot and bring the mixture to a boil over medium-high heat. Stir to dissolve the sugar. Add the pears, onion, raisins, cinnamon, cloves, and cayenne pepper; stir to combine. Return the mixture to a boil; reduce the heat, simmering the mixture until it thickens and the liquid reduces by one-third to one-half, about 2 to 2½ hours.

3 While your chutney is cooking, prepare your canning jars and two-piece caps (lids and screw bands) according to the manufacturer's instructions. Keep the jars and lids hot. (For information on water-bath canning and detailed instructions on preparing and filling your jars, releasing air bubbles, and testing the seals, see Chapter 4.)

4 Ladle the hot chutney into the prepared jars, leaving headspace of ½ inch. Release any air bubbles with a nonreactive tool, adding more chutney to maintain a headspace of ½ inch. Wipe the jar rims; seal the jars with the two-piece caps, hand-tightening the bands. Process your filled jars in a water bath for 15 minutes from the point of boiling. Remove the jars from the boiling water with a jar lifter. Place them on a clean kitchen towel or paper towels away from drafts. After the jars cool completely, test the seals. (If you find any jars that haven't sealed, refrigerate them and use them within two months.)

Vary It! *If you have the luxury of chile powder from New Mexico, use your favorite intensity of heat. My personal favorite is Chimayo chile powder, available seasonally from The Chile Shop in Santa Fe, New Mexico (see Chapter 18).*

Toasting nuts

Toasted nuts are delicious and simple to make. Pay close attention during the toasting process. If the nuts become overtoasted (very dark), there's no going back. You'll have to start over. Toast more nuts than your recipe calls for and use them in salads. Store cooled nuts in an airtight container in the refrigerator.

This process takes only minutes (literally), so stay right by the oven.

1. Spread your nuts evenly on a baking sheet and place it in a preheated 350-degree oven. The size of the nut determines the toasting time. Set your timer for 3 minutes.

2. Check the nuts; shake or stir them. If they're a color you're looking for, usually a light golden brown, remove them from the oven and cool them on the baking sheet. If they're not quite done, return them to the oven; check them in 2 minutes. Toasting takes place quickly.

3. You'll know your nuts are done, or close to being done, when you smell their wonderful aroma. If the skin is on the nut, it'll split to show you the color of the nut.

To resoften brown sugar, place it in an airtight container with an apple slice for one or two days. Discard the apple after the brown sugar softens and becomes moist.

Nectarine Chutney

This chutney was adapted from a recipe passed on to me from a fellow judge, Kyle Kimbell, at the San Diego County Fair. It's simply scrumptious!

Preparation time: *30 minutes*

Cooking time: *1 hour, 10 minutes*

Processing time: *10 minutes*

Yield: *5 pints*

2½ pounds white or yellow nectarines

1⅔ cups golden raisins

1 cup packed brown sugar

1 cup apple cider vinegar

½ cup finely diced onions (about ½ of a large onion)

¼ cup crystallized ginger (¼-inch dice or baker's cut, precut pieces in a ¼ inch dice)

1 tablespoon kosher or pickling salt

1 teaspoon powdered mustard

1 teaspoon red chile powder

⅛ teaspoon ground cinnamon

⅛ teaspoon ground cloves

½ cup toasted slivered almonds

1 Peel your nectarines (refer to Figure 5-1), discard the pits, and dice the fruit into ½-inch pieces. Place the fruit in a 4- to 5-quart pot. Add the raisins, brown sugar, vinegar, onions, ginger, salt, mustard, chile powder, cinnamon, and cloves; stir to combine.

2 Bring the mixture to a simmer over medium heat. Turn the heat to low, cover, and simmer for 30 minutes. Remove the lid, increase the heat to medium, and cook for 30 minutes longer, until the mixture thickens. Stir your chutney every 7 to 10 minutes to prevent any sticking. Add the almonds and cook 2 minutes more.

3 While your chutney is cooking, prepare your canning jars and two-piece caps (lids and screw bands) according to the manufacturer's instructions. Keep the jars and lids hot. (For information on water-bath canning and detailed instructions on preparing and filling your jars, releasing air bubbles, and testing the seals, see Chapter 4.)

4 Ladle the hot chutney into your prepared jars, leaving headspace of ½ inch. Release air bubbles with a nonreactive tool (refer to Figure 8-1), adding more chutney to maintain a headspace of ½ inch. Wipe the jar rims; seal the jars with the two-piece caps, hand-tightening the bands. Process your filled jars in a water bath for 10 minutes from the point of boiling. Remove the jars from the boiling water with a jar lifter. Place them on a clean kitchen towel or paper towels away from drafts. After the jars cool completely, test the seals. If you find any jars that haven't sealed, refrigerate them and use them within 2 months.

Reveling in Your Relish

Relish wears many hats and complements a wide variety of foods, from hamburgers and hot dogs, to meat and poultry. Relish is a cooked mixture of fruit or vegetables preserved with vinegar. Flavor can be sweet to savory and hot to mild with textures ranging from smooth to finely chopped or chunky.

Drunken Cranberry Relish

This is more of a traditional cranberry sauce with an added boost of flavor. If you don't use alcohol in your cooking, it's all right to omit it.

Preparation time: *10 minutes*

Cooking time: *10 minutes*

Processing time: *10 minutes*

Yield: *4 half-pints*

2 cups granulated sugar

½ cup water

4 cups (about 1 pound) fresh cranberries, rinsed (discard any bruised or soft fruit)

½ orange, peeled, membrane removed, and finely chopped

Zest from 1 orange

3 whole cloves

3-inch cinnamon stick

½ cup apricot brandy (optional)

1 Prepare your canning jars and two-piece caps (lids and screw bands) according to the manufacturer's instructions. Keep the jars and lids hot. (For information on water-bath canning and detailed instructions on preparing and filling your jars, releasing air bubbles, and testing the seals, see Chapter 4.)

2 Combine the sugar and water in a 5- to 6-quart pot. Stir to wet the sugar and bring the contents to a boil. Boil for 3 minutes without stirring. Add the cranberries, orange pieces, orange zest, cloves, and cinnamon stick. Bring the mixture to a simmer over medium heat, stirring occasionally, until the cranberries burst, about 5 to 6 minutes. Remove the pot from the heat and stir in the apricot brandy. Remove the cinnamon stick before canning your relish.

3 Ladle your hot relish into the prepared jars, leaving headspace of ¼ inch. Release air bubbles with a nonreactive tool (refer to Figure 8-1), adding more relish to maintain a headspace of ¼ inch. Wipe the jar rims; seal the jars with the two-piece caps, hand-tightening the bands. Process your filled jars in a water bath for 10 minutes from the point of boiling. Remove the jars from the boiling water with a jar lifter. Place them on a clean kitchen towel or paper towels away from drafts. After the jars cool completely, test the seals. (If you find jars that haven't sealed, refrigerate them and use them within 2 months.)

Summer Squash Relish

I discovered this tasty relish when my best friend, Judy, planted six zucchini plants in her garden. At that time, we had no idea of the amount of squash those plants would produce! Including an overnight soak, this recipe takes two days to make.

Preparation time: *45 minutes (not including soaking time)*

Cooking time: *40 minutes*

Processing time: *15 minutes*

Yield: *6 pints*

5 pounds (about 10 to 12) medium zucchini	*2 4-ounce jars pimientos, undrained*
6 large onions	*2 teaspoons celery seed*
½ cup kosher or pickling salt	*1 teaspoon powdered mustard*
Cold water to cover the vegetables (about 4 to 5 quarts)	*½ teaspoon ground cinnamon*
	½ teaspoon ground nutmeg
2 cups white wine vinegar	*½ teaspoon freshly ground black pepper*
1 cup granulated sugar	

1 On the first day, finely chop the zucchini and onions, in three batches for each vegetable, in a food processor fitted with a metal blade. Place them in a 5- to 6-quart mixing bowl and sprinkle them with the salt. Add water to cover the vegetables. Place a cover on the bowl and refrigerate overnight or at least 12 hours.

2 On the second day, drain the vegetables in a colander in batches. Rinse well with running water; drain. Transfer the vegetables to a 5- to 6-quart pot. Add the vinegar, sugar, pimientos, celery seed, mustard, cinnamon, nutmeg, and pepper. Stir to combine.

3 Bring the vegetables to a boil over medium-high heat, stirring occasionally. Reduce the heat and simmer, uncovered, until the mixture reduces to 3 quarts, about 30 to 40 minutes. Stir the vegetables every 10 minutes to prevent any sticking. The zucchini color turns a dull shade of green.

4 While your relish is cooking, prepare your canning jars and two-piece caps (lids and screw bands) according to the manufacturer's instructions. Keep the jars and lids hot. (For information on water-bath canning and detailed instructions on preparing and filling your jars, releasing air bubbles, and testing the seals, see Chapter 4.)

5 Spoon the hot relish into your prepared jars. Remove any air bubbles with a nonreactive tool (refer to Figure 8-1). Add more relish and lightly compact it with a spoon, releasing any additional air bubbles and allowing headspace of ¼ inch. Wipe the jar rims; seal the jars with the two-piece caps, hand-tightening the bands. Process your filled jars in a water bath for 15 minutes from the point of boiling. Remove the jars from the boiling water with a jar lifter. Place them on a clean kitchen towel or paper towels away from drafts. After the jars cool completely, test the seals. (If you find jars that haven't sealed, refrigerate them and use them within 2 months.)

Vary It! Use 3 pounds of zucchini and 2 pounds of patty pan or yellow crookneck squash.

Satisfying Your Sassy Salsas and Sauces

Salsa is the Mexican word for "sauce." Traditionally, salsa was made with tomatoes, cilantro, chilies, and onions and served at room temperature. Today, it's readily available in most supermarkets in mild, hot, or fiery intensities and is used on almost any food.

Tomatillo Salsa

Here's a welcome change from a traditional tomato-based salsa. Use this mild salsa for a chip-dipping sauce or a topper for your tacos or cheese enchiladas.

Preparation time: *20 minutes*

Cooking time: *10 minutes*

Processing time: *15 minutes*

Yield: *2 pints*

2 pounds tomatillos, husks removed, cored	*2 teaspoons ground cumin*
1 large onion, peeled	*½ teaspoon kosher or pickling salt*
4 large Anaheim chilies, seeds and stem removed	*½ teaspoon crushed red peppers*
4 garlic cloves, peeled	*1 cup distilled white vinegar*
2 tablespoons finely chopped fresh cilantro	*¼ cup fresh lime juice (2 or 3 limes)*

1 Prepare your canning jars and two-piece caps (lids and screw bands) according to the manufacturer's instructions. Keep the jars and lids hot. (For information on water-bath canning and detailed instructions on preparing and filling your jars, releasing air bubbles, and testing the seals, see Chapter 4.)

2 Cut the tomatillos into quarters and finely chop them in a food processor fitted with a metal blade. Transfer the tomatillos to a 5- to 6- quart pot. Finely chop the onion, chilies, and garlic cloves in two batches in the food processor. Add them to the tomatillos. Stir in the cilantro, cumin, salt, peppers, vinegar, and lime juice. Bring the mixture to a boil over high heat. Reduce the heat and simmer 10 minutes.

3 Ladle your hot salsa into the prepared jars, leaving headspace of ¼ inch. Wipe the jar rims; seal the jars with the two-piece caps, hand-tightening the bands. Process the filled jars in a water bath for 15 minutes from the point of boiling. Remove the jars from the boiling water with a jar lifter. Place them on a clean kitchen towel or paper towels away from drafts. After the jars cool completely, test the seals. (If you find jars that haven't sealed, refrigerate them and use them within 2 months.)

Tomatillos look like small green tomatoes with parchmentlike husks and light-green flesh with small seeds. Remove the husks before using them.

Jalapeño Salsa

This salsa isn't for those with sensitive mouths. The heat of the jalapeños grows stronger when the salsa cools and the flavors blend.

Preparation time: *30 minutes*

Cooking time: *10 minutes*

Processing time: *15 minutes*

Yield: *3 pints*

2 pounds tomatoes, peeled and chopped, to measure 3 cups

7-ounce can diced jalapeño chilies or 12 fresh jalapeño chilies, finely chopped, seeds removed

1 onion, peeled and chopped

6 garlic cloves, minced

2 tablespoons finely chopped fresh cilantro

2 teaspoons ground oregano

1½ teaspoons kosher or pickling salt

½ teaspoon ground cumin

1 cup apple cider vinegar

1 Prepare your canning jars and two-piece caps (lids and screw bands) according to the manufacturer's instructions. Keep the jars and lids hot. (For information on water-bath canning and detailed instructions on preparing and filling your jars, releasing air bubbles, and testing the seals, see Chapter 4.)

2 Place all the ingredients in a 5- to 6- quart pot. Bring the mixture to a boil over high heat, stirring to combine. Reduce the heat to low; simmer, uncovered, for 10 minutes.

3 Ladle your hot salsa into the prepared jars; leaving headspace of ¼ inch. Wipe the jar rims; seal the jars with the two-piece caps, hand-tightening the bands. Process the filled jars in a water bath for 10 minutes from the point of boiling. Remove the jars from the boiling water with a jar lifter. Place them on a clean kitchen towel or paper towels away from drafts. After the jars cool completely, test the seals. (If you find jars that haven't sealed, refrigerate them and use them within 2 months.)

Plum Sauce

You won't find a better dipping sauce for egg rolls or stuffed wontons. For something out of the ordinary, top a scoop of steamed rice with plum sauce and soy sauce.

Preparation time: *20 minutes*

Cooking time: *1 hour to 1 hour and 30 minutes*

Processing time: *15 minutes*

Yield: *4 to 5 pints*

4 pounds fresh, ripe plums, any variety, skins left on	*1 tablespoon ground ginger*
	1 tablespoon powdered mustard
1 medium onion, coarsely chopped	*1 teaspoon ground cinnamon*
1 garlic clove, peeled	*1 teaspoon crushed red peppers*
3½ cups granulated sugar	*½ teaspoon ground cloves*
2 cups apple cider vinegar	

1 Remove the pits from the plums and cut the fruit into quarters. Process the plums, onion, and garlic in two or three batches in the bowl of a food processor fitted with a metal blade until smooth. Transfer the mixture to a 5- to 6-quart pot while you work. Add the sugar, vinegar, ginger, mustard, cinnamon, peppers, and cloves. Bring the mixture to a boil over high heat, stirring occasionally. Reduce the heat and simmer the mixture, uncovered, to reduce the liquid by one-third, about 1 hour to 1 hour and 30 minutes.

2 While the mixture is cooking, prepare your canning jars and two-piece caps (lids and screw bands) according to the manufacturer's instructions. Keep the jars and lids hot. (For information on water-bath canning and detailed instructions on preparing and filling your jars and testing the seals, see Chapter 4.)

3 Ladle your hot sauce into the prepared jars; leaving headspace of ¼ inch. Wipe the jar rims; seal the jars with the two-piece caps, hand-tightening the bands. Process the filled jars in a water bath for 15 minutes from the point of boiling. Remove the jars from the boiling water with a jar lifter. Place them on a clean kitchen towel or paper towels away from drafts. After the jars cool completely, test the seals. (If you find jars that haven't sealed, refrigerate them and use them within 2 months.)

Mixed Fruit Sauce

Use this fruit mixture for an ice-cream topper or combine it with plain yogurt or sour cream for a tasty addition to a slice of cantaloupe, honeydew melon, or a grapefruit half.

Preparation time: *25 minutes*

Cooking time: *5 minutes*

Processing time: *20 minutes*

Yield: *3 pints*

4 cups fresh strawberries, hulled and diced, reserving all juice

3 mangoes, peeled and diced

2 kiwis, peeled and diced

2 cups granulated sugar

½ cup orange or kumquat marmalade

2 tablespoons orange liqueur

2 tablespoons fruit-flavored brandy (your flavor choice)

1 Prepare your canning jars and two-piece caps (lids and screw bands) according to the manufacturer's instructions. Keep the jars and lids hot. (For information on water-bath canning and detailed instructions on preparing and filling your jars and testing the seals, see Chapter 4.)

2 Combine all the ingredients in a 4- to 5-quart pot. Bring the mixture to a boil over high heat. Reduce the heat and simmer, uncovered, stirring constantly, until the sugar dissolves. Remove the mixture from the heat. Remove any foam from the surface with a foam skimmer.

3 Ladle your hot sauce into the prepared jars, leaving headspace of ½ inch. Wipe the jar rims; seal the jars with the two-piece caps, hand-tightening the bands. Process the filled jars in a water bath for 20 minutes from the point of boiling. Remove the jars from the boiling water with a jar lifter. Place them on a clean kitchen towel or paper towels away from drafts. After the jars cool completely, test the seals. (If you find jars that haven't sealed, refrigerate them and use them within 2 months.)

Tip: *Frozen strawberries may be substituted for fresh strawberries. Thaw them according to the package instructions and include all of the liquid.*

Raspberry Syrup

I love pure maple syrup, but I can't resist this for a flavor change. It's delicious on thick, grilled French toast sprinkled with ground cinnamon and powdered sugar.

Preparation time: *15 minutes*

Cooking time: *25 minutes*

Processing time: *10 minutes*

Yield: *6 half-pints*

5 cups fresh raspberries, hulled and cut in half

3 cups water

1 tablespoon grated lemon zest

2½ cups granulated sugar

3½ cups corn syrup

2 tablespoons fresh lemon juice (about ½ of a lemon)

1 Place the raspberries in a 4- to 5-quart pot. Crush the berries with a potato masher. Add 1½ cups of the water and the lemon zest. Bring the mixture to a boil; reduce the heat and simmer 5 minutes. Strain the hot mixture through a jelly bag or a cheesecloth-lined mesh strainer (refer to Figure 6-3).

2 While the berries drain, prepare your canning jars and two-piece caps (lids and screw bands) according to the manufacturer's instructions. Keep the jars and lids hot. (For information on water-bath canning and detailed instructions on preparing and filling your jars and testing the seals, see Chapter 4.)

3 Place the sugar and the remaining 1½ cups of water in a 4-quart saucepan. Bring the mixture to a boil over high heat, stirring to dissolve the sugar. Cook the mixture until the temperature registers 260 degrees on a candy thermometer. Add the strained berries and the corn syrup and return the mixture to a boil, boiling the syrup for 4 minutes. Remove the pan from the heat and stir in the lemon juice. Remove any foam from the surface with a foam skimmer.

4 Ladle your hot syrup into the prepared jars, leaving headspace of ¼ inch. Wipe the jar rims; seal the jars with the two-piece caps, hand-tightening the bands. Process the filled jars in a water bath for 10 minutes from the point of boiling. Remove the jars from the boiling water with a jar lifter. Place them on a clean kitchen towel or paper towels away from drafts. After the jars cool completely, test the seals. (If you find jars that haven't sealed, refrigerate them and use them within 2 months.)

Vary It! *Substitute other berries, or a combination of berries, for different syrup flavors.*

Chapter 8

Pickle Me Timbers!

*P*ickling is used for a wide range of foods, including fruit and vegetables. Although pickling isn't practiced much today, don't overlook this rewarding process. This chapter gives you an overview of pickling, describing the ingredients, the utensils, and the methods used. In no time, you'll be making easy-to-prepare pickled food and condiments to wow your taste buds.

The Art of Pickling

Pickling preserves food in a *brine solution,* a strong mixture of water, salt, vinegar, and sometimes sugar or another sweetener, like corn syrup. The perfect balance of salt, vinegar, water, and herbs and spices safely preserves your pickled food. You can achieve this balance by precisely measuring your ingredients and following each step in your recipe.

The ingredients

The four basic ingredients for pickling are salt, vinegar, water, and herbs and spices. Use high-quality ingredients for the best results.

Salt

Salt is used as a preservative. It adds flavor and crispness to your food, especially pickles. Use a pure, additive-free, granulated salt. Acceptable salts are: *pickling and canning salt* (a fine-grained salt containing no additives), most kosher salt, and *sea salt,* salt produced from evaporated seawater.

Additives in salt cause cloudy liquid. Always read the ingredient label on your salt container to ensure it's additive-free.

Salts *not* suitable for brining and pickling solutions are:

- ✔ **Table salt and iodized salt:** These contain *anti-caking agents,* additives that keep the salt from sticking together. These cloud your liquid. Iodine darkens food.

- ✔ **Rock salt:** Rock salt keeps roads free of ice and isn't made for use with food. It's okay in an ice-cream freezer because it never touches the food.

- ✔ **Salt substitutes:** These products contain little or no sodium.

Vinegar

Vinegar is a tart liquid that prevents the growth of bacteria. Always use a vinegar with an acidity level of 5 percent. If the level of acidity isn't on the label, don't use the vinegar — the strength of the acid may not be adequate for safe food preservation.

The preferred vinegar for pickling is distilled white vinegar with a sharp, tart flavor. It maintains the color of your food and is relatively inexpensive. Use apple cider vinegar for a milder flavor.

Never dilute or reduce the amount of vinegar in a recipe. If the flavor's too tart, add ¼ cup granulated sugar for every 4 cups of vinegar. Treating flavors in this manner won't upset the balance of your vinegar. If you don't like the flavor when you make the recipe a second time, try another recipe.

Water

Soft water is the best water for your brine solution. *Distilled water,* water with all minerals and other impurities removed, is also a good choice. If you use tap water, make sure it's of drinking quality; if it doesn't taste good to you, it won't taste better in your food. Also, avoid using sparkling water.

To soften tap water, boil it in a large kettle for 15 minutes. Cool the water and allow it to stand for 24 hours. Remove any scum on the surface with a foam skimmer. Ladle the water into a measuring cup without disturbing the sediment on the bottom of the kettle. Add 1 tablespoon of vinegar to each gallon of water. Boil the water before using it.

Herbs and spices

Use the exact amount of herbs or spices called for in your recipe. If your recipe calls for a fresh herb, use the fresh herb. If your recipe calls for a dried spice, use one with a strong aroma. (For more information on herbs and spices, check out Chapter 7.)

Pickling spices are blends of many spices including allspice, bay leaves, cardamom, cinnamon, cloves, coriander, ginger, mustard seeds, and peppercorns. They're mixed by the manufacturer and vary in flavor.

The equipment and the utensils

In addition to the basic equipment for water-bath canning (refer to Chapter 4), you'll need nonreactive utensils and equipment for handling, cooking, and brining your food. *Nonreactive* items are made of stainless steel, nonstick-surfaced items (without a damaged nonstick surface), enamelware, or glass.

Items made from, or containing, zinc, iron, brass, copper, galvanized metal, or enamelware with chips or crack in the enamel react with the acids and salt during the pickling process. This reaction alters the color of your food and produces a finished product that tastes bad.

Don't use equipment or utensils made from copper or iron, and *definitely* don't use galvanized products, which contain zinc. Copper turns your pickles green. Iron produces a black color in your food. *Galvanized items,* metal coated with zinc, produces a poison when the acid and the salt touch the zinc and transfers to your food causing serious illness (or worse).

Brining Education

The brining process is part of the pickling process. The brining solution extracts juice and sugar from your food, forming *lactic acid,* a bitter-tasting tart acid. Lactic acid is the preservative in your pickled food.

Be sure to keep your food completely submerged in the brine solution, whether it's for a few hours or longer. Accomplish this by placing a sealed, water-filled glass jar on top of your food. The jar applies pressure to keep the foods submerged when you cover your brining container.

Stoneware crocks are excellent choices for brining food. You can find them at specialty cookware stores or where canning supplies are sold.

The brining process

The brining process safely converts your low-acid foods (those with a pH level over 4.6) to high-acid foods (with a pH level of 4.6 or less). This conversion is accomplished with an acid, usually vinegar. Preparing your recipe as it's written makes processing your food in a water-bath canner safe.

Preparation methods for your pickled food include the following:

✔ **Long brine:** This process is primarily used for making pickles from cucumbers. The brine solution is quite heavy with salt and may contain some vinegar and spices.

The food is submerged in the brine solution, where it *ferments* (stays in the solution) for anywhere from 5 days to 6 weeks. (Your recipe gives you the details.) After fermenting, follow your recipe and make a fresh brine solution for filling your jars.

✔ **Short brine:** The soaking period for this method is 24 hours or less. Follow your recipe for the correct proportions in your brine solution. Prepare a fresh solution for filling your jars.

✔ **Complete precooking:** In this method, you cook your food completely before filling your jars.

✔ **A fresh (or raw) pack:** In this method, fresh raw vegetables are placed in prepared jars and then covered with hot, flavored liquid, usually a spicy vinegar, and processed in your water-bath canner. This process is used in the Dilly Beans recipe in this chapter.

Old-time canning recipes may instruct you to "soak your pickles in salt brine strong enough to float an egg." This equates to a 10-percent brine mixture of 1 pound (about 1½ cups) of salt dissolved in 1 gallon of water.

Adding crunch to your food

The best method for maintaining crispness, crunch, and firmness in your vegetables during the soaking period is to add ice, preferably crushed ice, to your soaking solution. This works best for short brine soaking.

After the soaking period, drain your vegetables in a colander, following your recipe instructions for any rinsing. Some recipes instruct you to roll the drained food in clean kitchen towels to dry it. This works well for larger pieces of food (it isn't for finely chopped relishes).

Note: In older pickling recipes, you may see the addition of alum or pickling (slaked) lime. My recipes don't add either of these products because they aren't necessary when you're using modern canning methods.

Packing and Filling Your Jars

The most important thing to do when you're filling your jars is to release trapped air bubbles between the food pieces (see Figure 8-1). This may seem unimportant, but air bubbles can play havoc with your final product:

✔ **Jar seals:** Too much air in the jar from trapped air bubbles produces excessive pressure in the jar during processing. The pressure in the jar is greater than the pressure outside the jar during cooling. This imbalance interferes with the sealing process.

✔ **Liquid levels:** Air bubbles take up space. When there's trapped air between your food pieces before sealing the jars, the liquid level in the jar drops when the food is heated. (For releasing air bubbles, refer to Figure 8-1.) In addition, floating and discolored food results from packing your food without the proper amount of liquid in the jars. Snuggly packed food eliminates air and allows enough liquid to completely cover the food with proper headspace (refer to Figure 2-14).

Never skip the step of releasing air bubbles. No matter how carefully you pack and fill your jars, you'll always have some hidden bubbles.

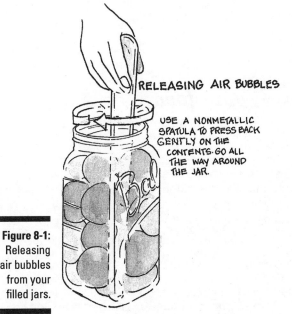

RELEASING AIR BUBBLES

USE A NONMETALLIC SPATULA TO PRESS BACK GENTLY ON THE CONTENTS. GO ALL THE WAY AROUND THE JAR.

Figure 8-1:
Releasing air bubbles from your filled jars.

Pickled Toppers

Use this pickled treat anytime you'd use a relish, on a hamburger or hot dog, in tuna salad, or anytime you want to add flavor to a sandwich.

Sweet Pickle Relish

One advantage of homemade relish is mixing flavors you don't find in commercially produced relishes. My family actually prefers this relish to store-bought.

Preparation time: *25 minutes (not including soaking time)*

Cooking time: *30 minutes*

Processing time: *10 minutes*

Yield: *7 half-pints or 3 pints*

5 to 6 medium cucumbers	*3 cups granulated sugar*
3 to 4 green and/or red bell peppers	*2 cups apple cider vinegar*
3 to 4 medium onions	*2½ teaspoons celery seeds*
Cold water, about 4 to 6 quarts	*2½ teaspoons mustard seeds*
¼ cup kosher or pickling salt	*½ teaspoon turmeric*

1 Peel the cucumbers and remove the seeds (see Figure 8-2). Finely chop them in a food processor fitted with a metal blade, to measure 6 cups.

2 Remove the stems and seeds from the bell peppers. Finely chop them in a food processor fitted with a metal blade, to measure 3 cups.

3 Remove the skin of the onions. Finely chop them in a food processor fitted with a metal blade, to measure 3 cups.

4 Combine the vegetables in a 5- to 6-quart bowl. Sprinkle them with salt and add cold water to cover the veggies. Cover the bowl; let the veggies stand at room temperature for 2 hours. Rinse the veggies with running water in batches in a colander. Drain well.

5 Combine the sugar, vinegar, celery seeds, mustard seeds, and turmeric in a 5- to 6-quart pot. Bring the liquid to a boil over high heat, stirring occasionally to dissolve the sugar. Add the drained vegetables and return the mixture to a boil. Reduce the heat to medium-high and simmer, uncovered, stirring occasionally, for 20 to 30 minutes or until most of the excess liquid has evaporated.

6 While your relish is cooking, prepare your canning jars and two-piece caps (lids and screw bands) according to the manufacturer's instructions. Keep the jars and lids hot. (For information on water-bath canning and detailed instructions on preparing and filling your jars, releasing air bubbles, and testing the seals, see Chapter 4.)

7 Spoon and lightly compact the hot relish into the prepared jars. Release any air bubbles (refer to Figure 8-1); add more relish and liquid to maintain headspace of ½ inch.

8 Wipe the jar rims; seal the jars with the two-piece caps, hand-tightening the bands. Process your filled jars in a water bath for 10 minutes from the point of boiling. Remove the jars from the boiling water with a jar lifter. Place them on a clean kitchen towel or paper towels away from drafts. After the jars cool completely, test the seals. If you find jars that haven't sealed, refrigerate them and use them within 2 months.

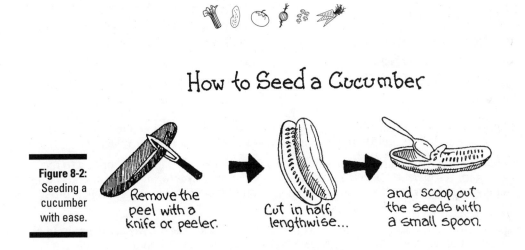

How to Seed a Cucumber

Figure 8-2: Seeding a cucumber with ease.

Remove the peel with a knife or peeler.

Cut in half, lengthwise...

and scoop out the seeds with a small spoon.

Pickled Cucumbers Are Just Pickles

So what's so important about what kind of cucumber you use for pickles? After all, a cucumber is a cucumber, right? This is definitely not the case. The common salad cucumber has a thick, dark-green, waxy skin. Don't use this cucumber for making pickles because the brine solution won't penetrate the waxy coating. Use this cucumber when your recipe doesn't specify "pickling cucumbers," like the Mixed Pickled Veggies in this chapter.

A pickling cucumber is the only cucumber to use for making pickles. The skin of a pickling cucumber is thin, not waxy, and is left on the cucumber. Pickling cucumbers are about 4 inches in length, smaller than salad cucumbers. Don't eat pickling cucumbers raw; their flavor is extremely bitter.

Speedy Dill Pickles

This recipe makes an old-fashioned dill pickle in almost the blink of an eye.

Preparation time: *30 minutes*

Cooking time: *5 minutes*

Processing time: *Quarts, 15 minutes; pints, 10 minutes*

Yield: *3 quarts or 6 pints*

4 pounds pickling cucumbers

6 tablespoons kosher or pickling salt

3 cups distilled white vinegar

3 cups water

1 tablespoon whole mixed pickling spices

18 black peppercorns

3 tablespoons dill seed

Fresh dill springs (optional)

1 Wash your cucumbers. Leave them whole if they're smaller than 4 inches in diameter. For larger cucumbers, cut them into slices or lengthwise, in halves or quarters.

2 Prepare your canning jars and two-piece caps (lids and screw bands) according to the manufacturer's instructions. Keep the jars and lids hot. (For information on water-bath canning and detailed instructions on preparing and filling your jars, releasing air bubbles, and testing the seals, see Chapter 4.)

3 Combine the salt, water, and vinegar in a to 3- to 4-quart saucepan. Bring the liquid to a boil over high heat, stirring occasionally to dissolve the sugar. Keep the liquid hot.

4 Snuggly pack the cucumbers into your prepared jars. To each quart jar, add 1 teaspoon of pickling spices, 6 peppercorns, and 1 tablespoon of dill seed. To each pint jar, add ½ teaspoon of pickling spices, 3 peppercorns, and 1½ teaspoons of dill seed. If you're using fresh dill, add a sprig or two to each quart or pint jar in between the inside edge of the jar and the cucumbers.

5 Ladle the hot liquid into your filled jars, leaving headspace of ½ inch in the quart jars and headspace of ¼ inch in the pint jars. Completely submerge the cucumbers in the liquid. If they protrude from the jar, adjust them until you have the proper headspace, because the lids may not properly seal from the internal pressure. Release any air bubbles with a nonreactive tool (refer to Figure 8-1). Add more liquid to the jar if the level drops from releasing the air bubbles.

6 Wipe the jar rims; seal the jars with the two-piece caps, hand-tightening the bands. Process your filled jars in a water bath — for quart jars, 15 minutes; for pint jars, 10 minutes; both from the point of boiling. Remove the jars with a jar lifter. Place them on a clean kitchen or paper towel away from drafts. After the jars cool completely, test the seals. If you find jars that haven't sealed, refrigerate and use them within 2 months.

Vary It! *For kosher-style dill pickles, add 2 cloves of peeled, halved garlic to each jar of pickles.*

Bread and Butter Pickles

Wait until you try these tartly sweet pickles. The onion pieces are an added bonus of flavor. It's certainly not what you find at your supermarket.

Preparation time: *30 minutes (not including the soaking time)*

Cooking time: *5 minutes*

Processing time: *15 minutes*

Yield: *4 to 5 pints*

4 pounds pickling cucumbers

4 small to medium onions

Ice water, about 4 to 6 quarts

½ cup kosher or pickling salt

5 cups granulated sugar

4 cups distilled white vinegar

2 tablespoons mustard seed

2½ teaspoons celery seed

1½ teaspoons turmeric

1 Slice the cucumbers into ¼ inch thick rounds. Peel the onions and cut them in half lengthwise from the tip to the bottom core. Lay them on a cutting board, cut side down and slice them, starting at the top of the onion, to a thickness of ¼ inch. Place the cucumber and onion slices in a pickling crock or two 5- to 6-quart bowls. Sprinkle them with salt. Add ice water to cover the vegetables. Stir them once, then cover the bowl and let the veggies stand at room temperature for 3 hours. Transfer the veggies to a colander and rinse them thoroughly with running water (you may need to do this in more than one batch). Drain well. Roll the pieces in a clean, dry kitchen towel to partially dry them.

2 Prepare your canning jars and two-piece caps (lids and screw bands) according to the manufacturer's instructions. Keep the jars and lids hot. (For information on water-bath canning and detailed instructions on preparing and filling your jars, releasing air bubbles, and testing the seals, see Chapter 4.)

3 Combine the sugar, vinegar, mustard and celery seed, and turmeric in an 8- to 10-quart pot. Bring the liquid to a boil over high heat, stirring occasionally to dissolve the sugar and mix the spices. Add the vegetables and return the mixture to a boil. Reduce the heat to medium-high and simmer, uncovered, for 5 minutes.

4 Pack the hot pickles into the prepared jars, leaving headspace of ¼ inch. Add the hot liquid, leaving a headspace of ¼ inch. Release any air bubbles with a nonreactive tool (refer to Figure 8-1). Add more pickles and liquid to the jar, leaving ¼ inch of headspace for both the pickles and the liquid.

5 Wipe the jar rims; seal the jars with the two-piece caps, hand-tightening the bands. Process your filled jars in a water bath for 15 minutes from the point of boiling. Remove the jars with a jar lifter. Place them on a clean kitchen or paper towel away from drafts. After the jars cool completely, test the seals. If you find jars that haven't sealed, refrigerate and use them within 2 months.

Pickled Vegetables

Pickled vegetables are delicious additions to green salads or a relish plate. Enjoy these treats for a change of pace from plain, raw vegetables.

Mixed Pickled Veggies

The vibrant colors and the variety of vegetables in this recipe are sure to please all tastes. Prepare your vegetables and get them soaking the night before you can them. After putting them into the brine solution, forget about them until the next day!

Preparation time: 30 minutes (not including overnight soaking)

Cooking time: 15 minutes

Processing time: 15 minutes

Yield: 6 pints

4 quarts water, at room temperature

1 cup kosher or pickling salt

4 cups (1 small) cauliflower, cut into florets

4 cups (about 2 large) cucumbers, peeled, seeds removed, cut into 1-inch-thick slices, then quartered (refer to Figure 8-3)

2 cups (about 4) carrots, cut into 1½-inch pieces

2 cups (¾ to 1 pound) green beans, cut into 1½-inch slices

2 cups (about 10 ounces) pearl onions, peeled (refer to Figure 5-1)

1 each green, red, and yellow bell peppers, cut into wide strips

6½ cups distilled white vinegar

2 cups granulated sugar

¼ cup mustard seeds

2 tablespoons celery seeds

7 spicy, dried red chile peppers (one for the vinegar mixture and one for each jar)

1 On the first day, dissolve the salt in the water in a 5- to 6-quart bowl. After the salt dissolves, add the vegetables. Cover the bowl; leave it in a cool place for 12 to 18 hours. On the second day, thoroughly drain your vegetables in a colander. Do not rinse them. Prepare your canning jars and two-piece caps (lids and screw bands) according to the manufacturer's instructions. Keep the jars and lids hot. (For information on water-bath canning and detailed instructions on preparing and filling your jars, releasing air bubbles, and testing the seals, see Chapter 4.)

2 Combine the vinegar, sugar, mustard seeds, celery seeds, and one chile pepper in an 8-quart pot. Bring the liquid to a boil over high heat; boiling for 3 minutes to dissolve the sugar and soften the seeds and the chile. Add your vegetables; return the liquid to a simmer, heating the veggies until they're hot throughout, about 5 minutes depending on the size and temperature of your vegetables.

3 Pack your hot vegetables into the prepared jars, leaving headspace of ¼ inch. Add one dried red chile to each jar, gently sliding it between the veggies and the inside of the jar, so it may be seen. Ladle the hot liquid over the vegetables, leaving headspace of ¼ inch. Release any air bubbles with a nonreactive tool (refer to Figure 8-1), adding more vegetables and liquid to maintain a headspace of ¼ inch.

4 Wipe the jar rims; seal the jars with the two-piece caps, hand-tightening the bands. Process your filled jars in a water bath for 15 minutes from the point of boiling. Remove the jars from the boiling water with a jar lifter. Place them on a clean kitchen towel or paper towels away from drafts. After the jars cool completely, test the seals. If you find jars that haven't sealed, refrigerate them and use them within 2 months.

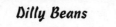

Dilly Beans

Serve these beans in a Bloody Mary in place of a piece of celery. For a variation, use a combination of green and yellow string beans.

Preparation time: *15 minutes*

Cooking time: *1 minute*

Processing time: *10 minutes*

Yield: *4 to 5 pints*

2½ pounds fresh green beans, washed, with the ends and strings removed (refer to Figure 10-1)

2½ cups distilled white vinegar

2½ cups water

¼ cup coarse kosher or pickling salt

4 stalks fresh dill, washed and drained

4 cloves garlic, peeled

4 dried whole red chile peppers

1 teaspoon cayenne pepper

1 teaspoon dill seed

1 Prepare your canning jars and two-piece caps (lids and screw bands) according to the manufacturer's instructions. Keep the jars and lids hot. (For information on water-bath canning and detailed instructions on preparing and filling your jars, releasing air bubbles, and testing the seals, see Chapter 4.)

2 Combine the vinegar, water, and salt in a 6- to 8-quart pot. Bring the liquid to a boil over high heat; boil for 1 minute, stirring to dissolve the salt. Reduce the heat to low and keep the mixture hot.

3 Pack your washed beans into the prepared jars (see Figure 8-3), leaving headspace of ¼ inch. Trim the tops of the beans, if necessary. During the packing process, add the following to each jar: a sprig of dill, 1 garlic clove, 1 dried red chile pepper, ¼ teaspoon cayenne pepper, ¼ teaspoon dill seed.

4 Ladle the hot liquid over the beans, leaving headspace of ¼ inch, covering the tops of the beans. Release any air bubbles with a nonreactive tool (refer to Figure 8-1), adding more liquid to maintain a headspace of ¼ inch.

5 Wipe the jar rims; seal the jars with the two-piece caps, hand-tightening the bands. Process your filled jars in a water bath for 10 minutes from the point of boiling. Remove the jars from the boiling water with a jar lifter. Place them on a clean kitchen towel or paper towels away from drafts. After the jars cool completely, test the seals. If you find jars that haven't sealed, refrigerate them and use them within 2 months.

Figure 8-3:
Packing
raw beans
into a jar.

PACK RAW BEANS INTO A JAR
BY HOLDING THE JAR AT AN
ANGLE ON IT'S SIDE.

Avoid long boiling periods for your vinegar solution. Lengthy boiling reduces the acetic-acid level in vinegar, changing the pH level of the food. This change may compromise the safety of your pickled food.

Spiced Pickled Beets

Use beets that are small and tender, not larger than 2 inches in diameter. Purchase beets with the top leaves attached. If the leaves are wilted and quite dark, the beets aren't fresh; continue your search for fresher beets.

Preparation time: *1 hour and 10 minutes*

Cooking time: *25 minutes*

Processing time: *30 minutes*

Yield: *4 to 5 pints*

4 pounds beets

3 cups thinly sliced white or yellow onions (about 3 medium)

2½ cups apple cider vinegar

1½ cups water

2 cups granulated sugar

1 tablespoon mustard seeds

1 teaspoon kosher or pickling salt

1 teaspoon whole allspice

1 teaspoon whole cloves

3 cinnamon sticks, broken into pieces

1 Trim your beets, leaving the taproots and 2 inches of the stems (refer to Figure 10-2). Wash and drain the beets, using a stiff brush to remove any clinging soil. Cover the beets with water in a 5- to 6-quart pot. Bring the water to a boil over high heat and cook the beets until they pierce easily with a fork, about 20 to 30 minutes. Drain the beets. Run cold water over them and remove the skin. Remove the stem and taproot. Slice the beets into ¼-inch-thick slices. Place the beets in a bowl; set them aside.

2 Prepare your canning jars and two-piece caps (lids and screw bands) according to the manufacturer's instructions. Keep the jars and lids hot. (For information on water-bath canning and detailed instructions on preparing and filling your jars, releasing air bubbles, and testing the seals, see Chapter 4.)

3 Place the onions, vinegar, water, sugar, salt, mustard seeds, allspice, cloves, and cinnamon sticks in a 5- to 6-quart pot. Bring the liquid to a boil over high heat; reduce the heat and simmer the mixture for 5 minutes. Add your beet slices and simmer the mixture to heat the beets, about 3 to 5 minutes. Remove the cinnamon stick pieces.

4 Pack the hot beets and onions into the hot jars, leaving headspace of ¼ inch. Ladle the hot liquid over the beets, leaving headspace of ¼ inch. Release any air bubbles (refer to Figure 8-1); add more beets and liquid to maintain headspace of ¼ inch.

5 Wipe the jar rims; seal the jars with the two-piece caps, hand-tightening the bands. Process your jars in a water bath for 30 minutes from the point of boiling. Remove the jars with a jar lifter. Place them on a clean kitchen or paper towel away from drafts. After the jars cool completely, test the seals. If you find jars that haven't sealed, refrigerate them and use them within 2 months.

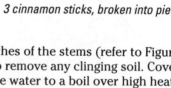

Part III
Pressure Canning

The 5th Wave   By Rich Tennant

"Jane start drying fruit. Before that we just eat cheetah. Too much fast food not good."

In this part . . .

The chapters in this part explore the world of pressure canning, the lesser used of the two home-canning methods. Use this method for preserving vegetables, meat sauce, soups, and other low-acid foods. Preserving low-acid foods requires more care than processing high-acid foods (discussed in Part II), but your rewards are well worth the additional effort.

You'll need a special piece of equipment, a pressure canner, for processing these foods because they require a temperature higher than the maximum temperature (212 degrees) achieved in a water-bath canner to kill the stubborn microorganisms low-acid foods contain. With the chapters in this part, you'll be safely preserving your favorite low-acid foods in no time. Having jars of spring and summer vegetables or ready-to-heat soups in your pantry is a welcome treat when winter rolls around.

Chapter 9

Don't Blow Your Top: Pressure Canning

*W*hen I talk about pressure canning, people often ask me, "Is it safe?" or, "Won't the pressure canner explode?" These concerns are certainly valid ones, but rest assured, when you know the right way to use a pressure canner, you can safely process a variety of low-acid foods (primarily vegetables).

Pressure canning requires a specific piece of equipment for safe food preservation: a pressure canner with an accurate gauge. If you don't use a pressure canner, your food won't be superheated to kill the microorganisms that cause your processed food to spoil, making it unsafe for consumption.

This chapter leads you step by step through the pressure-canning process, including an explanation of pressure canning, what to look for when purchasing a pressure canner, and how to fill your canner and safely process your filled jars.

Making Sense of Pressure Canning

Pressure canning is a process for preserving food with a low-acid content (check out "Understanding the Fuss about Low-Acid Foods," in this chapter) by exposing the food to a high temperature (240 degrees) under a specific pressure, for a specific period of time in a pressure canner. A *pressure canner* is a heavy kettle made for processing home-canned food. It includes a locking, tight-fitting cover that makes the kettle airtight. The purpose of this process is to sterilize the food by destroying hard-to-kill microorganisms, especially the bacteria that cause botulism (see Chapter 3).

Pressure canners, shown in Figure 9-1, come in many sizes and prices. In the "Knowing That All Pressure Canners Are Not Created Equal" section, later in this chapter, you can determine which features you prefer, taking into consideration the cost of the canner. In my experience, the type of pressure canner you choose doesn't matter as long as the model is made and approved for processing home-canned foods.

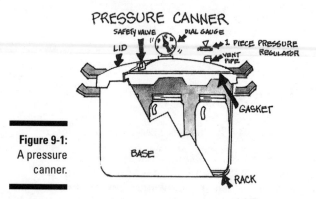

Figure 9-1: A pressure canner.

Don't confuse pressure canners with pressure cookers. A pressure canner (the subject of this chapter) is used to process and sterilize home-canned, low-acid foods. The purpose of a pressure cooker is to cook food fast. Check out *Pressure Cookers For Dummies,* by Tom Lacalamita (Wiley Publishing, Inc.), for the low-down on pressure cooking. Pressure canners and pressure cookers are not interchangeable.

Understanding the Fuss about Low-Acid Foods

Low-acid foods contain little natural acid and require more care during the canning process than other types of foods. (If you're a techie, note that low-acid foods are foods with a *pH factor* — that's a measure of acidity in food — higher than 4.6.) Foods in this category include vegetables, meats, poultry, seafood, and combination foods (like soups, meat sauces, and salsas), that contain low-acid and high-acid ingredients. Exceptions to these low-acid foods include tomatoes (which are really a fruit) and vegetables converted to high-acid foods (refer to Chapter 8) such as sauerkraut, pickles, or pickled vegetables.

In a water-bath canner, the temperature of boiling water never increases above 212 degrees (that's the boiling point for water). In order to increase the temperature to 240 degrees and superheat your filled jars of low-acid food, use a pressure canner that's approved for pressure canning by the United States Department of Agriculture (USDA).

Low-acid foods require pressure canning to kill microorganisms that are harmful if not destroyed before ingesting the food. Pressure canning kills the botulism bacteria at 240 degrees. If this temperature isn't achieved and the bacteria isn't destroyed, one taste of this spoiled food can kill you. And to make matters worse, these botulism-causing bacteria are odorless, have no taste, and actually thrive in low-acid foods that are in a moist environment and not in contact with air — the exact condition provided in a jar of canned food.

Knowing That All Pressure Canners Are Not Created Equal

No matter which type or size of pressure canner you choose, the goal is always the same: to superheat and process low-acid food at a high temperature (240 degrees) that destroys microorganisms.

Only one form of canning — pressure canning — is approved for safely processing low-acid foods. And only one piece of equipment — a pressure canner — is approved for safely processing low-acid foods. Don't allow yourself to think you can use a substitute process or piece of equipment.

Size

Use a pressure canner with a capacity of 16 to 22 quarts. This size holds seven 1-quart jars and permits good air circulation during processing.

Features

All pressure canners (not pressure cookers) — regardless of features — safely process your filled jars of low-acid food in the same manner because a pressure canner operates in only one way. Each pressure canner has a locking cover, a pressure gauge, and an overpressure plug. Manufacturers of pressure canners, however, slightly vary the same features and add accessories in much the same way car manufacturers add extras to a basic car model.

Cover: With a gasket or without

You can find two types of covers for pressure canners: a lock-on cover and a metal-to-metal cover that's attached with wing nuts. The difference is that one has a rubber gasket, and the other doesn't.

Lock-on cover

A lock-on cover (see Figure 9-2) securely fastens to the pressure canner by rotating the cover on the base to the locked position (matching up the handles or matching arrows or other markings on the unit) or with a type of clamping handle. There's usually a rubber gasket between the cover and the base unit. To ensure that the pressure canner is properly closed, refer to your owner's manual for precise instructions.

LOCK-ON COVER

Figure 9-2:
A lock-on cover and rubber gasket.

RUBBER GASKET

 Over time, the rubber gasket may stretch out of shape or begin to rot and deteriorate (indicated by cracking or splitting). If your gasket is in this condition, don't use your pressure canner until you've replaced the gasket. A gasket in poor condition may prevent the canner from reaching the pressure required to superheat the food and kill microorganisms.

 After each use, carefully remove the gasket from the cover. Thoroughly wash the gasket in hot, soapy water and dry it well. After the gasket is completely dry, put it back on the cover so that your pressure canner is always ready for use. Some manufacturers suggest lightly coating the gasket with cooking oil, but check your owner's manual before doing this.

Metal-to-metal cover with wing nuts

A metal-to-metal cover (see Figure 9-3) doesn't require a gasket to create a tight seal because of the design of this pressure canner; it uses wing nuts.

 To secure a cover with wing nuts, tighten two wing nuts on opposite sides of the canner at the same time. Repeat this process for the remaining wing nuts. Never tighten one nut at a time.

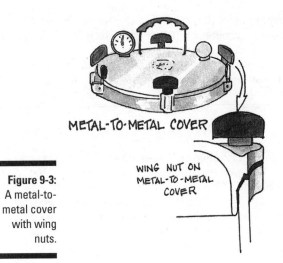

Figure 9-3:
A metal-to-metal cover with wing nuts.

Gauges

Gauges are located on the top of the pressure canner cover and regulate pressure within the canner. Two types of gauges are available: a weighted gauge and a dial gauge (see Figure 9-4).

Figure 9-4:
The two types of gauges available on pressure canners: a dial gauge and a weighted gauge.

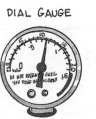

Weighted gauge

A *weighted gauge* is simple and accurate. It's sometimes referred to as an *automatic pressure control* or a *pressure regulator weight*. This gauge allows you to cook without looking: The weighted gauge automatically controls the pressure by jiggling as the canner reaches the correct pressure. When the pressure in the canner is too high, the weighted gauge jiggles faster, and may hiss, as it releases excess steam from the canner.

A weighted gauge has a preset control that needs no service or testing to ensure an accurate pressure measurement. The pressure settings are indicated by three numbers marked on the gauge (refer to Figure 9-4): 5, 10, and 15. The numbers represent the pounds per square inch (psi) of pressure created by the trapped steam from the boiling water in the pressure canner. The most common pressure used in pressure canning is 10 pounds, but never guess — always refer to your recipe.

Dial or steam pressure gauge

A *dial* or *steam pressure gauge* (refer to Figure 9-4) is a numbered instrument that indicates the pressure in the canner. Unlike the weighted gauge that requires no service, this control must be checked for accuracy each season or at least once every year of use. To obtain service, refer to your owner's manual for service locations, check with the store where you purchased the canner, or contact your local Cooperative Extension Services (check the phone book, possibly under the name of your county).

If your annual service shows that your dial gauge is off by 5 or more pounds, replace the gauge. An inaccurate reading may not produce the temperature required to kill all microorganisms.

Vent tube, pipe vent, or petcock

Whatever the name — *vent tube, pipe vent,* or *petcock* — the function is the same. These terms refer to an opening in the pressure-canner cover (shown in Figure 9-5) for emitting steam. Sometimes the weighted gauge sits on the vent tube.

Pressure canning at altitude

If you're canning at an elevation higher than 1,000 feet above sea level, adjust the pounds of pressure used during processing, according to the following table. Your pressure-canner processing time will remain the same.

Altitude (in feet)	Weighted Gauge	Dial Gauge
0 to 1,000	10	11
1,001 to 2,000	15	11
2,001 to 4,000	15	12
4,001 to 6,000	15	13
6,001 to 8,000	15	14
8,001 to 10,000	15	15

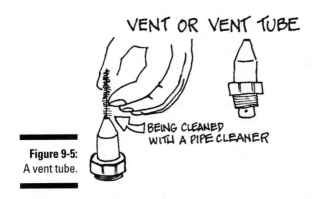

VENT OR VENT TUBE

BEING CLEANED
WITH A PIPE CLEANER

Figure 9-5:
A vent tube.

Make sure that the vent tube opening is never obstructed with food or other matter. Obstructions in this vent may interfere with the operation of the canner by restricting the optimum pressure and temperature required for your recipe. To check the vent for obstructions, hold it up to the light. If the vent appears to be clogged, insert a piece of wire (or other item suggested in your owner's manual) into the tube. Rinse the vent with hot water. Repeat the procedure if you still see an obstruction.

Overpressure plug

An *overpressure plug* (see Figure 9-6) releases if an overpressure condition exists in your pressure canner due to a blocked vent tube. The overpressure plug is a safety feature that's solely for your protection. If you follow the instruction manual for your pressure-canner operation, chances are this plug will never release.

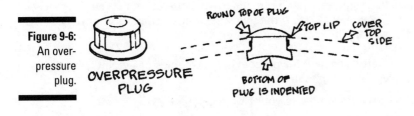

Figure 9-6:
An over-
pressure
plug.

ROUND TOP OF PLUG

TOP LIP   COVER
TOP
SIDE

OVERPRESSURE
PLUG

BOTTOM OF
PLUG IS INDENTED

Rack

Your pressure canner should come with a rack. (If the rack is missing, contact the store where you made your purchase.) The perfect rack will lie flat in the bottom of your canner and has lots of holes and openings that allows steam to circulate around your filled jars. Figure 9-7 is an example of a canner rack.

Figure 9-7:
A rack for holding jars in the bottom of your pressure canner.

A RACK FOR HOLDING JARS IN THE BOTTOM OF YOUR PRESSURE CANNER

Make sure your rack is stable when you place it in the bottom of the canner. A stable rack holds jars in place, thus preventing the jars from tipping, touching other jars, or touching the sides of the canner.

Price

The cost of a pressure canner can vary from $100 on the low end to upwards of $300. Some reasons for the variance are size, features, and reputation of the manufacturer. When making your purchasing decision, study your options and estimate how frequently (or infrequently) you plan to pressure can. You may even consider co-owning a pressure canner with a friend.

Putting Additional Equipment in Order

In addition to equipment that's specific to pressure canners (see the preceding section), you may also find the following items helpful (for more detailed descriptions of any item, refer to Chapter 2):

- ✔ A large kettle (or two) for precooking vegetables or heating your liquid and keeping your jars hot.
- ✔ A food scale for weighing your raw vegetables.
- ✔ Measuring cups and measuring spoons (preferably, heatproof ones).
- ✔ Plenty of canning jars for your food (no chips, cracks, or stains).
- ✔ Two-piece caps (lids and screw bands) made for your canning jars. The lids should be brand-new without dents or scratches. The screw bands should be in good condition, with no signs of corrosion or dents.
- ✔ A ladle for adding liquid to the jars.

✔ A wide-mouth funnel for quickly and neatly filling your jars.

✔ A lid wand for removing the lids from the hot-water kettle.

✔ A jar lifter for transferring the hot jars into and out of your canner.

✔ Dishtowels or paper towels.

A Canning You Will Go: Instructions for Successful Pressure Canning

In order to ensure a processed product of high quality, free from microorganisms, be sure to follow each step in this section. Don't omit or modify any part. You may spend a bit more time canning low-acid foods with a pressure canner than you would canning high-acid foods in a water-bath canner, but the end result is worth the extra effort.

Always read the manufacturer's instructions for your pressure canner and follow them to the letter.

Gearing up

Check your pressure canner at least a week before you want to use it, replacing any gasket or missing part, having a dial gauge checked professionally, or replacing a missing manual. Also, select your recipe, count your jars and two-piece caps, inventory your pantry for any nonperishable ingredients, and add any needed items to your shopping list.

Preparing your food

Wash all food prior to packing it in the jars or precooking it. (For detailed instructions on washing your food, refer to Figure 3-1.) Thoroughly cut away all evidence of spoilage or discard any inferior products.

Always start with food of the highest, freshest quality. Food that's spoiled or bruised doesn't improve in quality during the pressure-canning process!

Work in manageable batches. You may determine this by considering how much food fills one canner load at a time. Most recipes are geared for manageable batches, but if you're in doubt, check the yield for the recipe.

Filling your jars

Always place your product into hot jars. Keep your clean jars hot by submerging them in a kettle of hot water (see "Getting step-by-step instructions for canning low-acid foods" in this chapter) until you're ready to fill them. Then remove the jars from the kettle, one at a time. Always work quickly, stopping for nothing. Time is of the essence!

You may choose to fill your jars with raw food, or you may want to precook the food (see Chapter 10). If you're precooking your low-acid food before filling your jars, don't discard the cooking liquid; use this liquid for filling your jars. Be sure to divide the cooking liquid evenly among the jars. That way, if you run short of the cooking liquid, you won't have one jar filled with only boiling water.

Placing the jars in the canner

Place your filled and closed jars carefully on the rack in the pressure canner. Don't crowd the jars or place more jars in the canner than is recommended for your size of pressure canner. Place them so that they're stable, won't tip, and don't touch each other or the side of the canner.

Unlike water-bath canning (see Chapter 4), you can process a second layer of pint or half-pint jars at the same time as long as your canner accommodates the height of the two layers. To build the second layer, place a second rack on top of the first layer of jars. Stagger the second layer of jars so they aren't directly above the bottom layer. This permits proper air circulation for achieving the proper pressure and temperature.

Closing the canner

Closely follow your owner's manual when closing and locking the pressure canner. You must allow steam to steadily escape from the canner for the specified period for optimum performance. This process is called *exhaustion*.

Releasing the pressure after processing

I can't emphasize enough the importance of following the instructions in your owner's manual, step by step, for releasing the pressure in the canner after your processing time is concluded. There's no quick-release method for a pressure canner as there is for a pressure cooker. Don't confuse the two!

Running water over your pressure canner to reduce the pressure is a definite no-no. The sudden change in temperature can cause the jars to burst.

Cooling the jars

Remove your jars from the canner and place them on a dry towel away from drafts. A jar lifter (refer to Figure 2-7) is the perfect tool for this job.

The jars may take as long as 24 hours to completely cool. Don't be tempted to play with the lids or adjust the bands. After verifying a successful seal (refer to Figure 4-2), remove the bands and wash the jars and the bands in warm, soapy water. Dry them well and store them in a cool, dry place after labeling each jar with the product and the date of processing.

As your jars cool, you'll hear a popping noise coming from them, indicating a vacuum seal. I refer to this sound as *canning music*. After more than 20 years of successful canning, I was taught by my friend Joyce (a canning guru with more than 50 years of experience) to say "thank you" each time I hear one of my jar lids pop. Joyce told me that saying "thank you" ensures the sealing of all of the jars. I now thank each and every jar for singing to me.

Getting step-by-step instructions for canning low-acid foods

In this section, you begin your journey of pressure canning low-acid foods. Avoid any temptation to omit any step or portion of any step in the process. Each step is important to produce safe, home-canned foods.

1. **Assemble your prechecked equipment and utensils.**

   After examining the jars for nicks or chips, the screw bands for proper fit and corrosion, and the new lids for imperfections and scratches, wash them in warm, soapy water, rinsing well to remove any soap residue. Discard any damaged items immediately.

2. **Place your clean jars and lids in a kettle of hot — not boiling — water until you're ready to fill them.**

   Never boil the lids because the sealant material may be damaged and won't produce a safe vacuum seal.

3. **Ready your canner by filling it with 2 to 3 inches of water and heating the water.**

   Refer to your owner's manual for specific instructions.

4. **Prepare the food by precisely following your recipe.**

5. **Fill the jars, packing the food into one jar at a time, so that the food is snug, yet loose enough for liquid to circulate into the open spaces.**

6. **Ladle boiling water (or the liquid from precooking the vegetables) into the jars.**

   Leave the amount of headspace (refer to Figure 2-14) stated in your recipe.

7. **Release any air bubbles with a nonmetallic spatula or a tool to free bubbles (refer to Figure 8-1).**

   If the headspace drops, add additional food and liquid to the jar.

8. **Wipe the jar rims with a clean, damp cloth.**

9. **Place a lid on the jar (seal side down) and secure the lid in place with a screw band.**

   Hand-tighten the band without overly tightening it.

10. **Place the jars on the rack in the bottom of the canner, making sure you have the recommended amount of simmering water in the bottom of the canner.**

11. **Following the instructions in the owner's manual, lock the cover.**

12. **Allow a steady stream of steam to escape from the pressure canner for 10 minutes or the time recommended in your manual.**

13. **Close the vent, bringing the pressure to the amount specified in your recipe.**

    Processing time starts when your canner reaches the required pressure. The pressure must remain constant for the entire processing time.

    If your pressure drops at any time during processing, so will your temperature. To remedy this problem, return the pressure to the specified amount by increasing the heat. After your pressure has been regained, start your processing time from the beginning.

14. **After the processing time has passed, turn the heat off and allow the pressure to return to 0.**

    Allowing the pressure to return to 0 may take as long as 30 minutes. Don't disturb the canner; jars that are upset may not seal properly.

15. **Approximately 15 minutes after the pressure returns to 0, or at the time stated in the manual, remove the lid, opening the cover away from you and allowing the steam to flow away from you.**

16. **After 10 minutes, remove the jars from the pressure canner with a jar lifter, placing them on a clean towel, away from drafts with 1 to 2 inches of space around the jars.**

    Don't adjust the bands or attempt to check the seals.

17. **Completely cool the jars.**

    Cooling the jars may take 12 to 24 hours.

18. **Test the seals on completely cooled jars by pushing on the center of the lid (refer to Figure 4-2).**

    If the lid feels solid and doesn't indent, you've produced a successful seal. If the lid depresses when applying pressure, this jar isn't sealed. Refrigerate any unsealed jars immediately, using the contents within two weeks or the period stated in your recipe.

19. **Remove the screw bands of the sealed jars.**

20. **Remove any residue by washing the jars, lids, and bands in hot, soapy water.**

21. **Label your jars including a date.**

22. **Store the jars without the screw bands, in a cool, dark, dry place.**

Taking Precautions after Processing

Although you may follow all the steps and procedures for pressure canning low-acid foods (see the preceding section), you still have a chance for spoilage. Knowing the signs to look for is part of the food-preservation process. The following sections show you the basics.

Paying attention to your canned foods

Here are some visual signs that may indicate a spoiled product:

- A bulging lid or a broken seal
- A lid that shows signs of corrosion
- Food that has oozed or seeped under the lid
- Gassiness, indicated by tiny bubbles moving upward in the jar
- Food that looks mushy, moldy, or cloudy
- Food that gives off an unpleasant or disagreeable odor when the jar is opened
- Spurting liquid from the jar when the seal is broken

Storing your sealed jars without the bands allows you to see any signs of food seepage that indicates a potentially spoiled product.

As discussed in Chapter 3, botulism poisoning can be fatal. Because botulism spores have no odor and can't be seen, you can't always tell which jars are tainted. *If you suspect that a jar of food is spoiled, never, never, never taste it.* Proceed to the following section and dispose of the food responsibly.

Responsibly disposing of spoiled food

Occasionally, you'll need to dispose of spoiled low-acid foods. Here are two disposal methods, one for sealed jars and one for jars with broken seals.

If your jar is still sealed

If the jar has the seal intact, you can simply discard the unopened container in the trash or bury it deeply in the soil. This keeps the product from coming in contact with any human or animal and eliminates the transfer of bacteria.

If your jar has a broken seal

If you see signs that the seal is broken or not tight, place the jar, the lid, the screw band, and the contents of the jar in a deep cooking pot. Cover the items with 1 to 2 inches of water, taking care not to splash any of the contents outside of the pot, which can cause cross-contamination with other foods in your household.

Cover the pot with a tight-fitting cover. Bring the contents to a boil. Keep the contents boiling for 30 minutes. Turn off the heat and allow the contents to cool while remaining covered. Discard the contents in a sealed container in the trash or bury them deeply in the soil.

Never pour the contents into a water source, a sink or garbage disposal, or down the toilet, because the contents may come into contact with humans or animals through a water-reclamation process.

Using a solution made up of one part household chlorine bleach to four parts *tepid* water (that's lukewarm water), thoroughly wash all equipment, working surfaces, clothing, and body parts that may have come in contact with the jar or spoiled food. You may also add dishwashing soap. Dispose of the jar, the lid and screw band, and any sponges or dishcloths used in any phase of this process by wrapping the items in a trash bag, sealing the bag, and placing it in the trash.

Chapter 10

Preserving the Harvest: Just Vegetables

. . . .

In This Chapter

▶ Organizing your vegetables

▶ Filling your jars: raw packing versus hot packing

▶ Processing vegetables perfectly

▶ Preparing nutritious meals from your canned vegetables

. . . .

D on't you just love the time of year when you're starting your garden —
preparing the soil, sowing seeds, pulling weeds, looking for pests, and
asking the gardening gods for perfect weather and an abundant harvest?
Then, after months of hard work and dirty fingernails, you're rewarded with
fresh vegetables. At first, your garden produces enough each day for one or
two meals, and then the explosion starts. Tomatoes, zucchini, and beans, to
name a few, abound. You wonder, "How can just a few plants produce so
many vegetables?" You're proud to share your bounty with friends, neigh-
bors, and coworkers, but there's a limit to how much you can give away!

Now, reality sets in. You have to do something with this harvest or it will go
to waste! It's time to get out your pressure canner, check your equipment,
and get busy pressure canning. You must act quickly if you plan to preserve
these vegetables for use in the winter and spring.

Even if you don't have a garden (or access to one), you can find vegetables of
high quality at your local farmers' market or supermarket. Purchasing vegetables in season (when they're abundant) is usually the best time to find the
best pricing. Look for vegetables that are locally grown — they'll taste fresher
and won't be covered with wax that prolongs the life of veggies.

This chapter gives you basic information on selecting and preparing your
vegetables, understanding which packing method (raw or hot) works best,
knowing the correct pressure and processing times, and using the proper jar
sizes for your vegetables.

Selecting Your Vegetables

When choosing your vegetables, be picky. The quality of your final product is affected by the quality of the food you start with. Whether harvesting your vegetables from the garden or shopping at a farmers' market or your local supermarket, follow these guidelines when selecting your vegetables:

- ✔ **Before choosing your food, read the vegetable selection guidelines in the "Pressure Canning Your Vegetables" section of this chapter.**

- ✔ **Select vegetables that are free of bruises and imperfections.** These marks could encourage the growth of bacteria in your food.

  My basic rule for evaluating damage on vegetables for canning is "If I won't eat that portion of the vegetable, I won't buy it and can it."

- ✔ **Process the vegetables the day of harvesting or purchasing — the sooner the better.** If you need to wait a day, store the items in your refrigerator to preserve the quality and prevent deterioration of your food. Don't make your vegetables wait longer than one day!

Cleaning your vegetables

Properly cleaning your vegetables is important to your finished product (refer to Figure 3-1). The method and amount of cleaning required is determined by where the vegetables were grown: above the ground (like beans or squash) or in the ground (like carrots or beets).

Vegetables growing above the ground

These vegetables usually have a thinner, more tender skin than vegetables grown in the ground. Remove any stems and leaves. Run water over them, gently rub the skin with your fingers and remove any dirt. Shake off the excess water and place your food on clean kitchen or paper towels.

Gathering your supplies

During the canning season (summer), canning supplies may be in short supply and challenging to find. Inventorying your products early and purchasing missing items keeps you ready to can on a moment's notice. Jars, lids, and screw bands don't have a shelf life or expiration date.

About one week before you begin pressure canning, assemble and check your equipment (see Chapter 9). Locate your recipe and review the ingredients you'll need to have on hand. Stopping at any stage of food preparing or processing adversely affects the quality of your final product.

Vegetables growing in the ground

Root vegetables, such as carrots and beets, may require soaking to loosen any clinging soil. After first rinsing the vegetables, immerse them in a basin of cool water. Using a stiff brush (a new toothbrush works well), scrub the surface of the vegetables, removing any clinging soil. Rinse thoroughly with running water, placing the vegetables on clean kitchen or paper towels to drain.

Knowing which vegetables are not recommended for pressure canning

Some vegetables shouldn't be preserved by pressure canning because the food may discolor, produce a stronger flavor when canned, or just lose its look (meaning it disintegrates or falls apart when placed under high heat and high pressure). Other methods, such as pickling (see Chapter 8) or freezing (see Chapter 14), may be better preserving choices for these foods. Table 10-1 lists some vegetables you may be tempted to pressure can but that will preserve better in other ways.

Table 10-1	Vegetables Not Recommended for Pressure Canning
Vegetable	**Suggested Preservation Method**
Broccoli	Freezing
Brussels sprouts	Freezing
Cabbage	Pickling (to make sauerkraut)
Cauliflower	Pickling
Cucumbers	Pickling
Eggplant	Pickling
Mushrooms	Pickling (They must be an edible variety. For safety, use ones that are commercially grown; don't go out and pick some yourself.)
Onions	Pickling
Parsnips	Pickling
Rutabagas	Pickling
Turnips	Pickling

Understanding Preparation Methods before Filling Your Jars

You can prepare your clean vegetables for filling your jars in two ways: raw or hot. Not all vegetables are suited for both methods. Follow your recipe instructions or check out the "Pressure Canning Your Vegetables" section in this chapter.

Raw (cold) packing

The *raw packing* method uses raw, unheated vegetables for filling your prepared jars. Filling the jars with raw vegetables keeps them firm without being crushed during processing. Refer to your recipe instructions to decide whether to remove the skin or cut the vegetables into pieces.

Disadvantages of using raw vegetables include the following:

- **Floating food:** During the pressure-canning process, air is removed from the vegetable fiber, causing the food to shrink. With more room in the jars, the vegetables have room to float toward the top of the jar (this is called *floating food*). Floating food doesn't affect the quality of your final product, but it may be unattractive.

- **Discoloring:** *Discoloring* occurs when the food comes in contact with air in the jar, causing a color change in your food after two or three months of storage. The flavor of your product is not affected, but the change in color in a portion of the food may appear odd.

To fill your jars using a raw packing method, follow these instructions:

1. **Wash your vegetables.**

2. **Prepare the hot liquid (refer to your recipe) for filling your jars.**

3. **Fill the hot, prepared jars with your raw vegetables.**

4. **Add the hot liquid.**

5. **Release any air bubbles with a nonreactive tool (refer to Figure 8-1).**

   If the headspace in your jar drops, add additional food and liquid to maintain the headspace stated in your recipe.

6. **Wipe the jar rims; add the two-piece caps, and process the filled jars (see Chapter 9).**

Hot packing

Hot packing is precooking or heating your vegetables prior to placing them in your prepared canning jars. It's the preferred method for the majority of vegetables, particularly firm ones, such as carrots and beets. Using precooked vegetables improves the shelf life of the processed food by increasing the vacuum created in the jar during the pressure-canning period.

Precooking your vegetables in a boiling liquid, usually water, preshrinks the food and makes it more pliable, which allows you to pack more food into your jars. This results in using fewer jars. The method is a simple one:

1. **Wash your vegetables.**

2. **Heat your liquid to a boil in a large pot.**

3. **Add the vegetables; precook them as directed in your recipe.**

4. **Immediately fill your prepared jars with the hot vegetables, followed with the hot cooking liquid (see Chapter 9).**

5. **Release any air bubbles with a nonreactive tool (refer to Figure 8-1).**

   If the headspace in your jar drops, add additional food and liquid to maintain the headspace stated in your recipe.

6. **Wipe the jar rims, add the two-piece caps, and process the filled jars (see Chapter 9).**

Processing tips for successful results

In addition to the pressure-canner-processing steps in Chapter 9, use these tips for producing a product of high quality that's safe for eating.

- ✔ **Add salt.** Using or not using salt in your vegetables is a personal preference. Add ½ teaspoon to a 1-pint jar and 1 teaspoon to a 1-quart jar before adding the hot liquid.

  Use salt without additives (check the label), such as pickling or canning salt. This eliminates cloudiness in the liquid.

- ✔ **Cover the vegetables with liquid, allowing the proper headspace (refer to Figure 2-14).** This prevents discoloration and spoilage.

- ✔ **Release air bubbles.** Releasing all trapped air bubbles between the food pieces prevents a decrease in the liquid level of your final product, keeping the correct air space in the jar. After releasing air bubbles, you may need to add additional food or liquid to the jar (see Figure 8-1).

✔ **Be ready to process your jars immediately after filling them.** This decreases the opportunity for microorganisms to re-enter the jars.

✔ **Cool your jars.** Let your jars cool naturally. This may take as long as 24 hours.

Pressure Canning Your Vegetables

In this section, you get instructions and guidelines for pressure canning some of the more common fresh vegetables. Included are tips for selecting your vegetables, determining the approximate amounts of fresh vegetables for yielding 1 quart of a finished product, and which method is preferred.

Before you begin, take a few minutes to acquaint yourself with the steps for pressure-canner processing in Chapter 9. Always check your recipe to ensure you're processing your food for the correct time, pressure, and jar size.

When canning at altitudes over 1,000 feet above sea level, refer to the altitude chart in Chapter 9 for pressure adjustments.

Packing food raw or hot doesn't change your processing time. Reaching the required pressure in your canner, usually 10 pounds, takes the same amount of time, regardless of the temperature of your raw- or hot-packed jars.

If it's safe to use either quart jars or pints jars for your vegetables, I list the correct processing time for each size. Quarts take longer to process than pints because there's a larger amount of food to heat to properly destroy all microorganisms.

Use only one size jar (pints or quarts) for each batch of food. This allows you to complete the correct processing time required to evenly heat the jars and destroy microorganisms.

Asparagus

Select firm, bright-green stalks with tightly closed tips. Stalks with small diameters indicate a young, tender vegetable. Cut stalks into 1-inch pieces or can them whole, placing the tips of the stalks toward the top of the jar.

✔ **Quantity guide:** 3 to 4 pounds for a 1-quart jar.

✔ **Hot pack preferred:** Submerge asparagus in boiling water for 2 to 3 minutes. When the food is cool enough to handle, pack the food into the prepared jars.

✔ **Headspace:** 1 inch for asparagus and liquid.

✔ **Processing time:** At 10 pounds for 30 minutes (pints), 40 minutes (quarts).

Beans

Whether the beans you use are fresh or dried, thoroughly examine them. Select fresh beans free from bruising, rust, or mushiness; discard any beans fitting this description. Examine dried beans for any nonbean material, such as stems or stones.

Green (pole or bush), string, Italian, or wax

Choose tender, small beans. Remove the ends and strings from the beans, as shown in Figure 10-1. Can them whole or cut them into 1- to 2-inch pieces.

✔ **Quantity guide:** 1½ to 2 pounds for a 1-quart jar.

✔ **Raw pack:** Place the washed beans into your prepared jars, packing them tightly and covering them with boiling water.

  • **Headspace:** ½ inch for beans and liquid.

  • **Processing time:** At 10 pounds for 20 minutes (pints), 25 minutes (quarts).

✔ **Hot pack:** Add the beans to boiling water; continue boiling for 5 minutes. Pack the beans into the prepared jars, adding the boiling cooking liquid.

  • **Headspace:** ½ inch for beans and liquid.

  • **Processing time:** At 10 pounds for 20 minutes (pints), 25 minutes (quarts).

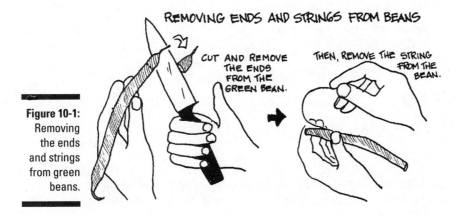

REMOVING ENDS AND STRINGS FROM BEANS

CUT AND REMOVE THE ENDS FROM THE GREEN BEAN.

THEN, REMOVE THE STRING FROM THE BEAN.

Figure 10-1: Removing the ends and strings from green beans.

Lima or butter

Purchase beans in the shell to ensure freshness, discarding any beans showing signs of rust or mushiness.

- ✔ **Quantity guide:** 4 to 5 pounds for a 1-quart jar.
- ✔ **Hot pack preferred:** Shell the beans by popping open the casing and placing the loose beans in a colander for washing. Add the beans to boiling water, removing them after 3 minutes. Pack the hot beans into the prepared jars, filling with boiling cooking liquid.
- ✔ **Headspace:** 1 inch for beans and liquid.

  Use a wire or bamboo strainer to quickly remove the beans from the boiling water.
- ✔ **Processing time:** At 10 pounds for 40 minutes (pints), 50 minutes (quarts). Increase the processing time for beans over ¾ inch in diameter by 10 minutes for pints and quarts.

Dried (kidney, navy, pinto, split peas, and so on)

Rinse the beans before you soak them to remove any dust or dirt particles. You can easily accomplish this by placing the beans in a colander and running cold water over them while stirring them with your hands or a spoon.

- ✔ **Quantity guide:** 1 to 1¼ pounds dried beans for a 1-quart jar.
- ✔ **Hot pack preferred:** Place the beans in a large pot. Fill the pot with enough cold water to cover the beans. Place a cover on the beans, allowing them to soak, undisturbed, for 12 to 18 hours. Drain the beans, adding fresh cold water to the pot to cover the beans by 2 inches. Bring the liquid to a boil and continue boiling for 30 minutes. Pack the hot beans into your prepared jars, adding the boiling cooking liquid.
- ✔ **Headspace:** 1 inch for beans and liquid.
- ✔ **Processing time:** At 10 pounds for 1 hour and 15 minutes (pints), 1 hour and 30 minutes (quarts).

Beets

Select beets with a deep red color. A beet with a diameter of 1 to 2 inches is the most desirable size for this method. Larger-size beets are best pickled (refer to Chapter 8).

Preserving the bright, red color of the beet is achieved by adding 1 tablespoon of vinegar (with an acidity of 5 percent) to each quart of liquid.

✔ **Quantity guide:** 2½ to 3½ pounds for a 1-quart jar.

✔ **Hot pack preferred:** Remove all but 2 inches of the stem, leaving the *taproot* (the main root growing downward into the ground from the bottom of the beet) intact (see Figure 10-2). Scrub any clinging dirt from the beet with a stiff brush. Add the beets to boiling water, cooking them until they're easily pierced with a fork (about 10 to 20 minutes, depending on the size of the beet) and the skins peel off easily. Slice, dice, or leave the beets whole before filling your prepared jars. Add clean, boiling water.

✔ **Headspace:** 1 inch for beets and liquid.

✔ **Processing time:** At 10 pounds for 30 minutes (pints), 35 minutes (quarts).

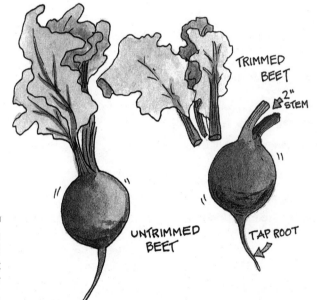

Figure 10-2:
A trimmed beet ready for precooking.

Bell peppers (green, red, orange, yellow)

Sweet, firm bell peppers produce the best results. Because of the extremely low acid level in this vegetable, you must adjust the acidity level of the bell peppers by adding bottled lemon juice. Use only pint or half-pint jars for this extremely low-acid vegetable.

✔ **Quantity guide:** 1 pound for a 1-pint jar.

✔ **Hot pack preferred:** Remove the bell pepper stem, core, and seeds. Cut the bell peppers into large (about 2- to 3-inch), uniform pieces. Boil the bell peppers for 3 minutes, draining and packing them immediately after cooking. (You can remove the skin by plunging the cooked bell peppers into cold water and peeling off the loose skins, but this is optional.) Pack the bell peppers into your prepared jars. Add 1 tablespoon of bottled lemon juice to each jar, and then fill with the boiling cooking liquid.

✔ **Headspace:** 1 inch for bell peppers; ½ inch for liquid.

✔ **Processing time:** At 10 pounds for 35 minutes (pints).

Carrots

Use carrots with a diameter of 1 to 1½ inches. Remove clinging dirt from carrots with thin, tender skins by rinsing and scrubbing with a brush. If you prefer carrots without the skin, remove the outer layer with a vegetable peeler. Always remove the tops.

✔ **Quantity guide:** 2½ to 3 pounds (cleaned and peeled, if desired, with tops removed) for a 1-quart jar.

✔ **Hot pack preferred:** Slice, dice, or keep the carrots whole. Simmer the carrots in boiling water for 5 minutes. Pack the hot carrots into your prepared jars, using the cooking liquid to fill the jars.

✔ **Headspace:** 1 inch for carrots and liquid.

✔ **Processing time:** At 10 pounds for 25 minutes (pints), 30 minutes (quarts).

Corn, whole kernel

Starting with corn that has the husks on and the silk attached allows you to assess the freshness of the corn. Choose ears with brightly colored husks that are free of spots and moisture; silks should be golden, not matted or brown.

My mother-in-law, Phyllis, taught me this method for selecting corn that's always sweet and tender: Slightly peel back the husk to check for any pests. If all is clear (no bugs or mold), use your thumbnail to depress a kernel about an inch below the top of the corn. If the ear has adequate moisture, liquid will squirt out, sometimes hitting you in the eye (see Figure 10-3). Buy this ear! If no spitting occurs, select another ear and repeat the test.

- ✔ **Quantity guide:** 4 to 5 pounds (weighed with husks on) for a 1-quart jar.

- ✔ **Hot pack preferred:** Remove and discard the husks and silk. Using a sharp knife, cut the kernels from each ear. Measure the corn to calculate water for cooking: For each pint of corn, add 1 cup of boiling water; for each quart of corn, add 2 cups of boiling water. Bring the measured corn and water to a boil, cooking for 5 minutes. Transfer the corn to your prepared jars, adding the boiling cooking liquid.

- ✔ **Headspace:** 1 inch for corn and liquid.

- ✔ **Processing time:** At 10 pounds for 55 minutes (pints), 1 hour and 25 minutes (quarts).

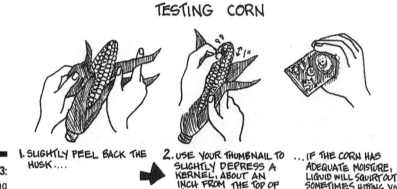

TESTING CORN

1. SLIGHTLY PEEL BACK THE HUSK....

2. USE YOUR THUMBNAIL TO SLIGHTLY DEPRESS A KERNEL, ABOUT AN INCH FROM THE TOP OF THE EAR OF CORN.

...IF THE CORN HAS ADEQUATE MOISTURE, LIQUID WILL SQUIRT OUT, SOMETIMES HITTING YOU IN THE EYE! ☆ BUY THIS ONE!

Figure 10-3: Testing corn.

Greens (beet, collard, kale, mustard, spinach, Swiss chard, turnip)

Select tender stems and leaves to produce a superior product after cooking and pressure canning. Large, older stems and leaves tend to produce a strong-tasting or stringy product.

- ✔ **Quantity guide:** 3 to 4 pounds for a 1-quart jar.

- ✔ **Hot pack preferred:** After washing, wilt the greens in batches by immersing them in just enough boiling water in a pot to prevent sticking. Wilting times vary from 2 to 5 minutes because of the size of the leaf and the quantity in each batch. Turn the leaves to cook evenly. Slice the wilted leaves before filling the prepared jars for a tight pack — this eliminates trapped air bubbles. Add boiling water, including any left from the wilting process.

✔ **Headspace:** 1 inch for greens and liquid.

✔ **Processing time:** At 10 pounds for 1 hour and 10 minutes (pints), 1 hour and 30 minutes (quarts).

Okra

Fresh okra is a pod that's best used when under 4 inches in length.

✔ **Quantity guide:** About 1½ pounds for a 1-quart jar.

✔ **Hot pack preferred:** Remove the stems, leaving the caps on for precooking and packing whole (see Figure 10-4). Cover the okra with boiling water; cook for 1 minute and drain. If you're cutting the pods into 1-inch pieces, remove the caps before packing. Fill your prepared jars, adding the boiling cooking liquid.

✔ **Headspace:** 1 inch for okra and liquid.

✔ **Processing time:** At 10 pounds for 25 minutes (pints), 40 minutes (quarts).

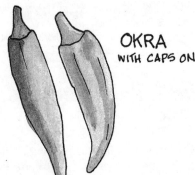

OKRA
WITH CAPS ON

Figure 10-4:
Okra pod
with the
cap on.

Peas

Use peas with a diameter smaller than ⅓ inch. If you use peas larger than ⅓ inch, add an additional 10 minutes of processing time for pints or quarts.

✔ **Quantity guide:** 4 to 5 pounds for a 1-quart jar.

✔ **Hot pack preferred:** After removing the peas from the pods, add them to boiling water, cooking as follows: small peas (diameter smaller than ¼ inch) for 3 minutes; medium peas (with a diameter of ¼ to ⅓ inch) for 5 minutes. Remove the peas from the boiling water and place them in a colander, rinsing them with hot water. Pack the peas in your prepared jars, adding the boiling cooking liquid.

✔ **Headspace:** 1 inch for peas and liquid.

✔ **Processing time:** At 10 pounds for 40 minutes (pints and quarts).

Potatoes

The only potatoes recommended for pressure canning are sweet potatoes, yams, and white, or Irish, potatoes. Using any other potatoes yields inferior results because of their chemical makeup (texture and composition).

Sweet potatoes and yams

Sweet potatoes are roots and yams are tubers — so they're actually from two different plant species. Even though sweet potatoes and yams are unrelated, they're suitable for the same uses.

Sweet potatoes have skin colors ranging from light yellow to dark orange and flesh colors ranging from pale yellow to medium orange and are sweeter than yams. Yams contain more natural sugar and have a higher moisture content than sweet potatoes; they're white to deep red in flesh color with skin colors ranging from creamy white to deep red. Small potatoes may be left whole; cut larger ones into quarters before removing the skins.

✔ **Quantity guide:** 2½ to 3 pounds for a 1-quart jar.

✔ **Hot pack preferred:** Precook vegetables in boiling water until the peels can be rubbed off, about 5 to 15 minutes. Pack hot food into your prepared jars, adding clean boiling water or a boiling sweet syrup (2½ cups granulated sugar and 5¼ cups water brought to a boil, yielding about 6½ cups of liquid).

✔ **Headspace:** 1 inch for potatoes and liquid.

✔ **Processing time:** At 10 pounds for 1 hour and 5 minutes (pints), 1 hour and 30 minutes (quarts).

White or Irish

These potatoes are round and white with a thin skin. Peel the potatoes prior to precooking. Small potatoes (2 to 3 inches in diameter) may be left whole; cut larger potatoes into quarters before precooking.

- ✔ **Quantity guide:** About 5 pounds for a 1-quart jar.
- ✔ **Hot pack preferred:** Cover the potatoes with water in a large pot, bring the contents to a boil, and boil for 10 minutes. Drain the potatoes, reserving the cooking liquid. Pack the cooked potatoes into your prepared jars, adding the reserved boiling cooking liquid.
- ✔ **Headspace:** 1 inch for potatoes and liquid.
- ✔ **Processing time:** At 10 pounds for 35 minutes (pints), 40 minutes (quarts).

Summer squash

Summer squash include crookneck, zucchini, and patty pan, to name a few. The skins are thin and edible, eliminating the need to peel them.

- ✔ **Quantity guide:** 2 to 2½ pounds for a 1-quart jar.
- ✔ **Hot pack preferred:** Cut the squash into even-sized slices or cubes. Steam or boil the squash for 2 to 3 minutes. Pack the hot pieces into your prepared jars, filling the jars with boiling water including any left-over from precooking.
- ✔ **Headspace:** ½ inch for squash and liquid.
- ✔ **Processing time:** At 10 pounds for 30 minutes (pints), 40 minutes (quarts).

Winter squash and pumpkins

Other squash that's good for canning includes banana, butternut, Hubbard, spaghetti, and turban squash. Because pumpkins are similar in texture, you can use these instructions also. This process is a bit labor-intensive, but the rewards are oh, so good!

- ✔ **Quantity guide:** 2 to 3 pounds for a 1-quart jar.
- ✔ **Hot pack preferred:** Cut the squash into pieces (about 1 inch by 3 inches), scraping out the fiber and the seeds. Place the pieces in a large pot, adding just enough water to cover the pieces. Boil the squash

until it's soft and is easily pierced with a fork, about 10 to 30 minutes depending on the variety you're using. Scrape the pulp from the softened skin and mash it or run it through a food mill. Return the squash to the pot and bring the contents to a boil, stirring constantly to keep it from sticking. Upon boiling, transfer the squash to your prepared jars.

- **Headspace:** 1 inch.
- **Processing time:** At 10 pounds for 55 minutes (pints), 1 hour and 30 minutes (quarts).

Using Canned Vegetables

Seeing a shelf lined with pressure-canned vegetables is quite rewarding, knowing all the care and effort applied to the process. Are you wondering, though, what you can do with all this nutritious food? Here are a few suggestions for using your pressure-canned vegetables to create easy, nutritious meals:

- **Beans with beef:** Brown ground beef (or any ground meat) in a skillet, stirring and breaking it into pieces. Season with salt, pepper, and your favorite herbs or spices. While the meat is cooking, bring any variety of pressure-canned dried beans to a boil in a large pot, boiling for 10 minutes. Drain the meat, adding it to the beans. Simmer to combine the flavors. Serve over hot noodles with canned peach slices for dessert.

- **Baked chicken with peppers:** Boil 1 pint of bell peppers in a pot for 10 minutes. Pour the bell peppers and the liquid over four to six boneless, skinless chicken breasts placed in an ovenproof pan. Season as you desire. Tightly cover the pan with aluminum foil to seal in all the moisture. Bake the chicken in a preheated 350-degree oven for 30 to 45 minutes, or until the chicken is done. Serve the chicken with the bell pepper pieces over your favorite rice, with a salad on the side.

- **Vegetable soup:** Combine one jar each of corn, carrots, peas, and bell peppers (or your favorite vegetable mix). After boiling your vegetables for 10 minutes, add 1 or 2 cups of dried pasta. Continue boiling the soup until the pasta is tender. Serve the soup in large bowls, topping it with Parmesan cheese shavings and passing a plate of sourdough bread.

When using low-acid, pressure-canned vegetables, always boil your food for 10 minutes *before you taste the food.* For altitudes over 1,000 feet above sea level, extend the boiling period 1 minute for each increase of 1,000 feet.

Chapter 11

Combining the Harvest: Soups, Sauces, and Beans

*W*ith a little bit of advanced planning during the growing season, you'll keep your shelves stocked with a variety of meals for people on the go. In this chapter, I give you tips for combining vegetables and other low-acid foods into savory soups, delectable sauces, or hearty one-pot meals. After your family gets a whiff of the aroma coming out of the kitchen, they'll think you've been slaving over the stove all day!

Combining Foods for Convenience

Pressure canning soups, sauces, and one-pot meals is the answer for healthy, quick meals without filling up your freezer. I find pressure canning a major timesaver in the long run: I spend one day (or even a weekend) preparing soups, sauces, and other hearty meals. Later, I can get a hot meal on the table in a flash and keep my freezer for ice cream and other treats!

Mixing low-acid foods and high-acid foods

In Chapters 4 and 9, you discovered the only processing methods approved by the United States Department of Agriculture (USDA) for safely home-canning food:

✔ **Water-bath canning:** For canning high-acid foods (like fruit and tomatoes)

✔ **Pressure canning:** For canning low-acid foods (including vegetables and meat)

So, knowing that a pot of chili or spaghetti sauce contains both high-acid and low-acid foods (the chili contains tomatoes and vegetables, and the spaghetti sauce contains meat, tomatoes, and vegetables), how do you determine which method is right while still ensuring a safe product? Quite simply, adding low-acid foods to high-acids foods raises the acidity level of the food being processed above 4.6 pH (see Chapter 3). Therefore, pressure canning is the only safe processing method when combining low-acid and high-acid foods.

Don't be tempted to add or adjust the ingredients in your recipe. Any variation changes the acidity level as well as the processing time (and sometimes the processing method) needed to destroy the microorganisms that cause botulism (refer to Chapter 3), the most serious form of food poisoning.

Adding meat, fish, poultry, and seafood

Meat, fish, poultry, and seafood fall into the category of low-acid foods. Although pressure canning is the proper processing method for preserving low-acid foods, freezing is the preferred method (see Chapter 12) for preserving steaks, roasts, poultry, or fish.

When combining meat, fish, poultry, or seafood with other low-acid or high-acid foods, pressure-canner processing is the correct method to use. Sometimes you precook the meat before adding it to your recipe; other times you add the meat raw and it's cooked while the ingredients simmer.

For detailed instructions for pressure canning meat, fish, poultry, or seafood, refer to the *Complete Guide to Home Canning and Preserving,* Second Revised Edition, U.S. Department of Agriculture (Dover Publications, Inc.). This book was originally published as a consumer service of the USDA.

Incorporating pasta and rice

Pasta and rice are wonderful additions to soups, but here's a tip: Don't add uncooked pasta or rice to your food before pressure canning your jars. The intense heat of this process disintegrates your pasta or rice. For example, if your pasta cooking time in boiling water is 8 to 10 minutes and you extended the period to 30 minutes or longer at a temperature higher than boiling water (as occurs in the pressure canner), you'd end up with something that doesn't resemble pasta or rice.

For best results when adding uncooked pasta or rice to your soup, do the following:

1. Complete the 10-minute boiling period for your canned food.

2. Add the pasta (or rice) to the boiling soup, cooking the pasta (or rice) for the time recommended on the pasta (or rice) package.

3. Test the pasta (or rice) for doneness.

Pressure Canning Combination Foods

Process all low-acid combination foods in a pressure canner. Before preparing your product, review the step-by-step instructions in Chapter 9.

For best results, use these tips when making combination foods:

✔ **Cut all ingredients uniformly to ensure even heating.**

✔ **Use the longest processing time given when combining low-acid foods.** For example, the processing time for only corn in a 1-quart jar is 1 hour, 25 minutes, and for only lima beans in a 1-quart jar is 50 minutes. Therefore, the correct processing time for combining corn and lima beans in a 1-quart jar is 1 hour, 25 minutes.

✔ **Always use the jar size recommended in your recipe.** Some combination foods may be canned in either pints or quarts; other foods may be suited only for pints. Use the jar size stated in your recipe.

Stocking Up on Soup

Soup is the ultimate comfort food. The road to great soup starts with a flavorful *stock,* which is water infused with the flavors of vegetables and/or the bones from beef, poultry, or fish. A *reduced stock* is boiled rapidly, thus reducing the amount of liquid by evaporation and producing an intense flavor.

Getting your meal on the table

After selecting a jar from your pantry, follow these simple steps for quick, timesaving meals:

1. Bring your canned food to a boil in a large pot, boiling the food for 10 minutes.

   Don't be tempted to taste your food until after the boiling period has elapsed.

2. Add your seasonings, such as salt, pepper, and fresh herbs.

3. Serve and enjoy!

Veggie Stock

Every vegetarian loves this stock, which is a perfect substitute for chicken stock.

Preparation time: *15 minutes*

Cooking time: *4 hours*

Processing time: *Pints, 30 minutes; quarts, 35 minutes.*

Yield: *About 8 pints or 4 quarts*

7 quarts water	2 small to medium turnips, diced
1 pound carrots, cut into 1-inch pieces	3 garlic cloves, crushed
6 stalks celery, cut into 1-inch pieces	3 bay leaves
3 medium to large onions, quartered	1 tablespoon fresh or 1 teaspoon dried whole thyme
2 red, orange, or yellow bell peppers, cut into 1-inch pieces	8 peppercorns
2 to 4 medium tomatoes, diced	

1 Combine all the ingredients in a 10- to 12-quart sauce pot. Bring the mixture to a boil over high heat. Reduce the heat; simmer, uncovered, for 2 hours. Remove the lid and continue cooking for 2 hours more.

2 While the stock is simmering, prepare the canning jars and two-piece caps (lids and screw bands) according to the manufacturer's instructions. Keep the jars and lids hot. (For information on pressure canning and detailed instructions on preparing and filling your jars and testing the seals, see Chapter 9.)

3 Strain the stock by pouring it through a mesh strainer or several layers of cheesecloth. (Cheesecloth is available in cooking stores and most supermarkets.) Discard the vegetables and seasonings.

4 Ladle the hot stock into your prepared jars, leaving 1 inch of headspace. Wipe the jar rims; seal the jars with the two-piece caps, hand-tightening the bands. Process your filled jars in a pressure canner at 10 pounds for 30 minutes (pints), 35 minutes (quarts).

5 After the pressure in the canner has returned to 0, open the canner and remove the hot jars with a jar lifter. Place them on a clean kitchen towel or paper towels away from drafts. After the jars cool completely, test the seals. (If you find jars that haven't sealed, immediately refrigerate them and use them within one week.) Boil the contents of each jar for 10 minutes before tasting or eating.

Chicken Stock

You can either purchase chicken and reserve the meat for another use (such as the White Chili recipe in this chapter) or use the parts you may not normally eat, such as the neck, the back, the wings, or — as my Uncle Lennie used to call them — the engine parts (the heart, the liver, the gizzards, and so on). These pieces explode with flavor, but using or not using the engine parts is up to you.

Preparation time: 10 minutes

Cooking time: About 2 hours

Processing time: Pints, 20 minutes; quarts, 25 minutes

Yield: About 8 pints or 4 quarts

3 to 4 pounds chicken pieces	*2 medium onions, quartered*
4 quarts water	*15 peppercorns*
2 stalks celery, leaves attached, cut into 1-inch pieces	*3 bay leaves*
	Salt, to taste

1 Combine the chicken and water in a 6- to 8-quart pot; bring the mixture to a boil over high heat. Add the celery, onions, peppercorns, bay leaves, and salt. Reduce the heat; simmer, covered, about 2 hours or until the chicken is tender. Remove from the heat; skim off any foam. Remove the chicken pieces, reserving the chicken for another use.

2 While the stock is simmering, prepare your canning jars and two-piece caps (lids and screw bands) according to the manufacturer's instructions. Keep the jars and lids hot. (For information on pressure canning and detailed instructions on preparing and filling your jars and testing the seals, see Chapter 9.)

3 Strain the stock through a mesh strainer or several layers of cheesecloth. (Cheesecloth is available in cooking stores and most supermarkets.) Allow the stock to cool until the fat solidifies; remove the fat.

4 Return the stock to the pot, bringing it to a boil.

5 Ladle the hot stock into your prepared jars, leaving 1 inch of headspace. Wipe the jar rims; seal the jars with the two-piece caps, hand-tightening the bands. Process your filled jars in a pressure canner at 10 pounds for 20 minutes (pints), 25 minutes (quarts).

6 After the pressure in the canner has returned to 0, open the canner and remove the hot jars with a jar lifter. Place them on a clean kitchen towel or paper towels away from drafts. After the jars cool completely, test the seals. (If you find jars that haven't sealed, immediately refrigerate them and use them within one week.) Boil the contents of each jar for 10 minutes before tasting or eating.

Simmering Split Pea Soup

Whenever I serve ham as a main dish, I always buy one larger than I need. My husband, Chris, always looks forward to his favorite soup made with the leftover ham pieces.

Preparation time: *15 minutes*

Cooking time: *1 hour, 30 minutes*

Processing time: *Pints, 1 hour, 15 minutes; quarts, 1½ hours*

Yield: *About 5 pints or 2 quarts*

16-ounce package dried green or yellow split peas, washed	*1 cup cooked ham pieces*
	1 bay leaf
2 quarts water	*¼ teaspoon allspice*
1 cup chopped onion (about 1 medium onion)	*Salt, to taste*
1½ cups sliced carrots (about 3 carrots)	*Freshly ground pepper, to taste*

1 Place the peas in a 6- to 8-quart pot. Add the water and bring the beans to a boil over high heat. Reduce the heat; simmer, covered, about 1 hour or until the peas are soft. (If you like a smooth soup, press the mixture through a sieve or food mill and return the peas to the pot.

2 Add the onions, carrots, ham, bay leaf, allspice, salt, and pepper; simmer for 30 minutes, uncovered. Remove the bay leaf before filling your jars. (If you prefer a thinner soup, add boiling water to achieve the consistency you desire.)

3 While the soup is simmering, prepare your canning jars and two-piece caps (lids and screw bands) according to the manufacturer's instructions. Keep the jars and lids hot. (For information on pressure canning and detailed instructions on preparing and filling your jars and testing the seals, see Chapter 9.)

4 Ladle the hot soup into your prepared jars, leaving 1 inch of headspace. Wipe the jar rims; seal the jars with the two-piece caps, hand-tightening the bands. Process your filled jars in a pressure canner at 10 pounds for 1 hour and 15 minutes (pints), 1 hour and 30 minutes (quarts).

5 After the pressure in the canner has returned to 0, open the canner and remove the hot jars with a jar lifter. Place them on a clean kitchen towel or paper towels, away from drafts. After the jars cool completely, test the seals. (If you find jars that haven't sealed, immediately refrigerate them and use them within one week.) Boil the contents of each jar for 10 minutes before tasting or eating.

Teaming Up with Tomatoes

In Chapter 4, you discover that tomatoes are a high-acid food and may be safely processed in a water-bath canner. Combining high-acid tomatoes with low-acid vegetables changes the pH (acidity level). These combined foods must be treated and processed as low-acid foods.

Stewed Tomatoes

Homemade stewed tomatoes are perfect in soups or sauces, as a condiment on scrambled eggs, or spooned over steamed summer squash with a grating of cheddar cheese.

Preparation time: *20 minutes*

Cooking time: *15 minutes*

Processing time: *Pints, 15 minutes; quarts, 20 minutes*

Yield: *About 6 pints or 3 quarts*

5 to 6 pounds of peeled tomatoes to measure 4 quarts (refer to Figure 5-1), chopped, and cored, reserving all liquid

1 large stalk celery, chopped

½ medium onion, chopped

¼ green bell pepper, chopped

1 tablespoon granulated sugar

2 teaspoons salt

1 Prepare your canning jars and two-piece caps (lids and screw bands) according to the manufacturer's instructions. Keep the jars and lids hot. (For information on pressure canning and detailed instructions on preparing and filling your jars, releasing air bubbles, and testing the seals, see Chapter 9.)

2 Combine the tomatoes, celery, onions, bell pepper, sugar, and salt in a 5- to 6-quart pot. Bring to a boil over high heat; reduce heat, cover, and simmer for 10 minutes, stirring to prevent sticking.

3 Ladle the hot tomatoes into the prepared jars, leaving 1 inch of headspace. Release any air bubbles (refer to Figure 8-1). Add more tomatoes to maintain a headspace of 1 inch. Wipe the jar rims; seal the jars with the two-piece caps, hand-tightening the bands. Process your filled jars in a pressure canner at 10 pounds for 15 minutes for pints, for 20 minutes for quarts.

4 After the pressure in the canner has returned to 0, open the canner and remove the hot jars with a jar lifter. Place them on a clean kitchen towel or paper towels away from drafts. After the jars cool completely, test the seals. (If you find jars that haven't sealed, immediately refrigerate them and use them within one week.) Boil the contents of each jar for 10 minutes before tasting or eating.

Spaghetti Sauce with Meat

Everyone seems to have his or her favorite recipe for spaghetti sauce. After much recipe testing, this is the one my family likes the best.

Preparation time: *20 minutes*

Cooking time: *2 to 2½ hours*

Processing time: *Pints, 1 hour, 5 minutes*

Yield: *About 5 pints*

12 ounces Italian sausage, bulk or links, mild or hot	2 quarts canned stewed tomatoes, including the liquid
½ pound ground beef or turkey	1 cup red wine
2 medium onions, chopped	1 tablespoon fresh basil, chopped
4 garlic cloves, minced	1 cup chopped Italian flat-leaf parsley
2 carrots, peeled and finely chopped	1 teaspoon salt (omit if salt was added to your canned tomatoes)
2 stalks celery, finely chopped	
½ pound mushrooms, sliced	Freshly ground pepper, to taste
2 6-ounce cans tomato paste	

1 Remove the sausage casings if you're using link sausage. Brown the sausage in a 5- or 6-quart pot over medium heat, stirring to break up the sausage. Add the ground meat and the onions; continue cooking until the meat is brown and the onions are translucent. Drain off any fat.

2 Add the garlic, carrots, celery, and mushrooms; cook an additional 2 to 3 minutes. Add the tomato paste, tomatoes, wine, basil, parsley, salt, and pepper. Bring to a boil over high heat; reduce the heat and simmer, covered, for 1½ to 2 hours, stirring often, until the sauce has thickened.

3 While the sauce is simmering, prepare your canning jars and two-piece caps (lids and screw bands) according to the manufacturer's instructions. Keep the jars and lids hot. (For information on pressure canning and detailed instructions on preparing and filling your jars and testing the seals, see Chapter 9.)

4 Ladle the hot sauce into the prepared jars, leaving 1 inch of headspace. Wipe the jar rims; seal the jars with the two-piece caps, hand-tightening the bands. Process your filled jars in a pressure canner at 10 pounds for 1 hour and 5 minutes (pints).

5 After the pressure in the canner has returned to zero, open the canner and remove the hot jars with a jar lifter. Place them on a clean kitchen towel or paper towels away from drafts. After the jars cool completely, test the seals. (If you find jars that haven't sealed, immediately refrigerate them and use them within one week.) Boil the contents of each jar for 10 minutes before tasting or eating.

Vary it! *For a meatless sauce, follow all the recipe instructions, omitting the sausage and meat. Process your pints for 25 minutes at 10 pounds pressure.*

Rounding Out Your Meals with Beans

Yes, beans may cause gassiness, but today, many over-the-counter remedies can eliminate this problem. Beans are high in protein, calcium, phosphorus, and iron, and are a good source of fiber.

White Chili

This is a great alternative to a tomato-based chili. When you serve your chili, garnish it with shredded Monterey Jack cheese and diced red bell pepper.

Preparation time: *15 minutes (not including soaking the beans)*

Cooking time: *2 hours*

Processing time: *Pints, 1 hour, 15 minute; quarts, 1 hour, 30 minutes*

Yield: *About 5 pints or 2 quarts*

1 pound small white beans, soaked overnight in water, drained

2 quarts chicken stock

2 cloves garlic, minced

2 medium onions, coarsely chopped

7-ounce can diced green chilies

3 teaspoons ground cumin

1½ teaspoons dried oregano

¼ teaspoon cayenne pepper

⅛ teaspoon ground cloves

4 cups diced, cooked chicken

1 Combine the beans, stock, garlic, onions, green chilies, cumin, oregano, cayenne pepper, and cloves in a 6- to 8-quart pot. Bring the ingredients to a boil over high heat; reduce the heat and simmer, covered, until the beans are soft but don't disintegrate, about 30 minutes. Add the cooked chicken and simmer, uncovered, for 30 minutes longer.

2 While the chili is simmering, prepare your canning jars and two-piece caps (lids and screw bands) according to the manufacturer's instructions. Keep the jars and lids hot. (For information on pressure canning and detailed instructions on preparing and filling your jars and testing the seals, see Chapter 9.)

3 Ladle the hot chili into the prepared jars, leaving 1 inch of headspace. Wipe the jar rims; seal the jars with the two-piece caps, hand-tightening the bands. Process your filled jars at 10 pounds for 1 hour and 15 minutes (pints), 1 hour and 30 minutes (quarts).

4 After the pressure in the canner has returned to 0, open the canner and remove the hot jars with a jar lifter. Place them on a clean kitchen towel or paper towels away from drafts. After the jars cool completely, test the seals. (If you find jars that haven't sealed, immediately refrigerate them and use them within one week.) Boil the contents of each jar for 10 minutes before tasting or eating.

Baked Beans

Basic baked beans are the perfect accompaniment to any barbecue or outdoor meal. I just love a bowl of these beans with a hunk of cornbread dripping with honey.

Preparation time: *15 minutes (not including soaking the beans)*

Cooking time: *4 hours*

Processing time: *Pints, 1 hour, 20 minute; quarts, 1 hour, 35 minutes*

Yield: *About 6 pints or 3 quarts*

2 pounds dried navy beans	⅔ cup packed brown sugar
6 quarts water	4 teaspoons salt
½ pound bacon cut into pieces	2 teaspoons powdered mustard
3 large onions, sliced	⅔ cup molasses

1 Place the beans in a 6- to 8-quart pot. Add 3 quarts of water to cover the beans; cover the pot and allow them to soak for 12 to 18 hours. Drain the beans, but don't rinse them.

2 Return the beans to the pot; add the remaining 3 quarts of water (to cover the beans); bring the mixture to a boil over high heat. Reduce the heat; cover and simmer until the bean skins begin to split. Drain the beans, reserving the liquid.

3 Transfer the beans to a 4-quart or larger covered baking dish. Add the bacon and onions. Combine the brown sugar, salt, mustard, and molasses in a large mixing bowl. Add 4 cups of the reserved bean liquid (if needed, add water to make 4 cups). Pour the sauce mixture over the beans. Don't stir.

4 Cover the beans; bake in a preheated 350-degree oven for 3 to 3½ hours. The consistency should be like a thick soup. Add more liquid if the beans become too dry.

5 While the beans are baking, prepare your canning jars and two-piece caps (lids and screw bands) according to the manufacturer's instructions. Keep the jars and lids hot. (For information on pressure canning and detailed instructions on preparing and filling your jars, releasing air bubbles, and testing the seals, see Chapter 9.)

6 Ladle the hot beans into your prepared jars, leaving 1 inch of headspace. Release any air bubbles with a nonreactive tool (refer to Figure 8-1), adding more beans to maintain a headspace of 1 inch. Wipe the jar rims; seal the jars with the two-piece caps, hand-tightening the bands. Process your filled jars in a pressure canner at 10 pounds for 1 hour and 20 minutes (pints), 1 hour and 35 minutes (quarts).

7 After the pressure in the canner has returned to 0, open the canner and remove the hot jars with a jar lifter. Place them on a clean kitchen towel or paper towels away from drafts. After the jars cool completely, test the seals. (If you find jars that haven't sealed, immediately refrigerate them and use them within one week.) Boil the contents of each jar for 10 minutes before tasting or eating.

Part IV
Freezing

The 5th Wave By Rich Tennant

@RICHTENNANT

"Quit moping. You won first place in the
pickled beets category, and that's good.
I'm the only one that knows it was
strawberry preserves you entered."

In this part . . .

If you're looking for the simplest and easiest food-preservation method, then you're in the right place. With a minimum of time and expense, you'll fill your freezer with fresh fruits and vegetables, herbs, meals of convenience, and so much more. Before you know it, you'll be amazing your family with hot, nutritious meals and freshly baked treats. They'll think you've been in the kitchen all day!

Chapter 12

Baby, It's Cold Inside!: Freezing Food

. . . .

In This Chapter

▶ Exploring the freezing process

▶ Getting acquainted with the spoilers of frozen food

▶ Discovering packaging methods

▶ Perfectly thawing your frozen food

. . . .

*W*elcome to freezing, the simplest and least time-consuming method for preserving food. Freezing works well for almost any food. (I'll tell you what doesn't freeze well, also.) With a minimum of planning and equipment (you may already have most of it), proper storage containers, and basic freezing techniques, keeping food from spoiling and tasting as if you just took it out of the oven or brought it home from the store will be a piece of cake.

Defining Freezing

After the development of refrigerators, people have been able to prolong the life of fresh food at home. No longer did the iceman need to make deliveries; homes were equipped with units to store and preserve food at consistently cool temperatures.

Preserving food by freezing maintains many of its fresh qualities, like flavor and taste. The process of freezing uses a low temperature, of 0 degrees or colder, halting microorganism activity by slowing the growth of enzymes. Freezing doesn't sterilize food or destroy the microorganisms; it only stops the negative changes in the quality of your frozen food. Your goal is to preserve the fresh quality of your food.

Frozen food stored at 15 to 20 degrees may appear as solid as food stored at 0 degrees or colder, but the quality of your thawed food stored at the warmer temperature produces a poorer quality than food stored at 0 degrees or colder.

Freezing basics

Freezing food is easy, convenient, and relatively inexpensive. The results produced from freezing food are superior to canning or drying. When food is properly prepared, packaged, and quickly frozen, there's no better method for retaining its natural color, flavor, and nutritive value.

Follow these tips for best freezing results:

- ✔ **Prepare your food quickly.**
- ✔ **Package your food in *moisture- and vapor-proof wrappings,* products that don't permit the penetration of air or moisture.**
- ✔ **Keep your freezer at 0 degrees or colder.**
- ✔ **Properly thaw your food to preserve its quality and eliminate bacteria growth.**

Meeting the spoilers

Before getting started, you need to recognize what I refer to as the spoilers of frozen food. One or more of these may occur before, during, or after freezing. For detailed information on the spoilers, refer to Chapter 3.

Bacteria, molds, and yeast

All fresh food contains microorganisms or bacteria. When active microorganisms are present in food, they multiply quickly and destroy the quality of your food, sometimes right before your eyes. The best example of this is a loaf of bread that becomes covered with green mold.

Bacteria are microorganisms that have no chlorophyll. Some bacteria may cause disease; other bacteria are actually good and are required for the fermentation process, used for making beer.

Prevent the growth of bacteria, mold, or yeast in your food by following these guidelines:

  ✔ Select food of the highest quality.

  ✔ Freeze your food at a temperature of 0 degrees or colder.

  ✔ Use sanitary conditions when handling and preparing your food.

Enzymes

An *enzyme* is formed in the cells of plants and animals and is proteinlike. Enzymes speed up the ripening process and change the color and flavor of your food. Not all enzyme reactions are bad: When beef is *aged,* it sits in a chilled room for about one week. The enzymes naturally tenderize the meat, making it more desirable to consume.

Use these methods to retain the colors and the flavors in fresh fruits and vegetables before the freezing process:

  ✔ Add sugar and *antioxidants,* a commercial antidarkening agent (see Chapter 14), to keep fruit from darkening in color.

  ✔ *Blanch* your veggies by briefly plunging them into boiling water and then into cold water to stop the cooking process.

Freezer burn and oxidation

Freezer burn and oxidation result from air coming in contact with your frozen food. *Freezer burn* is a change in color, texture, and flavor in the food during the freezing period because the air in the freezer removes moisture from the food and dries it out.

Oxidation is a chemical change in your frozen food. This may occur from improper wrapping, an unsuitable freezer container, or incorrect storage (check out "Packaging Is Everything" later in this chapter).

Ice crystals

When I think of ice crystals, I think of winter and snowflakes. But in the world of freezing, ice crystals aren't charming at all. They cause your frozen food to lose liquid and darken. To eliminate the growth of ice crystals in frozen food, freeze your food quickly at a temperature of 0 degrees or lower.

Gearing Up to Fill Your Freezer

Whether food is fresh from your garden or fresh from a store, the selection choices you make have an effect on the quality of your food after it's thawed. Of course, packaging materials, packaging procedures, and thawing methods play an important role in your frozen-food quality.

Selecting food for freezing

In practice, any food can be frozen. In reality, not all food freezes well because of its texture or composition.

Here's a list of foods that don't freeze well:

- **Cakes with frosting:** Frosting of fluffy egg whites, whipped cream, or cooked frostings become soft and *weep* (emit a thick liquid). The cake portion may be frozen after the frosting is scraped off. Cakes with butter-based frostings freeze well (flip to Chapter 13.)

- **Cooked pasta:** Reheated cooked pasta is soft, mushy, and shapeless.

- **Custards and cream-pie fillings:** These foods turn watery and lumpy.

- **Egg whites and meringues:** These crack, toughen, and turn rubbery.

- **Mayonnaise:** This condiment breaks down and separates.

- **Raw fruits or vegetables with a high water content:** Some examples are lettuce, watermelon, citrus fruit, and cucumbers. Tomatoes are an exception to this if you're using them in cooked dishes, like stews.

    When freezing fresh tomatoes, cut them into quarters. Package them in one-cup portions for quick freezing and easy measuring.

- **Sauces and gravy:** Thickened sauces and gravies separate when they're frozen. Freeze your *pan drippings;* the juices produced from cooking a roast or turkey freeze without adding a thickener.

- **Yogurt, cream cheese, and sour cream:** These tend to separate.

Evaluating your freezer

Today, most freezers are *frostfree,* automatically defrosting any buildup of ice in the freezer. This feature is a great convenience, but your electricity usage may be higher than with a freezer you manually defrost. Freezers that don't automatically defrost require defrosting when the ice buildup is ¾ inch, or at least once a year. You'll need to empty your freezer before defrosting it. (Refer to your owner's manual for instructions for defrosting your freezer.)

Keep your freezer operating in top-notch condition with proper care and maintenance according to the manufacturer's recommendations (refer to your owner's manual). If you've misplaced your manual or have questions regarding maintenance or usage, contact your local appliance company or search on the Internet for the manufacturer's Web site.

Types of freezers

Select a freezer based on your needs, the size of your family, the space available to you, your budget, and the cost required for running the freezer.

Refrigerators with freezer compartments are the most common units in homes today. The preferred model has a separate door for the refrigerator and the freezer. This allows you to regulate the temperature in each compartment with individual built-in thermostats.

Upright freezers and chest freezers are made for freezing only. Upright freezers have a door on the front with shelves inside, while a chest freezer opens from the top and you reach into it. Sizes vary from 6 cubic feet of storage to 32 cubic feet of storage.

Add no more food to your freezer than can freeze solid in 24 hours, about 2 to 3 pounds of food for each cubic foot of freezer space. Adding a large quantity of food to your freezer at one time may raise the temperature in the freezer above 0 degrees. This stops the quick-freezing process and may affect the quality of your frozen food.

Purchase a freezer thermometer to monitor the internal temperature of your freezer. Adjust your freezer thermostat, as needed, to maintain a temperature of 0 degrees or colder.

Packaging Is Everything

Proper packaging is important for preserving the quality of your frozen food after it's thawed. Any excess air in your container may compromise the quality of your thawed food. Remove as much air as possible in bags and wraps. Allow the recommended headspace in rigid freezer containers.

Protecting foods during the storage period requires containers that are easy to seal, suitable for low temperatures, and, most importantly, moisture- and vapor-proof. Three types of packaging materials meet the criteria for properly freezing food: rigid containers, freezer bags, and freezer paper and wrap.

Rigid containers

Rigid containers are the perfect solution for freezing any soft or liquid food, such as casseroles and soups, and they're reusable. The most desirable material for rigid containers is plastic, although some glass jars are made for freezing. Container sizes range from ¼ of a cup to 1 quart with a variety of sizes in between. Purchase container sizes that fit your freezing needs.

Vacuum sealing machines

A vacuum sealing machine is a handy appliance that's great for packaging foods for the freezer. Air is almost completely removed from the package through a suction process, the trademark of this appliance. Most vacuum sealing machines use materials that are freezer-safe or even microwavable and boil-proof. (This is handy for single-serving meals for home or at work.)

Consider these additional items when you're purchasing a vacuum sealing machine:

✔ **Cost:** Prices range from a low of $50 to upwards of $300.

✔ **Replacement bags:** Most machines include bags to get you started. Consider the cost of replacement bags and the reputation of the manufacturer. Investing in a vacuum sealer that is limited by a certain make of bags may limit use of your machine in years to come.

✔ **Storage requirements:** Depending on the size of your kitchen, storing a vacuum sealing machine may or may not be an issue. The ideal location for a vacuum sealer is in the kitchen, usually on a counter, where you can use it at a moment's notice.

Square- or rectangular-shaped containers save space and fit better in your freezer than round containers.

Rigid containers approved for freezing prevent the spoilers from attacking your food as well as stopping moisture and vapors from penetrating your food. Allow room for expansion of your food or liquid (refer to Table 14-2).

Freezer bags

Freezer bags are readily available, require a minimum amount of storage space, and come in a variety of sizes. When using freezer bags (I prefer the locking zipper variety), purchase bags labeled for freezing, because the thickness is moisture-proof and protects the flavors of your food.

After placing your food in the bag, force out as much air as possible by folding the filled part of the bag against the nonfilled portion of the bag, pressing the air out while sealing the bag.

Freezer paper and wraps

Freezer paper comes coated or laminated and protects your wrapped food from air and freezer burn. Other freezer papers include heavy-duty foil, clear plastic wrap, and polyethylene (plastic) sheets.

These papers and wraps are especially useful when packaging irregularly shaped foods, such as steaks and roasts. Freezer paper is primarily used for meat, because tight wrapping forces out excess air. Use a piece of freezer paper about double the size of your food to ensure there are no exposed areas. After the paper is snugly around the food (see Figure 12-1), securely tape the ends with *freezer tape,* a tape suited for cold temperatures.

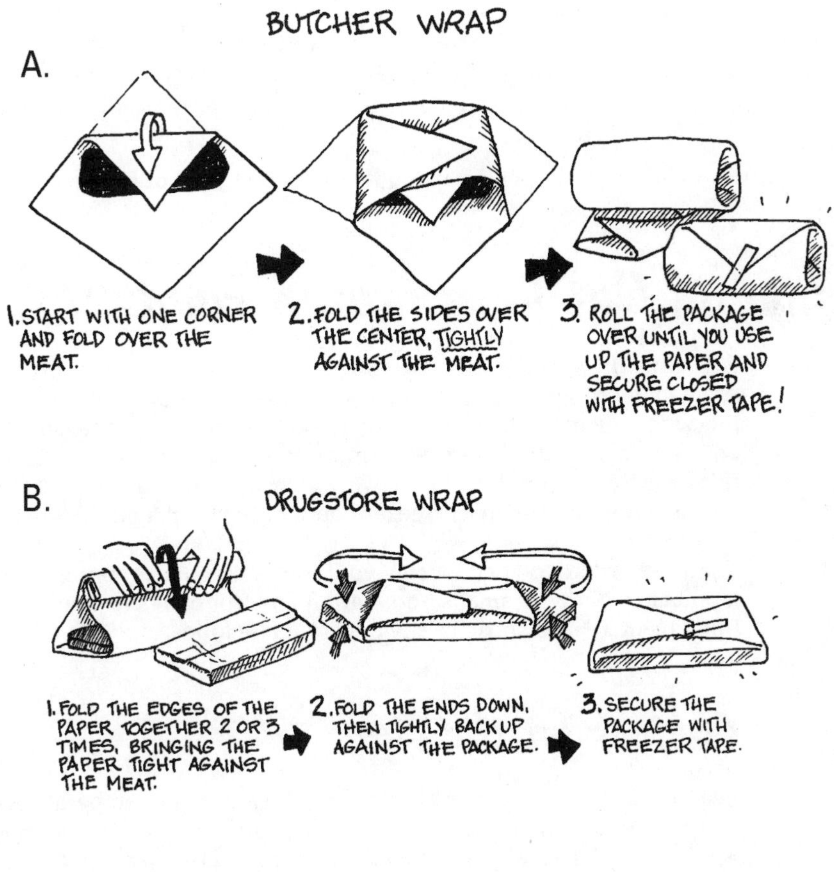

BUTCHER WRAP

A.

1. START WITH ONE CORNER AND FOLD OVER THE MEAT.

2. FOLD THE SIDES OVER THE CENTER, TIGHTLY AGAINST THE MEAT.

3. ROLL THE PACKAGE OVER UNTIL YOU USE UP THE PAPER AND SECURE CLOSED WITH FREEZER TAPE!

B. DRUGSTORE WRAP

1. FOLD THE EDGES OF THE PAPER TOGETHER 2 OR 3 TIMES, BRINGING THE PAPER TIGHT AGAINST THE MEAT.

2. FOLD THE ENDS DOWN, THEN TIGHTLY BACK UP AGAINST THE PACKAGE.

3. SECURE THE PACKAGE WITH FREEZER TAPE.

Figure 12-1: Freezer-paper wrapping techniques.

Tracking Your Frozen Food Trail

How many times have you looked in your freezer to the astonishment that it's full and yet you have no idea what's taking up so much space? Have you ever defrosted what you thought was soup, only to discover you're now having stewed tomatoes for dinner? Solve the dilemma of freezer mystery food by following these simple tips:

- ✔ **Label each package with the item and the date before placing your food in the freezer.** Also include the weight of a roast, the quantity of cut-up tomatoes, your preparation method, or the number of servings. Use an indelible marker or a waterproof pen, which won't rub off.

- ✔ **Keep an up-to-date written record of food in your freezer to help with your meal planning.** Any sheet of paper works well. Make columns with the following headings: date, item (roast, spaghetti sauce, and so on), quantity or weight (1 cup or 3 pounds, for example), and any recipe or preparation ideas. Keep the list on your freezer door, crossing off items you use them.

- ✔ **Rotate your food by using it within one year of freezing.**

Thawing Out Your Frozen Food

Following the guidelines for freezing won't guarantee a great product without practicing proper thawing methods. So what's the big deal about thawing? Freezing only halts the growth of microorganisms. After thawing, bacteria and enzymes in your food are free to multiply as if they hadn't been frozen. Keep this growth at a standstill by thawing your food at a low temperature, preferably in a refrigerator, in its freezer container or packaging.

Thaw only what you need, using your food immediately upon thawing. If your food tastes funny or smells odd, harmful microorganisms may be present. Don't hesitate to dispose of any questionable food.

Choices for thawing

Heat makes the spoilers grow faster, so the lower the temperature during the thawing period, the better for you and the quality of your food. Here are your best options for safely thawing and maintaining the quality of your food:

✔ **Thawing in your refrigerator:** This is the best and safest process for thawing your food because of the low temperature. Plan your meal the night before and place your choice in your refrigerator to thaw.

✔ **Thawing at room temperature:** Leave your frozen food at room temperature for 2 hours, then immediately place it in the refrigerator for the remainder of the thawing process. This option is a great alternative if you forgot to take your food out of the freezer the night before.

✔ **Thawing in the microwave:** Use this method only if your microwave has a defrost cycle. This is important because you want the food to defrost evenly, not be cooked in one portion and frozen in another part.

✔ **Thawing in water:** Immerse your packaged food in cold water, never hot or warm water. By maintaining the lowest temperature possible when thawing your food, you'll inhibit bacteria and enzyme activity.

Unplanned thawing

No matter how good technology is, everyone experiences a power failure at one time or another. This may be for a few minutes, a few hours, or, in the worst-case scenario, a few days. Don't panic, keep the freezer door closed and resist the temptation to open the door to check the temperature.

A fully loaded freezer at 0 degrees or colder usually stays cold enough to keep your food frozen for up to two days. A freezer that's half-full may not keep your food frozen for more than a day because air space doesn't maintain a constant temperature as efficiently as a piece of solidly frozen food.

If you do have a power outage, follow these tips for saving the contents of your freezer:

✔ **Check with your electric company to estimate the length of your power outage.**

If you find that your freezer is the only electric appliance that isn't operating, check the electrical cord and plug for a good connection. If this isn't the problem, check your electrical panel for a blown fuse.

✔ **If you receive advance warning that your electricity will be off, set your freezer temperature to its coldest setting.** The colder temperature delays thawing during the time the electricity is off.

✔ **In the worst-case scenario, your freezer may be out long enough for your food to defrost.** Locate a supplier of dry ice and pack your food in the dry ice before it defrosts completely. (Ask your dry-ice supplier for safe packing and handling instructions.)

Dry ice is a refrigerant of solid carbon dioxide. Handle dry ice with care and never touch it with your bare hands. Even a short exposure to dry ice may cause frostbite.

To refreeze or not to refreeze thawed food

From time to time, even the best-laid plans change and your defrosted food doesn't get used when you planned. If your food is only partially defrosted, indicated by the presence of ice crystals (see the "Ice crystals" section earlier in this chapter), it may be refrozen.

I don't suggest refreezing food as a regular practice, but if you're considering it for any reason, follow these guidelines:

✔ Don't refreeze completely defrosted low-acid foods, such as vegetables or meat sauces, after they reach room temperature. These foods may not be safe to eat.

✔ You may refreeze high-acid foods and most fruits and fruit products if they're still cold.

✔ You may safely refreeze partially thawed foods containing ice crystals if you were thawing your food in your refrigerator.

Refrozen foods have a shorter shelf life than when first frozen. They may also taste different from refrozen foods. If you refreeze an item, make a note on the package including the refreezing date. Use refrozen food as soon as possible.

Follow this simple rule when evaluating refrozen, thawed food: When in doubt, throw it out! Eating spoiled food can be quite dangerous.

Chapter 13

Meals and Snacks in a Snap: Freezing Prepared Foods

In This Chapter

▶ Keeping frozen food as tasty as fresh food

▶ Saving time and money by freezing prepared foods

▶ Freezing meat, poultry, and fish

Freezing is a great option for taking advantage of buying food in large quantities at bargain prices, making large quantities of food, or saving leftovers. Taking a few minutes to package your food in meal-sized portions allows you flexibility in the amount of food you thaw. In this chapter, I give you great tips on freezing food and hints for planning your meals.

Managing Your Time with Freezing Food

I never seem to have enough hours in my day to get everything done and get a nutritious meal on the table. Most families today seem to have the same predicament: work, children, school, after-school activities, and more! Filling your freezer with meals and snacks allows you plenty of nutritious choices.

If you make soup or a casserole, double your recipe and put one in the freezer. If you're baking cookies, freeze some for another day or freeze some of the raw dough and bake it later.

Here are some tips for meal planning:

✔ **Review your schedule for the upcoming week to determine your time available for preparing meals.** Use prepared meals, like soups or stews, on busy days. Cook meat or bake casseroles on not-so-busy days

✔ **Make a list of your planned meals, including snacks.** Keep a second list with a complete inventory of food in your freezer.

> ✓ Watch your weekly food ads for specials.
>
> ✓ Keep your lists on the front of the refrigerator. Cross off items as you use them.
>
> ✓ Get your family involved in the planning process.

The key to delicious frozen food

Excess air left in your freezer packaging is the number-one enemy causing damage in frozen food. Preserving the quality of your food during freezing requires quick freezing at a temperature of 0 degrees or colder.

Don't make the mistake of thinking packaged food from your store is in moisture- and vapor-proof packaging — this is rarely the case. To preserve the quality of store-bought food, repackage your food following the guidelines in Chapter 12.

Check your purchased foods for a sell-by or a use-by date. (Not all foods are dated.) If the food is still on the shelf after the date, don't buy it.

The key to thawing frozen food

Yes, there's a correct process for thawing frozen food. The preferred method is in the refrigerator, but there are exceptions. Some prepared frozen foods may be used in their frozen state; other foods may be used partially frozen.

Check out the "Choices for thawing" section in Chapter 12. If there are special thawing instructions for the foods listed in this chapter, they're described within the section for that food.

Freezing and Using Prepared Foods

There are many benefits of freezing food purchased from your supermarket or foods prepared in your home. These include:

> ✓ **Time saving:** Freezing allows you the luxury of making a double batch of soup or spaghetti sauce in less time than it takes to make the same recipe at two different times. Freeze what you don't use.

✔ **Cost saving:** By taking advantage of sale pricing and purchasing perishable food in large amounts, you'll reduce your food costs.

✔ **Convenience:** You'll always have a quick meal at hand for reheating, partial cooking, or complete cooking, depending on your time allowance.

Convenience meals

Meals of convenience include casseroles, soups, and sauces. Freezing them in family-sized portions or as single-servings provides options for meals, later.

Main dishes (casseroles, chili, and stew)

Prepare your recipe and transfer your food to rigid freezer containers. If you're making a casserole, prepare it in a baking dish (approved for the freezer) up to the point of baking. Wrap it in heavy-duty aluminum foil. Thaw the unbaked casserole in the refrigerator and bake it according to your recipe.

Soups and sauces

Ladle hot soup or sauce into rigid freezer containers, based on the portion you'll be using. Allow headspace of ½ inch for your pints and 1 inch for your quarts (refer to Figure 2-14). Here are some freezing tips:

✔ **Soups:** Use freezer containers no larger than 1 quart for quickly freezing your soups and preventing loss of flavor in your thawed product. If your workplace has a breakroom with a stove or microwave, freeze portions in single-serving containers and enjoy a hot lunch. (Potatoes frozen in soup and stew may darken or become mushy or mealy after freezing.)

✔ **Stocks (see recipes in Chapter 11):** Use rigid freezer containers or ice-cube trays. Transfer frozen stock cubes to a freezer bag for storing. Add one to a soup or sauce for added flavor.

✔ **Sauces:** Package your sauces in rigid freezer containers in quantities suited to your family's usage.

Don't add cooked pasta to your spaghetti sauce before freezing or freeze liquids with cooked grains and rice; their flavor and texture will be lost.

Snacks and other treats

Have your ever felt like you had to finish a birthday cake before it went bad or had a partial loaf of bread grow fuzzy, green mold? Well, here's the answer to these (and more) challenges using freezing for saving these foods.

Bread, buns, muffins, and rolls

Bread and bread products freeze well. Repackage them in moisture- and vapor-proof paper or freezer bags.

When you're making muffins at home, make two or three varieties at the same time, wrapping them individually and using them one at a time.

When making bread, prepare your loaves to the point of baking, including all of the rising periods. Place your dough into a baking container approved for the freezer; wrap it for freezing. To bake your bread, remove the wrapping, place the container of frozen dough into a preheated 250-degree oven for 45 minutes, and then bake your bread as stated in your recipe.

Cakes

Cakes with or without frosting may be frozen, but fillings can make your cake soggy. Butter-based frostings freeze well. Remove other types of frosting, including whipped-cream frosting, before freezing your cake.

Cheesecakes, whole or leftover, are my favorite cakes for freezing, keeping about 4 months in your freezer. Thaw the wrapped, frozen cheesecake in your refrigerator for 4 to 6 hours. Serve it chilled.

Freezing leftover cake in single-serving sizes keeps you from thawing more cake than you may want available to you at one time.

Cookies

Who can resist warm cookies fresh from the oven? You can freeze cookies in many forms: store-purchased or home-baked or raw dough to bake later. Use all of these within 3 months.

- ✔ **Store- or bakery-bought cookies:** Most purchased cookies freeze well, except cream- or marshmallow-filled cookies. Laying sheets of wax or parchment paper between your cookies keeps them from sticking together. Thaw them at room temperature.

- ✔ **Homemade cookies, baked:** Store cooled cookies in rigid freezer containers, placing layers of wax or parchment paper between the cookies. Thaw them at room temperature or place them on a baking sheet in a preheated 350-degree oven for 2 to 3 minutes to warm them.

- ✔ **Homemade cookies, raw dough:** Freeze raw dough in rigid freezer containers, freezer paper, or freezer bags.

  - • For slice-and-bake cookies: Form your cookie dough into a log, wrap the dough in freezer paper, and freeze it. Thaw your dough slightly for easy slicing. Bake according to your recipe instructions.

• For drop cookies: Drop your cookie dough onto a baking sheet, leaving 1 inch between each cookie. Place the baking sheet in your freezer and quick-freeze the dough. Place the frozen cookies in freezer bags for storage. To bake your cookies, place them (frozen is okay) on a baking sheet and bake them as your recipe states.

Label bags of frozen cookie dough with the baking temperature and time.

Pies

You may freeze pies at almost any stage in the preparation process. (Check out Chapter 14 for pie fillings.)

Cream pies and meringue pies aren't suitable for freezing.

✔ **Whole baked pies:** Wrap your pie with freezer wrap or place it in a freezer bag. Thaw it, wrapped, at room temperature for 2 hours; serve.

✔ **Whole unbaked pies:** This works best for fruit, mince, and nut pies. Prepare your pie in the pie pan you'll bake it in.

To reduce sogginess in your crust: Brush the inside of the bottom crust with shortening, add your filling, and brush the top crust with shortening. Cut vents and glaze the top right before baking. Wrap it for freezing.

For baking: Remove the freezer wrap and place your frozen pie on a baking sheet in a preheated 450-degree oven for 15 to 20 minutes. Reduce the temperature to 375 degrees; bake 20 to 30 more minutes or until the top is golden brown.

✔ **Pie shells, baked or unbaked:** Place your bottom piecrust in a pie pan for baking. Wrap the dough-lined pan in freezer wrap or place it in a freezer bag, stacking multiple filled pie pans on top of each other.

✔ **Pie dough, unrolled:** Form your pie dough into a flat, round disc. Wrap it tightly in a piece of plastic wrap and place it in a freezer bag.

To use your dough: Thaw it slightly in the refrigerator and roll it out while it's still chilled. This keeps your dough tender after baking.

When making dough for a double-crusted pie, separate it into two rounds before wrapping and packaging them for freezing.

Other foods

Buying butter, nuts, meat, and poultry at special prices can keep your food costs in line.

Dairy products

Not all dairy products are suitable for freezing. Here are your best choices:

- ✔ **Butter:** Unsalted and salted butter freeze well. Use salted butter within 3 months because the salt flavor disappears during the freezing process.

- ✔ **Hard cheese:** Freeze hard cheese as a last resort because it crumbles after freezing. Use this cheese within 6 months.

- ✔ **Soft cheese (like blue cheese):** Freezes better than hard cheese. Use soft cheese within one month.

Nuts

Freezing is perfect for keeping nuts fresh and ready-to-use. Freeze any size of shelled nut, raw or toasted, in rigid freezer containers or freezer bags.

Freezing meat, poultry, and fish

Purchase meat, poultry, and fish from stores that practice sanitary handling procedures. If you're buying at a butcher store or fish market, ask them to wrap it for the freezer. If your food is prepackaged, repackage it for the freezer.

Packing hints: Divide your food into meal-sized portions, always packaging steaks, chops, and chicken parts individually. Even though you may use more than one piece at a time, freezing and thawing time is less because you're working with a smaller mass. Freezer bags or freezer wrap are your best packaging materials for these foods.

Never freeze a whole stuffed bird because freezing time is increased and microorganisms may be passed from the poultry to the stuffing. If the stuffing doesn't reach a high enough temperature during cooking to kill the bacteria, it may be passed to your consumers, making them ill.

Fish and shellfish must be kept chilled from the time they're caught. Ideally, clean and freeze them immediately if you aren't using them within 24 hours.

Prepare your fish for your freezer based on its size:

- ✔ If it's under 2 pounds, remove the tail, head, fins, and internal organs; freeze it whole.

- ✔ If it's over 2 pounds, clean it as above. Cut it into fillets or steaks and wrap each piece separately for freezing.

Thawing tips: Thaw your food in its freezer packaging in the refrigerator. For meat, allow five hours for each pound; for poultry, allow two hours for each pound; and for fish, allow eight hours for each pound. If your time is limited, thawing it on the kitchen counter at room temperature will take about half the time of thawing it in the refrigerator, but this isn't the preferred method because bacteria may start to multiply at room temperature.

Chapter 14

Savoring the Days of Summer: Freezing Fruits and Vegetables

*F*reezing fruits and vegetables is the second best preserving method after canning. Preparing and processing fresh fruits and vegetables for the freezer takes about one-third of the time of water-bath or pressure canning.

Don't feel like you have to grow your own fruits and vegetables to get the best produce. Local farmer's markets, food producers, and your supermarket can assist you with selecting your food, telling you when it was harvested, or how long it's been on the shelf.

The equipment required for freezing food is more than likely already in your kitchen: a freezer, packaging materials (check out Chapter 12), pots, a colander, measuring cups, measuring spoons, and a food scale. After your equipment and food is in order, start freezing!

Mastering Freezing Fruit

Fresh fruits require a minimum of preparation before packaging them for the freezer. Fruits may be frozen raw, with added sugar, or with added syrup (a mixture of sugar and water). Occasionally, you'll add an *antioxidant* (an anti-darkening agent) to the liquid to keep your fruit from discoloring.

The key to a great frozen product starts with perfect, ripe fruit. Be prepared to process your fruit the day it's picked, or immediately after bringing it home from the store.

Packing methods for your fruit

The best choices for fruit packaging materials are rigid freezer containers and freezer bags (see Chapter 12). Use rigid freezer containers when you add liquid to the fruit. (Check out Table 14-1 for a variety of syrup concentrations and Table 14-2 for headspace allowances for your rigid freezer containers.) Use freezer bags when no liquid is added to your fruit.

Select your storage container size and fruit-packing method based on how you intend to use your final product. Adding sugar to your fruit isn't necessary, but it's preferred.

Here are your packing choices:

- ✔ **Dry or unsweetened pack:** When you'll be eating the fruit or using it for pies, jams, or jellies, use this method. No sugar or liquid is added. There may be minor changes in the color, flavor, or texture of your fruit.

- ✔ **Dry sugar pack:** This is preferred for most berries unless you're making pies, jams, or jellies (see the preceding bullet). Place your washed fruit on a shallow tray or a baking sheet. Evenly sift granulated sugar over the fruit (a mesh strainer works well).

  Transfer the berries to a bowl or a rigid freezer container and allow them to sit. The longer the berries sit, the more juice is drawn out. (It's not necessary for the sugar to dissolve as in the "Wet pack with sugar method," below.) When your berries are as juicy as you want them, transfer the berries, including the juice, to a rigid freezer container, allowing the recommended headspace (refer to Table 14-2).

- ✔ **Wet pack with sugar:** Place your fruit in a bowl and sprinkle it with granulated sugar. Allow the fruit to stand until the natural fruit juices drain from the fruit and the sugar dissolves. Transfer your fruit and the juice to a rigid freezer container, allowing the recommended headspace (refer to Table 14-2).

- ✔ **Wet pack with syrup:** Place your fruit in a rigid freezer container, adding syrup (refer to Table 14-1) to completely cover the fruit and allowing the recommended headspace (refer to Table 14-2). Your fruit needs to be fully submerged in the syrup before sealing the containers.

To solve the problem of *floating fruit,* fruit rising to the top of the liquid in the jar, wad a piece of moisture-proof paper (foil works well) into a ball. Place it on top of the fruit to force the fruit to stay completely submerged when the container is sealed. Remove the paper after thawing your fruit.

Table 14-1	Syrup for Freezing Fruit			
Type of Syrup	**Sugar Concentration**	**Sugar**	**Water**	**Syrup Yield**
Extra-light	20	1¼ cups	5½ cups	6 cups
Light	30	2¼ cups	5¼ cups	6½ cups
Medium *	40	3¼ cups	5 cups	7 cups
Heavy	50	4¼ cups	4¼ cups	7 cups

* ***Note:*** *Medium syrup is used for most fruits.*

Use these syrup estimates for planning the amount of syrup to make for filling your storage containers:

- **Sliced fruit or berries:** ⅓ to ½ cup of syrup for 1½ cups of fruit in a 1-pint container
- **Halved fruit:** ¾ to 1 cup of syrup for 1½ cups of fruit in a 1-pint container

Table 14-2	Headspace Guidelines for a Dry or Wet Pack		
Packing Method	**Jar Opening Size**	**Pints**	**Quarts**
Dry pack	Narrow mouth	½ inch	½ inch
Dry pack	Wide mouth	½ inch	½ inch
Wet pack	Narrow mouth	¾ inch	1½ inches
Wet pack	Wide mouth	½ inch	1 inch

How to thaw and use your frozen fruits

For retaining the best quality of your fruit after freezing, refer to Chapter 12 and follow these guidelines:

- **Open your container when a few ice crystals remain in your fruit.**
- **Use your fruit immediately after thawing.**
- **When cooking with sweetened, thawed fruits, you may need to reduce the amount of sugar your recipe calls for.**
- **Use your frozen fruit within one year.**

Step-by-step instructions for freezing fruit

When freezing fruit, follow these steps:

1. **Choose only perfect fruit, free of bruises and not overly ripe.**

2. **Work with small, manageable quantities, about 2 to 3 quarts.**

3. **Wash your fruit before packing it for freezing.**

4. **Prepare your fruit for freezing based on your final use.**

5. **If called for in your recipe, add an antioxidant (refer to Chapter 5).**

6. **Fill your container, allowing the proper headspace (refer to Table 14-2).**

7. **Label the package and let your freezer do the rest!**

In addition to the steps for freezing fruit, use any additional tips included in the list of fruit in this chapter. Not all packing methods are suitable for all fruits. Only methods recommended for each fruit are supplied.

Apples

Use crisp apples with a firm texture like Pippin or Golden Delicious.

- **Preparation:** Peel, core, and slice your apples into 12 or 16 pieces, dropping the slices into an ascorbic or citric acid solution or 3 tablespoons of lemon juice to 1 gallon of water.

- **Yield:** 1¼ to 1½ pounds fruit for 1 pint.

- **To pack in sugar:** Remove the apples from the antioxidant solution and place them in a shallow dish or on a baking sheet. Sprinkle the apple slices with granulated sugar, one part sugar to four parts apples. Fill your container and allow the proper headspace (refer to Table 14-2).

- **To pack in syrup:** Place your drained apple slices in rigid freezer containers, filling them with a cold heavy syrup (refer to Table 14-1), adding ½ teaspoon of an antioxidant solution to each container and allowing the proper headspace (refer to Table 14-2).

Apricots, nectarines, and peaches

All varieties freeze well. Use fully ripe fruit without any bruised areas.

- **Preparation:** Remove the skin from the fruit as shown in Figure 5-1, leaving it in the boiling water no longer than 1 minute.

- **Yield:** 1 to 1½ pounds fruit for 1 pint.

✔ **To pack in syrup:** Measure ½ cup of cold medium syrup (refer to Table 14-1) with an antioxidant added into each rigid freezer container. Slice or halve the fruit directly into the containers, discarding the fruit pits. Fill the containers with additional syrup, allowing the proper headspace (refer to Table 14-2).

Berries (except strawberries)

All berries (except strawberries) freeze well. Select firm berries.

✔ **Preparation:** Gently wash the berries, removing any stems.

✔ **Yield:** 1 to 1½ pounds fruit for 1 pint.

✔ **To pack whole:** Spread your washed berries on a baking sheet, placing it in your freezer. (This process is known as *quick-freezing* or *flash-freezing*.) Transfer the berries to freezer bags or rigid freezer containers.

Jams, jellies, and preserves made with frozen berries produce a product superior in color, flavor, and texture to one made with fresh berries.

✔ **To pack in syrup:** Place your berries into rigid freezer containers, covering them with cold medium syrup (refer to Table 14-1), allowing the proper headspace (refer to Table 14-2). If the berries float, add a ball of moisture-proof paper to keep the berries submerged.

Fruit purees

Use purees for making fruit leathers (see Chapter 16), fruit sauces (by adding water, fruit juice, or a teaspoon of your favorite liqueur), as a concentrated flavor in fruit smoothies, or as a topping for your favorite ice cream.

✔ **Preparation:** Cook or steam your fruit in water until the fruit is soft. Process your fruit in a food processor fitted with a metal blade or run it through a food mill (refer to Figure 2-5). Add granulated sugar and lemon juice to taste. Bring the mixture to a boil over medium-high heat, stirring constantly. Remove it from the heat after achieving a boil.

✔ **Yield:** Use any amount of fruit you have on hand; 2 to 4 cups of raw fruit is a good working quantity.

✔ **To pack in containers:** Ladle your puree into 1-cup or smaller rigid freezer containers, allowing the proper headspace (refer to Table 14-2).

Freeze small amounts of fruit puree in ice-cube trays. Remove the frozen cubes from the trays and transfer them to a freezer-storage bag.

Lemon and lime juice

Lemons and limes produce a superior juice that retains its flavor after juicing. Use freshly picked, fully ripe fruit.

✔ **Preparation:** Squeeze the juice from the fruit into a measuring cup.

If you prefer juice without pulp in it, place a small mesh strainer over the edge of your measuring cup; juice your fruit over the strainer.

✔ **Yield:** As much or as little as your prefer.

✔ **For freezing:** Pour the juice into 1-ounce freezer containers or ice-cube trays. After the cubes freeze, remove them from the ice-cube trays and store them in freezer bags.

Mangoes

Choose fully ripe mangoes that are slightly soft yet firm to the touch with a strong mango aroma.

✔ **Preparation:** Peel the skin from the fruit, slicing the flesh away from the seed (see Figure 14-1).

✔ **Yield:** 2 to 3 medium mangoes for 1 pint.

✔ **To pack in syrup:** Measure ½ cup of cold light syrup (refer to Table 14-1) into each rigid container. Slice the fruit directly into the containers. Press the slices to the bottom of the container, adding additional syrup to achieve the proper headspace (refer to Table 14-2). Add a ball of moisture-proof paper to keep the fruit submerged.

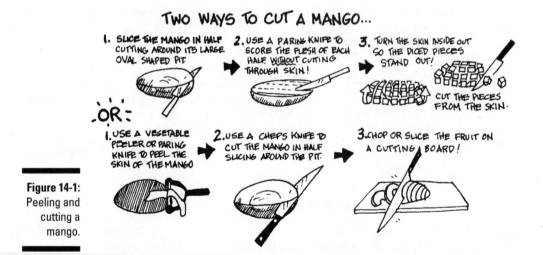

Figure 14-1: Peeling and cutting a mango.

Pie fillings (apple, blueberry, peach, or nectarine)

If you love homemade pies, you'll find this a real timesaver for assembling pies, especially when you have a pie shell in the freezer (see Chapter 13).

Prepare your favorite pie filling. Ladle the hot filling into rigid freezer containers, allowing ½ inch of headspace. Cool the filled containers on your kitchen counter up to 2 hours before sealing and freezing.

Pineapple

Selecting a ripe pineapple can be challenging because of the thick peel. Start by checking out the fronds (leaves) at the top. If they're dry and brown, don't buy it, this pineapple is old. Look for fresh green fronds, a strong sweet pineapple aroma, no mushy-soft areas, and a golden-yellow color on the peel.

I use the following technique for picking pineapples: After verifying that the pineapple isn't bruised or damaged, try to pull out a green frond. If it comes out easily, I buy the pineapple; if I have to struggle to pull one out, I put that pineapple back on the shelf and try another one.

- **Preparation:** Peel and core the pineapple (see Figure 14-2), cutting it into wedges or cubes.
- **Yield:** 1 pound of fruit for 1 pint.
- **To pack in syrup:** Pack your fruit into rigid freezer containers. Fill the containers with a cold light syrup (refer to Table 14-1), allowing the proper headspace (refer to Table 14-2).

TRIM AND CUT PINEAPPLE

Figure 14-2:
Removing the rind and the core from a pineapple.

1. LAY THE PINEAPPLE ON ITS SIDE. CUT OFF THE TOP FRONDS AND A SLICE OFF THE BOTTOM.

2. WITH THE PINEAPPLE UPRIGHT, CUT OFF THE EYES WITH A KNIFE.

3. CUT IN HALF

4. CUT AGAIN INTO WEDGES OR SLICES.

Strawberries

Strawberries are put in a category of their own for freezing. Cut them and treat them with sugar or pack them in syrup.

- **Preparation:** Wash your strawberries in water, being careful to not bruise them. Remove the hulls (stems).
- **Yield:** ¾ to 1½ pounds fruit for 1 pint.
- **To pack in sugar:** Slice the strawberries lengthwise into a bowl. Add ¾ cup granulated sugar for each quart of strawberries, stirring the berries to dissolve the sugar. Transfer your berries to rigid freezer containers, allowing the proper headspace (refer to Table 14-2).

> ✔ **To pack in syrup:** Place your sliced strawberries into rigid freezer containers. Fill the containers with a cold medium syrup (refer to Table 14-1), allowing the proper headspace (refer to Table 14-2).

Freezing Vegetables like a Pro

Like fresh fruit, fresh vegetables are quick and easy to freeze. The key to great frozen vegetables is a process called blanching. *Blanching* scalds the vegetables in boiling water, slows down the enzymes and the spoiling process, and preserves the color, flavor, texture, and nutritive value.

Blanching isn't necessary if you're using your frozen vegetables, like onions, in foods, like stock, where you're only concerned with flavor, and not color.

Blanching perfect vegetables

Blanching requires 100 percent of your attention. Vegetables blanched for too short of a time won't stop the enzymes in the vegetables, and microorganisms start where they were stopped after the vegetables thaw. Vegetables left in the boiling water too long start cooking and may become limp.

Follow these steps for successful blanching:

1. **Wash and drain your vegetables.**

2. **Remove any peel or skin, if needed.**

3. **If you're not freezing your vegetables whole, cut them now.**

4. **Bring a 5- to 6-quart pot of water to a boil.**

5. **Fill a large mixing bowl with ice water.**

   Add ice cubes to the mixing bowl because the hot vegetables increase the temperature of the ice bath. Cold stops the cooking process.

6. **Blanch your vegetables in batches, no more than 1 pound of vegetables in 1 gallon of water, accurately time the blanching.**

   Begin timing your vegetables as soon as they're in the boiling water; don't wait for the water to return to a boil.

7. **Remove your vegetables from the boiling water and plunge them into the ice-water bath, stirring the vegetables and circulating the ice water to stop the cooking process as quickly as possible.**

Don't leave your vegetables in the ice-water bath longer than they were in the boiling water.

8. **After the vegetables are chilled all the way through, remove them from the ice-water bath and drain them in a colander. If you're dry packing them, roll them in or lay them on clean, dry kitchen towels to remove excess moisture.**

9. **Pack your vegetables into your freezer containers as your recipe states, allowing the proper headspace (refer to Table 14-2).**

10. **Seal and label your containers and then add them to your freezer.**

Packing your vegetables

Pack your vegetables immediately after preparing them. Moisture-proof, vapor-proof freezer bags are the best choice for your vegetables. Don't season them before freezing them.

After filling your bags, place them in a single layer in your freezer. Quick freezing is important to the thawed quality of your vegetables. After the packages are frozen solid, you may stack them on top of each other. Removing all excess air is important to avoid the spoilers, such as freezer burn (refer to Chapter 12). To remove air from your containers, follow these guidelines:

- ✔ **Freezer bags:** Package your vegetable pieces as close together as possible at the bottom of the bag, without bruising or squashing the vegetables. Fold the unfilled upper portion of the bag over the vegetables, gently pushing any air out of the bag. Seal the bag.

- ✔ **Rigid containers:** Use this reusable container when you're adding liquid to the vegetables. Allowing the proper headspace exhausts the air because the liquid in the container expands when it freezes. For headspace allowances, refer to Table 14-2.

How to thaw and use your vegetables

Thawed vegetable results are best when your food is thawed in your refrigerator rather than on your kitchen counter. A package of vegetables containing a single serving size takes less time to thaw than a package containing 1 pound of vegetables. Properly thawing your vegetables completes the cycle of preserving your fresh vegetables by freezing.

Step-by-step instructions for freezing vegetables

In addition to the tips in Table 14-3, follow these steps for freezing vegetables:

1. **Choose only perfect vegetables, free of bruises and imperfections, not overly ripe.**

2. **Work with small, manageable quantities, about 2 pounds at a time.**

3. **Wash and drain your vegetables.**

4. **Prepare your vegetables according to your recipe, usually blanching the vegetables.**

5. **Chill your vegetables before packing them for freezing.**

6. **Fill your container, allowing the proper headspace if you're using rigid containers (refer to Table 14-2), or removing all of the excess air from freezer bags.**

7. **Label your package, adding it to your freezer.**

Freezing fresh herbs

The flavors fresh herbs impart in just about any dish are truly a gift from nature. Frozen herbs are a great compromise when fresh herbs aren't available.

Thawed herbs are great in cooked dishes, but they aren't suitable as a garnish because they're limp after freezing and thawing. If you grow your own herbs, harvest them early in the day before the sun wilts the leaves.

Some herbs that freeze well include basil, chervil, chives, cilantro, comfrey, dill, lovage, mint, parsley, savory, sweet fennel, and thyme.

To prepare fresh herbs for the freezer, follow these steps:

1. **Clean fresh herbs by holding the bottom of the stems (don't remove the leaves from the stems) and swish the herbs in a bowl of cool water.**

2. **Drain and dry the herbs, gently shaking off any excess water.**

   If you're blanching the herbs, you don't need to dry them.

3. **Optional: Blanch the herbs by holding onto the stems and immersing them in boiling water for a few seconds; shake off excess water.**

4. **Lay the herb sprigs flat, not touching each other, on a piece of wax paper.**

5. **Starting at one end, roll the wax paper snuggly over the herbs.**

   This keeps the herbs separate and easy to use one sprig at a time.

6. Place the rolled herbs in a freezer bag, label the package, and freeze.

There's no need to thaw the herbs before using them.

If you're still stumped for more ways you can freeze fresh herbs, try the following:

Herb cubes: After washing the herbs, remove the leaves from the stem and cut them into pieces. Place 1 teaspoon to 1 tablespoon of herbs in each opening of an ice-cube tray. Pour boiling water into the tray and freeze the herb cubes. After the cubes are frozen solid (usually 24 hours) pop them out of the tray and into a plastic freezer bag. When your recipe calls for 1 teaspoon or 1 tablespoon of an herb, add the ice cube to the dish and continue cooking!

Herbed butter: Add chopped fresh herbs to one cube of softened, unsalted butter. For a mild herb flavor, start with ¼ cup of herbs, adjusting the amount to your personal taste. Transfer the flavored butter to an ice-cube tray sprayed with no-stick cooking spray and freeze the butter. After the butter is frozen (about 24 hours), remove the butter cubes, placing them in a labeled freezer bag. Serve the flavored butter with bread or add one to a casserole.

Herbed butter logs: Flavor the butter as stated in the previous paragraph. Form the flavored butter into a log in a sheet of wax or parchment paper. Twist the ends, place the log in a freezer bag, and freeze it. Slice off what you need and return the log to the freezer.

WRAPPING HERBS FOR FREEZING

1. RINSE HERBS AND SHAKE OFF WATER.

2. LAY THE HERBS IN A SINGLE LAYER ON WAXED PAPER.

3. ROLL THE WAXED PAPER AROUND THE HERBS.

4. FOLD IN THE ENDS AND PLACE IN A FREEZER BAG...

Table 14-3

Vegetable Freezing Guide

Vegetable	Quantity for 1 pint	Piece Size	Blanching Time	Suggested Container
Asparagus	1 to 1½ pounds	Whole or pieces	2 to 4 minutes	Freezer bags
Beans, green, string, Italian, or wax	⅔ to 1 pound	1 inch, ends and strings removed	2 to 3 minutes	Freezer bags
Beans, lima or butter, shelled	2 to 2½ pounds	Loose beans	2 to 4 minutes	Freezer bags
Bell peppers, green, red, orange, or yellow	1 to 3 pounds	Stems and seeds removed; slices or uniform pieces	None	Rigid containers
Broccoli	1 pound	½ inch	3 to 4 minutes	Freezer bags
Brussels sprouts	1 pound	Whole, sorted by size, leaves removed	3 to 5 minutes	Freezer bags
Carrots	1¼ to 1½ pounds	Whole, sliced, or diced; remove tops and scrape or peel skin	Slices or diced, 2 minutes Whole, 5 minutes	Freezer bags
Cauliflower	1¼ pounds	1-inch pieces, broken, not cut	3 minutes, add 1 tablespoon of vinegar to 1 gallon of water	Freezer bags
Corn, whole kernels	2 to 3 pounds (6 to 8 ears)	Blanch ears whole; cut kernels from ears after cooling	4 minutes	Freezer bags
Greens, beet, spinach, Swiss chard	1 to 1½ pounds	Wash well, remove thick stems	1½ minutes, stir constantly to separate leaves	Freezer bags

Vegetable	Quantity for 1 pint	Piece Size	Blanching Time	Suggested Container
Okra	1 to 1½ pounds	Remove stems, leave whole for blanching; pack whole or slice	Small pods, 3 minutes Large pods, 4 minutes	Freezer bags
Onions, yellow or white	1 to 3 whole	Peel and chop	None	Freezer bags
Peas, shelled	2 to 3 pounds	Loose beans	1½ minutes	Freezer bags
Snow peas	⅔ to 1 pound	Whole, stems and blossom ends removed	1½ minutes	Freezer bags
Squash, summer (crookneck, patty pan, zucchini)	1 to 1½ pounds	½-inch slices, stems removed	3 minutes	Rigid containers
Squash, winter (banana, butternut, Hubbard) and pumpkins	1 to ½ pounds	Peel outer skin, scrape out seeds, cut into chunks	Cook in a small amount of water until soft (10 to 30 minutes); mash	Rigid containers

Part V
Drying

The 5th Wave   By Rich Tennant

"I SAID, I DON'T KNOW WHY WE NEED A FOOD DEHYDRATROR WHEN WE ALREADY OWN A CLOTHES DRYER!"

In this part . . .

In this part, you'll have the opportunity to experience the pleasures of drying food in the comfort of your home. You'll soon know the secrets behind great-looking dried fruit that tempts your tastebuds, adorns your meals, and satisfies a hungry appetite with a nutritious snack-on-the-run. As you discover the methods for achieving these fabulous dried foods, you'll be practicing the oldest food-preservation method using modern techniques. Just decide what fruit you'll try first and start drying!

Chapter 15

Dry, Light, and Nutritious: Drying Food

• •

In This Chapter

▶ Discovering the basics of drying food

▶ Unlocking the secrets for successful drying

▶ Mastering the drying process

▶ Preserving the quality of your dried food

• •

*I*n the world of food preservation, sun-drying is the oldest method known. Although canning and freezing require exact applications of processing procedures, drying food isn't exact or precise. Don't be surprised if you find yourself working by trial and error when it comes to knowing how long it takes for your food to reach its degree of doneness. Just follow the general guidelines provided and make adjustments. ***Remember:*** Drying isn't exact.

In this chapter, I explain the basic techniques for drying food, the best drying methods, and how drying food prevents spoilage. Drying is simple and easy to do in your home. Most of the equipment and tools you'll need, except an electric dehydrator, are probably just waiting for you in your kitchen.

Opening the Door to Successful Food Drying

Drying food is also referred to as *dehydrating*. The goal in this technique is removing moisture from your food. Achieving a successfully dried product requires removing 80 to 95 percent of the moisture in food. Removing moisture inactivates the growth of bacteria and other microorganisms but doesn't kill them.

The following factors affect your finished product:

- ✔ **Heat:** The correct temperature is important in drying food. It must be high enough to force out moisture but not so high that it cooks the food. If your temperature is too high, your food exterior cooks or hardens before the interior of the food dries, trapping moisture in your food — known as *case hardening*. If your temperature is too low or the humidity too high, your food dries too slowly. Both of these dilemmas may cause your food to spoil before you consume it.

  The temperature guidelines for drying food are as follows: 125 degrees for vegetables, 135 degrees for fruit, and 145 degrees for meat. Always follow the instructions for the correct drying temperature for your food in your recipe or the owner's manual for your dehydrator.

- ✔ **Dry air:** Dry air absorbs moisture that leaves the food in the drying process. The higher the humidity, the longer it takes for food to dry because of the additional moisture in the air.

- ✔ **Air circulation:** Circulating air carries away moisture absorbed by dry air. This keeps the humidity level constant in the drying chamber.

- ✔ **Uniform size:** Pieces of food uniform in size and thickness contain about the same amount of moisture.

Deciding Which Method to Use

The three approved methods for drying food are an electric dehydrator, using a conventional oven, and drying in the sun. All methods work well when you follow basic food-drying procedures, use high-quality fresh food, and practice good sanitation for food preparation.

An electric dehydrator

If you dry a lot of food, an electric dehydrator is a great investment. It's the most reliable method for achieving the most consistent results each time you dry food. This method dries your food evenly and quickly, doesn't tie up your oven, and produces great results in any weather.

An electric dehydrator dries your food by heating the air inside the chamber to a low temperature and circulating the warm air through the chamber with a fan, passing the heat evenly over your food for the entire drying process. After you place your food in your dehydrator, it needs little or no attention.

Dehydrator prices may start as low as $65 and go up to $200 or more. Figure 15-1 illustrates two types of electric dehydrators.

TWO ELECTRIC DEHYDRATORS

Figure 15-1:
Two examples of electric dehydrators.

If you're purchasing a dehydrator, carefully assess your needs. Then, consider the following factors when making your final decision:

✔ **Overall construction:** Purchase a unit that's approved for safe home use by the Underwriters Laboratory (UL). If the unit isn't UL approved, don't buy it — it may not be safe for use in your home. Choose one with insulated walls that's easy to clean. Drying trays need to move easily in and out of the dehydrator without disturbing the food.

✔ **Capacity:** Purchase a dehydrator whose size fits your needs for the amount of food you'll dry at one time. Typically, the most common-sized food dehydrator has four trays. Each tray holds about ¾ to 1 square foot of food. Some dehydrators expand to utilize 30 trays at one time. Snack-size dehydrators with two trays are also available.

✔ **Heat source:** Select one with an enclosed heating element. Wattage needs to accommodate about 70 watts for each tray the unit holds.

✔ **Fan:** The fan circulates the heated air around your food. Purchase a dehydrator with a quiet fan, because it runs for long periods of time. If your unit isn't equipped with a fan, you'll need to rearrange the trays during the drying period for an even drying.

✔ **Thermostat:** Purchase a dehydrator with an adjustable thermostat. Your temperature options need to range from 85 to 160 degrees.

✔ **Drying trays:** Check for trays that are sturdy and lightweight; made from a food-safe product like stainless steel, nylon, or plastic; and easy to clean. Some manufacturers offer dehydrator accessories like extra drying trays and trays for drying fruit leather and herbs.

✔ **Warranty:** Check out the warranty term (one year is a good average) and any restrictions the manufacturer has for your dehydrator.

A conventional oven

Drying food in your oven takes longer than using a dehydrator but less time than sun-drying. If you have an oven — gas or electric — that maintains a temperature between 130 and 150 degrees with the door propped open, you're ready to start drying.

To test your oven's temperature, put an oven thermometer in the center of your oven with the door propped open. Your oven must maintain a temperature of 130 to 150 degrees for one hour to safely dry food. Higher temperatures cook — they don't dry — the food.

The cost of oven-drying is higher than the cost of using an electric dehydrator because the oven uses a greater amount of electricity or gas than the amount of electricity a dehydrator uses. Keep in mind that if you use your oven for drying, it isn't available for any other use during that time.

The sun

The oldest drying method is dependent on perfect weather conditions to produce a safely dried product. Sun-drying is the least expensive of the three methods. It lets you dry large quantities of food at one time but can take days compared to hours in a dehydrator or a conventional oven.

Weather conditions must be perfect for sun-drying, making only a few climates suitable for this method. The ideal temperature for sun-drying fruit is 85 degrees or hotter for many consecutive days, with the humidity level low to moderate. If your temperature drops more than 20 degrees below your highest temperature during the drying period, your conditions are not suitable for this method. You also need good air circulation, a minimum of air pollution, and insect control around the food.

This method is less attractive for drying vegetables because the temperature needs to be at 100 degrees or above for a number of days with the lowest evening temperature never dropping below 80 degrees (even at night).

Sun-drying isn't safe for meats and fish because the low-acidity level of the food, the low drying temperature, and the long drying period (taking many days) don't destroy the bacteria that cause your food to spoil.

Gearing Up with Basic Tools

After you decide which drying method you want to use, assemble your basic tools to aid you in completing the drying process. If there's something on this list that you don't have, now may be a good time to buy it.

- ✔ **Blender:** Use this for pureeing fruit.

- ✔ **Candy thermometer:** From time to time, you'll need to heat your food to a specific temperature.

- ✔ **Colander or steaming rack:** Steam-blanching your food is simple when you suspend your food in one of these over your boiling water. The steam easily passes through the holes. You'll find a colander helpful for washing and rinsing your food. Collect a few different sizes.

- ✔ **Cutting board:** Cutting boards are relatively inexpensive, which allows you to have one for each kind of food — fruits, vegetables, meats, and fish. This eliminates any *cross-contamination,* transferring bacteria from one food to another, from using the same board for different types of food.

  In addition to flat cutting boards of wood and plastic, flexible cutting mats are available. They're easy to clean, come in colors, and roll up for compact storage. Use a different color for different foods, writing the food use on the edge of the mat with an indelible marker.

- ✔ **Food processor:** You'll make uniform slices in a blink of the eye.

- ✔ **Grater:** Either a box grater or a flat grater works well.

- ✔ **Measuring cups and spoons:** Measuring cups are made for measuring liquid or dry products (refer to Figure 2-1). Measuring spoons may be used for dry or liquid ingredients (refer to Figure 2-2).

- ✔ **Oven thermometer:** For safely drying food in your oven, it's critical to know the exact temperature of your oven chamber.

- ✔ **Paper bags:** Use either brown or white bags for drying fresh herbs.

- ✔ **Paring knife:** The knife must be sharp for smooth edges on your fruit.

- ✔ **Plastic wrap:** Purchase a heavy-duty wrap that's suitable for food products. You'll use this for drying and rolling your fruit leathers.

✔ **Racks and tray:** Your electric dehydrator provides the correct size of trays for your unit. For oven- or sun-drying, you can use oven racks, net-covered racks, or baking sheets. Racks with mesh bottoms or oven racks work well and provide air circulation. To prevent food from falling off the racks, tightly stretch and pin layers of cheesecloth or nylon netting over the racks. If you use baking sheets, you'll need to rotate the sheets and turn the food over for even drying.

✔ **Vegetable peeler:** This simple tool removes peels in easy, even strokes.

Drying fresh herbs

I love strolling through local farmers' markets and smelling the lingering aromas of rosemary, basil, parsley, lemon verbena, and whatever else was brought to market. Although I have herbs growing at home, I still buy more and then rack my brain with how to use them. Air-drying herbs is easy and the perfect solution for saving your fresh herbs.

Follow these steps for drying herbs and check out the figure as well:

1. **If you're harvesting herbs from a garden, cut the stems, don't pick them, leaving an extra inch or two for tying them in bunches.**

   Harvest the herbs in the morning after any moisture on the leaves has dried.

2. **Rinse your herbs quickly by dipping them in a bowl of cool water and shaking off the excess water.**

   Pat them dry with a paper towel, making sure they're completely dry to prevent mildew.

3. **Tie the herb stalks near the cut part of the stem in small bunches (no more than five or six stems) with cotton string or thread.**

   Don't mix your herb bunches because flavors transfer during the drying process.

4. **Either hang the herbs upside down in a warm room (the kitchen works well) near a south-facing window and out of direct sunlight or place the tied herb bundle in a paper bag with holes or slits cut in it for air circulation before hanging the bag in a warm room. Place the herb bundle upside down in the bag with the stems toward the top opening of the bag. Tie the top of the bag closed. The bag protects the herbs from light and catches any loose seeds for replanting your herbs.**

   Your herbs will dry in two to three weeks with good air circulation.

Herbs are dry when they crumble easily. Remove the leaves from the stems. Crush soft leaves (like basil, sage, and oregano) by hand. Store harder leaves (like rosemary, tarragon, and thyme) whole, crushing them with a rolling pin before using them.

Store your dried herbs in small containers. Glass jars with tight-fitting lids work best. For your herbs to maintain the best flavor during storage, keep them away from heat, light, and your refrigerator.

When adding dried herbs to your food, remember that less is best. Dried herbs are stronger than fresh herbs. You can always add flavor, but it's difficult to remove too much of a flavor.

Herb Blends: Combine your favorite herbs and roll a cube of butter in them to coat the stick, or soften the butter to room temperature and mix the dried herbs directly into the butter. Chill the butter; cut it into slices or make rounds with a melon baller for serving.

Rice Mix: Package ready-to-make mixes with your freshly dried herbs. Combine the following in a bowl: 1 cup of long-grain rice,

2 teaspoons bouillon granules (chicken, beef, or vegetable), 2 to 3 teaspoons of one or more dried herbs, and ¼ teaspoon kosher salt. Transfer the mix to a glass container or clear food-safe bag. Seal the jar or tie the bag closed. Add a card with the following instructions: Add the rice mix to 2 cups of water in a 2- to 3-quart saucepan. Bring the rice to a boil over high heat, stir, cover, and reduce the heat to medium-low. Cook for about 30 minutes without peeking. Remove the rice from the heat (don't lift that lid to peek) and let the rice stand for 30 minutes. Fluff the rice with a fork and serve immediately.

TWO WAYS TO AIR-DRY FRESH HERBS

1. TIE THE RINSED HERBS BY THE STEMS, IN SMALL BUNCHES. OR 2. PLACE HERB BUNCHES IN A PAPER BAG WITH SEVERAL ½" HOLES CUT, ON ALL SIDES.

STEM ENDS OUTSIDE OF THE BAG.

3. HANG HERBS BY THE STEMS, OUT OF DIRECT SUNLIGHT! ALLOW FOR GOOD AIR CIRCULATION...

Gathering and Preparing Your Food

Food of high quality that's ripe, mature, and in top condition is the best for drying. If you dry food during the peak of its season, you'll get high-quality food at a lower price because the food is more abundant.

Washing and eliminating blemishes

Always wash your food to remove dust, dirt, grime, or insects. When you clean your food, start with a clean sink and clean utensils. Any residue from a previous use may cross-contaminate your food. (For detailed information on bacteria and safe food handling, check out Chapter 3.)

Striving for uniform size

It's important to prepare your food in uniform sizes and thickness for the food to be done about the same time. If you have two different-size pieces of the same fruit, spread like sizes on one tray. Because one tray of food with smaller or thinner pieces will finish drying before the other tray with larger pieces, you won't spend time sorting through the food and disrupting the drying process.

Checking out spoilage

Keep an eye on your food while it's drying. The shorter the drying period, the less opportunity there is for mold to develop on your food. If mold does develop, remove it with a cloth moistened with distilled white vinegar with an acidity level of 5 percent. Wipe the mold from the food, and then wipe the area again with an unused area of the cloth. The vinegar kills mold spores.

The Finale: Your Dry Product

The length of time required for drying your food varies with the quality of your food, whether you're using a pretreating method, your climate and humidity, the size of the food pieces, the moisture content of the food, and the drying temperature.

The easiest method for checking your dried food for doneness is touching and tasting it. This may sound overly simplified, but there's nothing like using your senses. Follow the guidelines in your recipe for approximate drying times for your food. Check your recipe for a description of the degree of doneness like "leathery and pliable with no moisture pockets."

Drying food using an electric dehydrator

Each time you use your dehydrator, review the operating instructions including preheating the unit, filling the trays, setting the temperature, and the time recommended for drying your food.

Prepare your food according to your recipe and then follow the instructions for using your dehydrator. If you have any questions regarding the use or operation of your unit, contact the manufacturer. You can find this information in your owner's manual or check with the store you purchased it from.

Drying food in your conventional oven

To dry food in your oven, follow these steps:

1. **Preheat your oven to the temperature setting in your recipe.**

2. **Wash and prepare your food as directed in your recipe.**

3. **Place your food on the tray.**

   Leave spaces between the pieces of food so that they're not touching each other or the edge of the tray.

4. **Place your filled trays in the oven.**

   Leave the door propped open to allow moisture to escape from the oven.

5. **When your fruit appears to be done, completely cool one piece and test it for the level of doneness stated in your recipe.**

   If you use baking sheets or other trays without holes or openings in the bottom, you must turn your fruit to achieve an evenly dried product. After the first side of the fruit has absorbed all the liquid on the top of the food, turn it over and repeat this for the other side. After this has been done on both sides, turn the food occasionally until it's done.

6. **Store your cooled food in plastic bags, glass containers, or rigid plastic containers with airtight seals.**

7. **Label your bags or containers.**

Sun-drying your food

If you're willing to deal with the variances in weather conditions and the lengthy drying time, follow these step-by-step instructions for sun-drying in addition to the guidelines in "The sun" section earlier in this chapter:

1. **Wash and prepare you food as specified in your recipe.**

2. **Line your drying trays or racks with a double layer of cheesecloth or nylon netting.**

3. **Place your food on the tray.**

   Leave space between your pieces of food so they're not touching another piece or the edge of the tray.

4. **Cover your trays with a single layer of cheesecloth or nylon netting to protect your food from insects and dust.**

   Stretch the cover tightly over the trays, not touching the food.

5. **Place your filled trays on benches or tables in full sunlight.**

   Check your trays at different times of the day, keeping them in full sun at all times. If your nighttime temperature varies more than 20 degrees from the temperature at the hottest part of the day, move your trays to a warmer area (indoors or an enclosed patio area) for the evening, returning them outside when they can be in full sunlight. Relocate the trays if it rains, regardless of the temperature.

6. **Check your fruit daily for evidence of mold (refer to "Checking out spoilage" earlier in this chapter).**

7. **When your fruit appears to be done, completely cool one piece and test it for the level of doneness listed in your recipe.**

   If you use baking sheets or other trays without holes or openings in the bottom, you must turn your fruit to achieve an evenly dried product. After the first side of the fruit has absorbed all the liquid on the top of the food, turn it over and repeat this for the other side. After this has been done on both sides, turn the food daily until it's done.

8. **Store your cooled food in plastic bags, glass containers, or rigid plastic containers with airtight seals.**

9. **Label your bags or containers.**

Protecting the Life of Your Dried Food

You'll receive many months of rewarding flavor from your dried foods when they're protected from air, moisture, light, and insects. Generally speaking, food dried and stored properly can be kept from six months to one year.

Cooler air provides a longer shelf life for your food. The best storage temperature is 60 degrees or colder. This will hold your food for at least one year. Temperatures between 80 and 90 degrees will only preserve the quality of your dried food for about three to four months.

Check your unused dried food from time to time for any visible moisture or spoilage. If the food has signs of moisture, such as droplets of liquid in the containers, your food isn't completely dried. Use it immediately or repeat the dehydrating process and repackage it.

Suitable storage containers include the following:

- ✔ **Glass:** Home-canning jars with two-piece caps (see Chapter 2) are a perfect choice for storing dried food. Wash them with hot soapy water and rinse them well or wash them in a dishwasher. Dry and cool your jars completely before filling them and adding the two-piece caps.

- ✔ **Plastic:** Heavy-duty (freezer) plastic bags with locking zipper-style seals work well. After placing your dried food in the bag, roll the bag to remove any extra air and press the seal together, making the bag airtight.

- ✔ **Metal:** If you buy coffee in cans, line the inside of a clean can with heavy plastic wrap, place your food inside, and add the tight-fitting lid.

- ✔ **Vacuum sealers:** If you own one of these units, now's the time to use it. Check your owner's manual for operating instructions and start packaging your dried food.

Always label your container with the type of food it contains, the date of processing, and, if you measure your food before placing it into the storage container or bag, list the amount.

Drying vegetables

Vegetables are quite funny looking when they're all wrinkly and shriveled. Vegetables aren't commonly dried, but if you'd like to try your hand at it, follow these guidelines (and refer to Table 15-1):

- ✔ **Select vegetables of the best quality.** Anything less produces an inferior dried product.

- ✔ **Pretreat your vegetables as stated in your recipe or in Table 15-1.**

- ✔ **For the best results, use an electric dehydrator.** If you use an oven, set your temperature at 140 to 150 degrees with the door propped open by at least 4 inches and a small fan outside of the oven blowing air into the oven chamber. (Sun-drying isn't recommended because the required temperature is 100 degrees for consecutive days with low humidity; few locations fit these requirements.)

- ✔ **Follow your recipe and test for doneness.** Store dried veggies in an airtight container.

Rehydrate dried vegetables as follows: Add 1½ cups boiling water to 1 cup of dried vegetables. Let them stand for 20 to 30 minutes to absorb the water. If all the water is absorbed and they're not as plump as you'd like, add about 2 cups additional water and let stand until most of the water is absorbed. Use the vegetables as you would raw ones; cook them or add them to a soup or stew.

Table 15-1	Vegetable Drying Guidelines			
Veggie	Preparation	Pretreating	Temperature and Drying Time	Doneness Test
Beans, green and string (Water content 90 percent)	Wash, remove ends, cut into 1-inch pieces or smaller.	Steam blanch for 4 to 6 minutes.	125 degrees for 12 to 14 hours	Very dry and brittle
Carrots (Water content 88 percent)	Wash, trim tops, peel. Slice crosswise or dice.	Steam blanch for 3 to 4 minutes.	125 degrees for 8 to 12 hours	Almost brittle
Corn off the cob (Water content 73 percent)	Remove husks and corn silk, cut kernels from cob.	Steam blanch for 5 to 6 minutes.	125 degrees for 8 to 12 hours	Dry and brittle
Onions (Water content 89 percent)	Trims ends, remove peel, slice 1/4-inch-thick rounds.	None	145 degrees for 12 to 18 hours	Crisp and brittle
Peppers, bell (Water content 93 percent)	Slice or dice.	None	125 degrees for 12 to 18 hours	Leathery
Tomatoes (Water content 94 percent)	Peel (refer to Figure 5-1), core, slice 1/4- to 1/2-inch-thick.	None	145 degrees for 6 to 8 hours	Slightly leathery and crisp

Chapter 16

Snacking on the Run: Drying Fruit

In This Chapter

▶ Preventing your fruit from changing its color

▶ Managing the level of moisture in your dried fruit

▶ Utilizing your convection oven

▶ Returning life to your dried fruit

Recipes in This Chapter

▶ Dried Fruit Medley

▶ Fruit and Bran Muffins

▶ Fruit Leather

*I*n this chapter, I discuss the rewarding process of drying fruit. Dried fruit has many uses — from snacks to sauces, dessert toppings to baked-good fillings. Many of the best fruits for this method oxidize and brown easily when their flesh is exposed to air. I'll introduce you to the options available to you to prevent any color change in your fruit.

The times required for drying fruit may take anywhere from a few hours to many days. An electric dehydrator provides you with the shortest drying time and produces the best dried fruit of the three methods discussed in Chapter 15. Sun-drying is the lengthiest process and requires a lot of your attention as well as perfect weather conditions.

Putting Your Fruit in Order

Using the best, perfectly ripe fruit for drying is important for a dried fruit that's worthy of high marks and rave reviews. Most fruit is suited for this process with a few exceptions. Fruits *not* recommended for drying include avocados, citrus fruits (except for the peel), crab apples, guavas, melons, olives, pomegranates, and quinces.

Sizing up your preparation options

Drying time is determined by the moisture in your fruit, the size of your fruit pieces, the moisture in the air (even if you're using a dehydrator or an oven), and the pretreating method you choose. Larger pieces of fruit take longer to dry than smaller pieces of the same fruit. So, the smaller you cut your peaches or the thinner you slice your bananas, the less time you'll need to produce a safely preserved dried product.

Pretreating your fruit

Pretreating makes your fruit look good by preventing *oxidation* and *discoloration,* the darkening of the fruit flesh after it's exposed to air. This process retards the enzyme activity in the fruit that causes it to ripen.

Pretreating only slows down the ripening process in fruit; it doesn't stop it.

Using a pretreating method before drying your fruit isn't as important as when you're canning fresh fruit. In fact, it's not necessary at all, but it does assist you with the drying process by shortening the drying time.

Your pretreating choices are:

- ✔ **Water blanching:** This method is the best for maintaining the bright fruit color. Immerse the fruit in boiling water for a short period of time and then immediately plunge it into ice water to stop the cooking process started from the boiling water. Drain the fruit well.

- ✔ **Steam blanching:** This is the most common method used for fruit. The steam quickly heats the fruit, shortens the drying and rehydrating times, sets the color and flavor, and slows down the enzyme activity, in some cases killing microorganisms (refer to Chapter 3).

  Hang a colander on the inside edge of a pot of boiling water, making sure the colander doesn't touch the water. Place your fruit in the colander and heat it as directed in your recipe. Cool your fruit quickly in a bowl of ice water. Drain the fruit well.

  Fruit retains more of its water-soluble vitamins and minerals from steam blanching than water blanching.

- ✔ **Dipping:** This is a process of immersing your fruit into a liquid or a solution to control the darkening of your fruit. Dipping the fruit helps it retain vitamins A and C that are lost during the oxidation process. You can use any of the following liquids:

  - • **Lemon or lime juice:** Fresh citrus juice is the most natural of the dipping solutions. Mix 1 cup of juice with 1 quart of water. Soak the fruit no longer than 10 minutes; drain thoroughly before drying.

  - • **Ascorbic acid:** This white, powdery substance is available in drugstores. Its common name is vitamin C. Dissolve 1 tablespoon of powder in 1 quart of water. Don't soak your fruit longer than 1 hour; drain it well before drying.

- **Commercial antioxidants:** These products are found in supermarkets or where canning supplies are sold. Some common brand names are Fruit-Fresh and Ever-Fresh. Follow the directions on the product package for making your solution and determining the soaking time.

At one time, sulfuring fruit was popular for preserving fruit color and vitamins in dried fruit. Sulfur is unsafe for any drying method other than sun-drying because the sulfur produces dangerous fumes of sulfur dioxide when it's heated, such as drying fruit in an oven or a dehydrator. People with asthma or other allergies should avoid this product.

Detailing Your Fruit-Drying Expertise

Properly dried fruit produces a superior product for use at a later time. After your fruit is dried, properly labeled, and stored (check out Chapter 15), you'll find it hard to believe that 10 pounds of fresh apples produces only 1½ pounds of dried apples!

Evaluating dryness

Knowing when your fruit is properly dried is important. Normally, touching and tasting a cooled piece of fruit gives you the answer, but when you're in doubt and you positively, absolutely need to know the moisture in your fruit has reduced enough, follow these basic steps:

1. **Prepare your fruit and weigh the portion you'll be drying.**

2. **Look up the amount of moisture (water content) in your fruit from the fruit list in this chapter.**

3. **Determine the total water weight of your fruit.**

   Multiply the weight of your prepared fruit before drying by the water content percentage from the fruit list.

4. **Calculate the amount of water (by weight) that needs to be removed from the fruit during the drying process.**

   Multiply your total water weight (your answer from Step 3) by 0.8 (the minimum amount of water you want to remove from your fruit during the drying process).

5. **Weigh your fruit when you think it's done.**

   Subtract the amount of the water you want removed (your answer from Step 4) from the total weight of the fruit you prepared for drying (your answer from Step 1). If your fruit weighs this amount, or less, your processing is successful. If your fruit weighs more than this amount, return it for more drying.

Here's an example: You have 20 pounds of prepared peaches with a water content of 89 percent. Find the weight of your dried product with 80 percent of the moisture removed from your fruit.

The solution: 20 pounds of peaches × 0.89 water content = 17.8 pounds of water. A total water weight of $17.8 \times 0.8 = 14.24$ pounds of water to remove. Twenty pounds of prepared fruit − 14.24 pounds of water to remove = 5.76 pounds of dried fruit as your goal. If your fruit weighs more than this, keep drying.

Properly dried fruit has 80 to 95 percent of its moisture removed.

Drying fruit step by step

This procedure is simple and is detailed in Chapter 15 for the three drying methods. Here's a summary for drying fruit in a dehydrator or an oven:

1. **Preheat your oven or dehydrator and prepare your trays.**

2. **Prepare your fruit as directed in your recipe.**

3. **Place your fruit on your prepared trays or racks.**

4. **Place the filled trays in your dehydrator or oven and begin the drying process.**

   Don't stop or interrupt the process for any reason. Keeping your fruit at a consistent temperature for the entire drying period is important.

5. **At the end of your drying time, check your fruit for the proper degree of doneness as stated in your recipe.**

6. **Package your fruit in temporary containers, like plastic bags, and allow them to *condition* or *mellow*.**

   This process distributes any moisture left in the fruit pieces to other, drier pieces, reduces the chance of spoiled fruit, and may take up to one week.

7. **Package and label your product for storage.**

Don't add fresh fruit to partially dried trays of fruit. The fresh fruit increases the humidity in the drying chamber and adds moisture back to your drying fruit. This adjustment in the humidity level affects drying and increases the drying time for both fruits.

Talking about Drying Fresh Fruit

Patience is the key to successful drying. Preparation may take you less than an hour, but that's just the beginning of many hours until you have dried fruit. Refer to Table 16-1 for drying guidelines.

If you're using an electric dehydrator, verify the correct drying temperature for your fruit in your owner's manual. If it differs from the guidelines given in your recipe or this section, use the temperature in your manual.

Apples

- ✔ **Varieties:** Apples with tart flavors and firm texture dry best. Some good choices are Pippin, Granny Smith, Jonathan, and Rome Beauty.

- ✔ **Preparation:** Wash, peel, and core your apples. Slice into rings, ¼- to ½-inch thick (see Figure 16-1).

- ✔ **Pretreating:** Dipping (refer to "Pretreating your fruit" in this chapter).

- ✔ **Drying time:** Dehydrator or conventional oven: 130 to 135 degrees for 6 to 8 hours. Sun-drying: 2 to 3 days.

- ✔ **Testing for doneness:** Soft, pliable, leathery. Water content: 84 percent.

Figure 16-1:
Cutting
apple rings.

Apricots

- **Preparation:** Wash, cut in half, and discard the pits.
- **Pretreating:** Dipping (refer to "Pretreating your fruit" in this chapter).
- **Drying time:** Dehydrator or conventional oven: 130 to 135 degrees for 8 to 12 hours. Sun-drying: 2 to 3 days.
- **Testing for doneness:** Pliable, leathery, no moisture pockets. Water content: 85 percent.

Bananas

- **Preparation:** Use ripe, yellow-skinned fruit with a few brown speckles. Peel and slice to a thickness of ¼- to ½-inch.
- **Pretreating:** Dipping (refer to "Pretreating your fruit" in this section).
- **Drying time:** Dehydrator or conventional oven: 130 to 135 degrees for 6 to 8 hours. Sun-drying: 2 days.
- **Testing for doneness:** Pliable and crisp, almost brittle. Water content: 70 percent.

Blueberries and cranberries

- **Preparation:** Use plump berries that aren't bruised. Drop into boiling water for 30 seconds. Place the drained berries on paper towels to remove any excess water.
- **Pretreating:** None.
- **Drying time:** Dehydrator or conventional oven: 130 to 135 degrees for 12 to 24 hours. Sun-drying: 2 to 4 days.
- **Testing for doneness:** Leathery and hard but shriveled like raisins. Water content: 83 percent.

Cherries

- **Varieties:** Any sweet or sour cherries work well.
- **Preparation:** Wash, cut in half, remove pits.
- **Pretreating:** None.

✔ **Drying time:** Dehydrator or conventional oven: 165 degrees for 2 to 3 hours; reduce heat to 135 degrees for 10 to 22 hours. Sun-drying: 2 to 4 days.

✔ **Testing for doneness:** Leathery, hard, and slightly sticky. Water content: sweet cherries, 80 percent; sour cherries, 84 percent.

Citrus peel

✔ **Varieties:** Grapefruit, lemon, lime, oranges, or tangerines with unblemished skin. Don't use fruit with color added.

✔ **Preparation:** Wash and remove a thin layer of peel with a vegetable peeler. Use peel without any of the white, bitter pith attached.

✔ **Pretreating:** None.

✔ **Drying time:** Dehydrator or conventional oven: 135 degrees for 1 to 2 hours. Sun-drying: Not recommended.

✔ **Testing for doneness:** Crisp, not brittle. Water content: 86 percent.

Grapes

✔ **Varieties:** Use seedless varieties.

✔ **Preparation:** Dip in boiling water for 30 seconds. Remove stems before or after drying. Drain grapes on paper towels.

✔ **Pretreating:** None.

✔ **Drying time:** Dehydrator or conventional oven: 130 to 135 degrees for 24 to 48 hours. Sun-drying: 3 to 6 days.

✔ **Testing for doneness:** Shriveled and pliable with no moisture pockets. Water content: 81 percent.

Nectarines and peaches

✔ **Varieties:** Any ripe fruit works well. Clingstone or freestone varieties, where the fruit separates easily from the pit, are easier to work with.

✔ **Preparation:** Remove peels as directed in Figure 5-1 and discard the pits. Slice or leave in halves. (***Note:*** Peel may be left on nectarines, but place them skin side down, cut side up, on the tray.)

- **Pretreating:** Dipping (refer to "Pretreating your fruit" in this section).

- **Drying time:** Dehydrator or conventional oven: 130 to 135 degrees for 10 to 12 hours. Sun-drying: 2 to 6 days.

- **Testing for doneness:** Leathery, pliable, and shriveled with no moisture pockets. Water contents: Nectarines, 82 percent; peaches, 89 percent.

Pears

- **Preparation:** Wash, peel, and core. Cut into halves or quarters, or slice to a thickness of ½-inch.

- **Pretreating:** Dipping (refer to "Pretreating your fruit" in this section).

- **Drying time:** Dehydrator or conventional oven: 130 to 135 degrees for 12 to 18 hours. Sun-drying: 2 to 3 days.

- **Testing for doneness:** Leathery with no moisture pockets. Water content: 83 percent.

Pineapple

- **Preparation:** Use fully ripe fruit. Cut away the peel and the eyes and remove the core. Cut into ½-inch-thick rings.

- **Pretreating:** None.

- **Drying time:** Dehydrator or conventional oven: 130 to 135 degrees for 12 to 18 hours. Sun-drying: 4 to 5 days.

- **Testing for doneness:** Leathery, not sticky. Water content: 86 percent.

Drying fruit in a convection oven

If you happen to have a *convection* oven, try this out before investing in an electric dehydrator. **Remember:** Your oven will be out of commission for cooking until your fruit is dry.

Set your oven at 140 to 150 degrees and leave the door open about ½ inch. Rotate the trays or racks every few hours for even drying. Cool a piece of fruit before testing it for doneness.

Plums

- ✔ **Preparation:** Wash, cut in half, and discard pits. Leave in half or cut into ¼- to ½-inch-thick slices.

- ✔ **Pretreating:** None.

- ✔ **Drying time:** Dehydrator or conventional oven: 130 to 135 degrees for 12 to 18 hours. Sun-drying: 4 to 5 days. (*Note:* When drying fruit halves, place them skin side down, cut side up, on the drying tray.)

- ✔ **Testing for doneness:** Pliable and shriveled. Water content: 87 percent.

Strawberries

- ✔ **Preparation:** Wash and remove caps. Leave whole, cut in half, or slice to a thickness of ½-inch.

- ✔ **Pretreating:** None.

- ✔ **Drying time:** Dehydrator or conventional oven: 130 to 135 degrees for 8 to 12 hours. Sun-drying: 1 to 2 days.

- ✔ **Testing for doneness:** Pliable, hard, and almost crisp. Water content: 90 percent. (*Note:* Strawberries don't rehydrate well.)

Table 16-1	Fruit Drying Guidelines for a Convection Oven			
Fruit	*Preparation*	*Pretreat*	*Drying Time*	*Testing a Cooled Piece*
Apples	Peel, remove ends and core; slice into ⅛-inch-thick rings.	Yes	5 to 8 hours	Soft, leathery, pliable
Apricots	Wash, cut in half, discard pits.	Yes	18 to 24 hours	Soft, pliable, slightly moist in center
Bananas	Peel, cut into ⅛-inch-thick slices.	Yes	20 to 24 hours	Leathery and pliable

(continued)

Table 16-1 *(continued)*

Fruit	Preparation	Pretreat	Drying Time	Testing a Cooled Piece
Figs	Leave on tree until ripe and ready to drop; wash, cut in half or leave whole.	No	24 to 36 hours	Leathery but pliable exterior, slightly sticky interior
Grapes	Wash, leave whole with stems on.	No	16 to 24 hours	Wrinkled like raisins; discard stems
Nectarines and peaches	Wash, cut in half, discard pits; peeling is optional.	Yes	24 to 36 hours	Soft, pliable, slightly moist in center
Pears	Wash, peel, cut in half, core.	Yes	24 to 36 hours	Soft, pliable, slightly moist in center
Persimmons	Wash, cut into ½-inch-thick rings.	No	8 to 24 hours	Leathery

Enjoying the Labors of Your Drying

Most dried fruit is used just as it's stored after the drying process. It's great added to hot or cold cereal or baking batters. It's perfect if you're always on the go: It travels well and can be eaten right out of the container.

If you prefer your dried fruit a bit chewier, soften or rehydrate it. *Rehydrating* is the process of adding moisture back to the fruit. Use rehydrated fruit right away because it's not dry enough to go back on the shelf without spoiling.

Your rehydrating options are:

✔ **Boiling water:** Place the desired amount of fruit in a bowl. Cover the fruit with boiling water, allowing it to stand for 5 to 10 minutes to plump, or add moisture, to your fruit. Use this method when adding fruit to jams, chutney, or baked goods. Substitute fruit juice or wine for water.

✔ **Steaming:** Place your fruit in a steamer or a colander over a pot of boiling water (refer to steam blanching earlier in this chapter). Steam your fruit for 3 to 5 minutes or until the fruit plumps.

✔ **Sprinkling:** Put your fruit in a shallow bowl. Sprinkle the fruit with water or fruit juice. Allow it to soak in the moisture. Repeat the process until the fruit reaches the level of moistness you desire.

Dried Fruit Medley

This is a great blend for a quick and nutritious snack. Make up small packages for a grab-and-go snack.

Preparation time: *15 minutes*

Yield: *4½ cups*

½ cup toasted almonds

½ cup sunflower seeds

½ cup dried apples, cut into ½-inch pieces

½ cup dried apricots, cut into ½-inch pieces

½ cup dried banana slices

½ cup dried pears, cut into ½-inch pieces

½ cup dried pineapple, cut into ½-inch pieces

½ cup raisins

1 Place all the ingredients in a large bowl; stir to combine and distribute the fruit and nuts evenly.

2 Store your mix in home-canning jars or other airtight containers.

Vary It! *Substitute your favorite nuts or fruits, or use up small amounts of dried fruit.*

When chopping dried fruit, spraying your knife with no-stick cooking spray keeps the fruit from sticking to your knife.

Fruit and Bran Muffins

Personalize this hearty muffin by using your favorite dried fruits. Macadamia nuts offer a tropical twist, but if this isn't to your liking, substitute almonds, pecans, or walnuts.

Preparation time: *25 minutes*

Baking time: *20 to 25 minutes*

Yield: *12 to 16 muffins*

$1\frac{1}{2}$ *cups whole-bran cereal (not bran flakes)*

$\frac{1}{2}$ *cup boiling water*

1 egg, lightly beaten

1 cup buttermilk

$\frac{1}{2}$ *cup honey*

$\frac{1}{4}$ *cup melted unsalted butter*

$1\frac{1}{2}$ *cups mixed dried fruit, your combination choice*

$\frac{1}{2}$ *cup chopped macadamia nuts*

$\frac{1}{2}$ *cup whole-wheat flour*

$\frac{3}{4}$ *cup all-purpose flour*

$1\frac{1}{4}$ *teaspoon baking soda*

$\frac{1}{2}$ *teaspoon kosher salt*

1 Preheat the oven to 425 degrees. Spray a muffin pan with nonstick cooking spray.

2 Combine the bran cereal with water in a large mixing bowl. Stir to moisten the cereal. Cool the mixture until it's lukewarm. Stir in the egg, buttermilk, honey, butter, dried fruit, and nuts; mix well. Set aside.

3 Combine the flours, salt, and baking soda in a small mixing bowl. Add this to the wet ingredients, stirring just until the ingredients are evenly moist. Spoon the batter into your prepared muffin pan, filling each cup about ¾ full.

4 Bake the muffins for 20 to 25 minutes or until a toothpick inserted in the center of a muffin comes out clean. Cool the muffins for 5 minutes in the pan; remove them from the pan and place them on a rack to cool completely. Wrap them individually in plastic wrap or store them in an airtight container.

Fruit Leather

Fruit leather is dried pureed fruit, rolled up in plastic (see Figure 16-2). The result is a chewy, fruity, taffylike treat. Some good choices for fruit leathers are apples, apricots, berries, cherries, nectarines, peaches, pears, pineapple, and plums.

Preparation time: *20 minutes or longer (this is determined by the amount of fruit you're pureeing and the preparation involved preparing the fruit for pureeing)*

Drying time: *Depends on the amount of moisture in your fruit; allow 6 to 8 hours in an electric dehydrator or up to 18 hours in a conventional oven. Sun-drying isn't recommended.*

Yield: *1 cup of fruit puree makes 2 to 3 servings; 2½ cups covers an 18-x-14-inch area, ¼-inch thick (see Note at the end of this recipe)*

Fresh fruit of your choice

Water or fruit juice (optional)

Corn syrup or honey (optional)

Ground spices (optional): choose from allspice, cinnamon, cloves, ginger, mace, nutmeg, or pumpkin pie spice (Use ⅛ to ¼ teaspoon for 4 cups of puree.)

Pure extract flavors (optional): choose from almond, lemon, orange, or vanilla (Use ¼ to ½ teaspoon for 4 cups of puree.)

1 Cover your drying trays or baking sheets with a heavy-duty, food-grade plastic wrap. If your dehydrator comes with special sheets for your trays, use those.

2 Wash your fruit and remove any blemishes. Prepare your fruit as directed in the guidelines for preparing your fruit in this chapter.

3 Puree the fruit in a blender until smooth. Strain out any small seeds, if desired, with a mesh strainer or a food mill. If your puree is too thick, add water or fruit juice, 1 tablespoon or less at a time. If your puree is too tart, add corn syrup or honey, 1 teaspoon at a time. If you're adding spices or other flavorings, add them now.

4 Spread the puree evenly onto the prepared trays to a thickness of ⅛-inch in the center and ¼-inch-thick around the edges. If you use cooked fruit, it must be completely cool before spreading it on the trays.

5 Dry your fruit leather at a temperature of 135 degrees in a dehydrator or 140 degrees in a conventional oven. Dry the fruit until it's pliable and leatherlike with no stickiness in the center.

6 Roll the warm fruit leather, still attached to the plastic, into a roll. Leave the rolls whole, or cut them into pieces with scissors. Store the rolls in a plastic bag or an airtight container.

Note: Here's an idea of how much fresh fruit you'll need for one cup of puree: apples, ½ to ¾ pounds (about 2 to 3) for 1 cup; apricots or peaches, ¾ to 1 pound (about 6 apricots or 2 to 3 peaches) for 1 cup; strawberries, 1 pint of strawberries for 1 cup.

ROLLING FRUIT LEATHER

1. AFTER YOU REMOVE THE PEEL, STEMS OR CORES, BLEND THE FRUIT TO A SMOOTH PASTE.

2. SPREAD THE PURÉE EVENLY ON A LINED BAKING SHEET WITH TURNED UP SIDES.

3. DRY THE PURÉE UNTIL IT FEELS LEATHER-LIKE AND PLIABLE. REMOVE IT FROM THE TRAY WHILE IT'S STILL WARM. ROLL IT!

4. CUT EACH ROLL INTO 4 TO 6 PIECES. WRAP EACH PIECE IN PLASTIC WRAP OR WRAP EACH WHOLE ROLL IN PLASTIC WRAP.

Figure 16-2: Preparing and rolling fruit leather.

Part VI
The Part of Tens

The 5th Wave — By Rich Tennant

"I'm sure there are some canned staples in the food pantry. That's what it's there for. Just look next to the roller blades, below the bike helmets above the back packs but underneath the tennis balls."

In this part . . .

This part is packed full of helpful suggestions and ideas for making your canning and preserving time pleasurable and rewarding, from planning your day to giving creative and delicious gifts. Just in case you encounter a few bumps along your canning road, I help you determine what caused your problems and offer suggestions for avoiding these glitches in the future. You'll also find a list of my favorite suppliers for canning and preserving gear, seeds for growing your own food, and labels for adding character to your food. With all of this information for motivation, you'll find yourself canning and preserving year-round!

Chapter 17

Ten (Or So) Troubleshooting Tips for Your Home-Canned Creations

Canning and preserving is a science and, like any science, you must be precise when working in your lab, which in this case, is your kitchen. Although you follow your recipe instructions to the letter, accurately measure your ingredients, and properly process your filled jars, you aren't guaranteed a perfect product.

In this chapter, I fill you in on some problems you may encounter in canning and what can be done to remedy the situation. If it's not fixable, you'll understand how you can avoid these troubles in the future.

Your Jars Didn't Seal Properly

There may be several reasons your jar didn't seal after processing: Maybe you didn't follow the manufacturer's instructions for using the jars and two-piece caps; maybe a particle of food was left on the jar rim; maybe a piece of food was forced out of the jar during processing; maybe the processing timing was calculated incorrectly; or maybe your filled jars weren't covered by 1 to 2 inches of water in your water-bath canner.

Eliminate these problems by reviewing and following the manufacturer's instructions for preparing and using your jars and two-piece caps, cleaning the rims after filling your jars, leaving the proper headspace in the jar, timing your processing after reaching a boil or the correct pressure, and covering your filled jars with 1 to 2 inches of water in your water-bath canner.

But what if your jar seals and then comes open? If this happens, check for hairline cracks in the jar. If you find a crack in the jar, discard the food (just in case there's a piece of glass in it) and the jar. If your food wasn't processed correctly, microorganisms may be active. They'll produce a gas in the jar that expands and forces the seal to break loose. Because this indicates food spoilage, don't taste the food or use it; dispose of it properly (refer to Chapter 9 for instructions).

Your Jar Lost Liquid During Processing

Starchy food absorbs liquid — this is normal, and there's no way to correct it. Raw, unheated food also absorbs liquid during processing. Eliminate liquid absorption by using the hot-pack method.

Trapped air bubbles released during processing increase the air space in the jar while lowering the liquid level. Always release air bubbles before sealing and processing your jars (refer to Figure 8-1).

Longer-than-suggested processing times cause a loss of liquid in your jars. If you're water-bath canning, prevent this by covering your jars with 1 to 2 inches of water for processing. If you're pressure canning, keep the pressure constant during processing; then, let the pressure drop to 0 and wait 2 minutes before opening the canner.

Your Jar's Liquid Is Cloudy

Cloudy liquid occurs from using water with lots of minerals, salt containing additives, or ground spices. Remedy these problems by using soft water, pure salt (like canning and pickling salt), and whole spices.

If you didn't use one of the items mentioned in the previous paragraph and your jar's liquid is still cloudy, you probably have spoiled food. Dispose of it without tasting it.

Your Jar's Lid Has Dark Spots on the Underside

Occasionally, naturally occurring compounds (like acids and salts) in some food cause a brown or black deposit, along with some corrosion, on the inside of the lid. This deposit is harmless and doesn't spoil your food.

Your Jelly Doesn't Have the Right Consistency

Although you can't fix a batch of jelly that didn't set up or is too stiff, you may safely eat your jelly. Review the following tips to avoid future problems:

✔ Soft, runny, or syrupy jelly: The proportions of sugar, acid, and juice may not be correct. Accurately measure your ingredients.

✔ Work with smaller amounts of juice, no more than 4 to 6 cups at one time. Working with larger amounts of juice won't allow the juice to heat fast enough to reach its gel point, which can result in runny jelly.

✔ Store your sealed jars in a cool, dark place with a temperature between 50 and 70 degrees. Jelly may *break down* (become runny) in less-than-ideal storage conditions.

On the other end of the spectrum, stiff jelly results from using too little sugar or cooking the jelly too long before it reaches the gel point. When your recipe doesn't call for adding pectin, your proportion guideline for sugar and juice (for most fruit) is ¾ cup of sugar to 1 cup of fruit juice.

Your Jelly Is Cloudy or Has Bubbles

There's no solution for fixing cloudy jelly, but rest assured, it's safe to use. Poor straining is the most common cause of cloudy jelly. Carefully strain your fruit through a damp jelly bag (or cheesecloth). This keeps pulp out of the juice. Don't squeeze the jelly bag; let it drain slowly by gravity.

Overcooking fruit breaks down fruit pulp. And broken pulp is small enough to pass through your strainer. Be sure to cook your fruit just until it's tender.

And finally, don't allow your jelly to cool before filling your jars.

Although cloudy jelly isn't anything to worry about, moving bubbles in jelly indicates spoilage. This occurs when living microorganisms in the jar break the vacuum seal during storage. Discard your food without tasting it. Review the step-by-step instructions for preparing your food, readying and filling your jars, and processing your food. (**Note:** It's not uncommon to see a few small air bubbles lodged in a thick jam or butter. It's the moving bubbles you need to be concerned with.)

Your Jelly Has Mold on It

Mold on your jelly indicates an improper or a broken seal. Don't use or taste the jelly — just throw it out. Always clean your jar rims, allow the proper headspace, and process your jars for the correct amount of time.

Your Jelly Has Very Little Fruit Flavor

Jelly with weak flavor results from using fruit that's not ripe or fruit that's been stored too long after being picked. You can't add flavor to your jelly, but the next time, use tree-ripened fruit; store your sealed jars in a cool, dark, dry location; and consume your jelly within one year.

Your Jelly Contains Glasslike Particles

As long as your jar didn't break, you can safely use your jelly. Slow cooking evaporates liquid and allows particles to form in the jelly. Quickly heat the jelly to its gel point.

Ladle, don't pour, your jelly from the pot into the jars. Pouring transfers any undissolved sugar crystals from the inside edge of the pot into your jars.

Your Pickles Are Hollow, Shriveled, Discolored, or Slippery

Occasionally, pickling cucumbers develop hollow interiors as they grow or if they wait too long between harvesting and pickling. You can't fix hollow pickles, but you can identify them because they float when they're put in a sink of water. Use any hollow pickles for making relish.

If your pickles are shriveled, too much salt, sugar, or vinegar was added at once to the cucumbers. Start with a weaker solution and gradually add the full amount of ingredients called for in your recipe.

Discolored pickles may be from using hard water with minerals in it. Use soft water for your brine solution as well as for the liquid for filling your jars. Reactive metals like brass, iron, copper, aluminum, or zinc in pots and utensils cause darkening as well. Use nonreactive equipment such as enamelware with no chips or cracks, glass, stainless steel, or stoneware. Finally, your pickles may have absorbed ground spices. Prevent this by using whole spices rather than ground ones. These problems don't indicate spoilage, but your pickle flavor may be altered slightly.

Soft or slippery pickles indicate spoilage. Discard the pickles without tasting them. Prevent these problems by accurately measuring your salt, using a vinegar with 5 percent acidity, and completely covering your pickles with liquid during the brining process and in your filled jars.

Remove the scum from your brining solution daily, use a modern-day recipe, follow your recipe to the letter, and use a heating period long enough to destroy any microorganisms.

Your Pickle Jars Have White Sediment in the Bottom

Soft pickles in a jar with white sediment indicate spoilage. Don't taste these, simply discard them.

But, if the pickles are firm, they're safe to eat. The sediment is a harmless lactic acid or yeast that develops in the jar and settles to the bottom.

Your Food Floats in the Jar

Fruit weighs less than the syrup you pack it in. If your fruit isn't packed snuggly, it'll float to the surface. Use ripe, firm fruit, and pack it tightly — but don't crush it. Fill your jars with a light to medium syrup. You can't sink floating fruit, but with practice, you can improve your packing skills.

Raw-packed vegetables shrink during processing. This doesn't indicate food spoilage. Reduce shrinkage by packing your vegetables tightly or blanching or precooking them prior to packing them in the jars.

Your Food's Color Is Off

Fruit near the top of the jar may darken if it's not covered with liquid. This doesn't indicate food spoilage. Completely cover your fruit with liquid using the correct headspace for the fruit and the liquid. Too much headspace seals excess air in the jar. Trapped air bubbles change the liquid level in sealed jars when they're released during processing. Leave the correct headspace. Release any trapped air bubbles in the jar before sealing it.

If your fruit darkens after removing it from the jar, active enzymes may be to blame. Process your filled jars for the required length of time stated in your recipe to inactivate these enzymes. Start counting your processing time when the water in your kettle reaches a full rolling boil, with your jars covered by 1 to 2 inches of water.

You may notice your apples, pears, or peaches turning colors during processing. Heat causes chemical changes in fruit that may alter the color of the food. Don't be surprised if these fruits turn pink, blue, red, or purple — there's no way to avoid it. So just sit back, admire the colors, and enjoy your food.

Fruits and vegetables turn dark when the natural chemical substances in food (such as acids, tannins, or sulfur compounds) react with minerals in the water. Food making direct contact with reactive utensils (utensils made from brass, copper, iron, aluminum, zinc, or chipped enamelware) experiences a color change. Prevent this by using soft water and nonreactive equipment, like stainless steel, glass, or enamelware with no chips or cracks.

Heating green vegetables breaks down *chlorophyll,* the green coloring in plant materials. If your green vegetables lose their bright-green color, you can't do anything about it. You have to expose your canned food to heat to produce a safe vacuum seal.

Green vegetables can turn brown if they're overcooked before they're heated again during processing. Accurately monitor your precooking time.

Chapter 18

Ten (Or So) Sources for Canning and Preserving Supplies and Equipment

- -

In This Chapter

▶ Locating suppliers for canning and preserving gear

▶ Discovering suppliers of seeds and spices for the home canner

- -

*I*n this chapter, I share some of my favorite places for finding anything and everything I need for canning and preserving without leaving the comfort of my home. The part I enjoy most about shopping by catalog or online is that I never have to worry about finding a parking place or getting to the store before it closes!

Alltrista Consumer Products Company

This company manufactures Ball and Kerr home-canning products and supplies. It no longer offers an online ordering service, but it does provide retail stores carrying its products on the Web site. In addition to an archive of recipes, there's a help line for home canners (available weekdays from 8:30 a.m. to 4:30 p.m. EST).

P.O. Box 2729
Muncie, IN 47307-0729
Phone: 800-240-3340
Web site: www.homecanning.com

The Chile Shop

The Chile Shop is the place to purchase the best and the freshest chile from New Mexico, like the Chimayo chili powder I mention for the Pear Chutney in Chapter 7. In addition to its Web site, it produces one catalog a year.

109 East Water St.
Santa Fe, NM 87501-2132
Phone: 505-983-6080
Fax: 505-984-0737
Web site: www.thechileshop.com

Cooking.com

This is the place for out-of-the ordinary canning jars, as well as jars made in the United States. It also carries water-bath canners, pressure canners, and basic canning tools.

2850 Ocean Park Blvd., Suite 310
Santa Monica, CA 90405
Phone: 800-663-8810 or 310-450-3270
Web site: www.cooking.com

The Cook's Garden

If you have a garden or you're new to gardening, start your adventure here. Since 1983, the Cook's Garden has developed an impressive selection of vegetable, herb, and flower seeds along with kitchen and gardening supplies (including some canning equipment). Its collection of *certified-organic seeds,* seeds produced without the use of synthetic chemical fertilizers or pesticides, are easily identified in the 108-page catalog or on its Web site.

P.O. Box 535
Londonderry, VT 05148
Phone: 800-457-9703
Fax: 800-457-9705
Web site: www.cooksgarden.com

The Food Safety Network

This Web site is the gateway to government food-safety information. The database of federal and state government agencies includes anything and everything concerning safe food handling. From the Federal and State Government Agencies heading, go to the United States Department of Agriculture (USDA), then to the Cooperative State Research, Education, and Extension Services (CSREES).

Web site: www.foodsafety.gov

Home Canning Supply & Specialties

Hugh and Myra Arrendale are longtime home canners with extensive knowledge of canning equipment and supplies. They carry everything for the home preserver except the food. Their selection of canning equipment, canning supplies, canning tools, and dehydrators provides one-stop shopping for your home-canning and -preserving needs. Call to request a catalog or visit their Web site.

P.O. Box 1158-WW
Ramona, CA 92065
Phone: 800-354-4070 or 760-788-0520
Fax: 760-789-4745
Web site: www.homecanningsupply.com

Kitchen Krafts, Inc.

Kitchen Krafts carries a complete line of canning supplies, including hard-to-find tools and ingredients. Its Web site is updated with new items, exclusive items, and back-ordered items to save time when you're placing an order. Check out the selection of labels and decorative two-piece caps for dressing up your jars.

P.O. Box 442
Waukon, IA 52172-0442
Phone: 800-776-0575
Web site: www.kitchenkrafts.com

MyOwnLabels.com

Create personalized labels for your home-crafted food. This company specializes in small orders with no minimum. Follow the easy ordering instructions on its Web site, submit the order, and receive your labels in 7 to 12 days! This is an Internet-only company.

Web site: www.myownlabels.com

Penzeys Spices

Penzeys carries an extensive line of spices, herbs, and seasonings. Rest assured that you're getting fresh, high-quality products from this company. Their pickling spices are a must-try along with glass storage jars for your spices, herbs, and seasonings. In addition to its catalog and online store, there are numerous retail locations from Kansas to Connecticut.

P.O. Box 933
Muskego, WI 53150
Phone: 800-741-7787
Fax: 262-785-7678
Web site: www.penzeys.com

Sur La Table

In addition to carrying a water-bath and a pressure canner, Sur La Table offers stoneware crocks for pickling, food mills, Weck and Leifheit canning jars from Germany, high-quality pots and pans, and other basic equipment to simplify your kitchen tasks. For a listing of its retail store locations, check its catalog or Web site, or call its customer-service number (it's toll-free in the U.S.).

P.O. Box 34707
Seattle, WA 98124-1707
Phone: 800-243-0852 (to order) or 866-328-5412 (for customer service)
Web site: www.surlatable.com

Tupperware Corporation

Tupperware is well known for its line of plastic containers and other supplies for your home and kitchen. Check out its FreezeSmart line: It includes rigid containers designed for the cold temperatures of your freezer. Choose from a wide variety of shapes and sizes.

Phone: 800-366-3800, or check your phone book for a local number
Web site: www.tupperware.com

Appendix

Metric Conversion Guide

∙ ∙

*N**ote:* The recipes in this cookbook were not developed or tested using metric measures. There may be some variation in quality when converting to metric units.

Common Abbreviations

Abbreviation(s)	What It Stands For
C, c	cup
g	gram
kg	kilogram
L, l	liter
lb	pound
mL, ml	milliliter
oz	ounce
pt	pint
t, tsp	teaspoon
T, TB, Tbl, Tbsp	tablespoon

Volume

U.S. Units	Canadian Metric	Australian Metric
¼ teaspoon	1 mL	1 ml
½ teaspoon	2 mL	2 ml
1 teaspoon	5 mL	5 ml

(continued)

Volume *(continued)*

U.S. Units	Canadian Metric	Australian Metric
1 tablespoon	15 mL	20 ml
¼ cup	50 mL	60 ml
⅓ cup	75 mL	80 ml
½ cup	125 mL	125 ml
⅔ cup	150 mL	170 ml
¾ cup	175 mL	190 ml
1 cup	250 mL	250 ml
1 quart	1 liter	1 liter
1½ quarts	1.5 liters	1.5 liters
2 quarts	2 liters	2 liters
2½ quarts	2.5 liters	2.5 liters
3 quarts	3 liters	3 liters
4 quarts	4 liters	4 liters

Weight

U.S. Units	Canadian Metric	Australian Metric
1 ounce	30 grams	30 grams
2 ounces	55 grams	60 grams
3 ounces	85 grams	90 grams
4 ounces (¼ pound)	115 grams	125 grams
8 ounces (½ pound)	225 grams	225 grams
16 ounces (1 pound)	455 grams	500 grams
1 pound	455 grams	½ kilogram

Measurements

Inches	Centimeters
½	1.5
1	2.5
2	5.0
3	7.5
4	10.0
5	12.5
6	15.0
7	17.5
8	20.5
9	23.0
10	25.5
11	28.0
12	30.5
13	33.0

Temperature (Degrees)

Fahrenheit	Celsius
32	0
212	100
250	120
275	140
300	150
325	160

(continued)

Temperature (Degrees) *(continued)*

Fahrenheit	Celsius
350	180
375	190
400	200
425	220
450	230
475	240
500	260

Index

FOR DUMMIES®

A world of resources to help you grow

HOME, GARDEN & HOBBIES

Feng Shui For Dummies
0-7645-5295-3

Gardening For Dummies
0-7645-5130-2

Guitar For Dummies
0-7645-5106-X

Also available:

Auto Repair For Dummies
(0-7645-5089-6)

Chess For Dummies
(0-7645-5003-9)

Home Maintenance For Dummies
(0-7645-5215-5)

Organizing For Dummies
(0-7645-5300-3)

Piano For Dummies
(0-7645-5105-1)

Poker For Dummies
(0-7645-5232-5)

Quilting For Dummies
(0-7645-5118-3)

Rock Guitar For Dummies
(0-7645-5356-9)

Roses For Dummies
(0-7645-5202-3)

Sewing For Dummies
(0-7645-5137-X)

FOOD & WINE

Cooking For Dummies
0-7645-5250-3

Cookies For Dummies
0-7645-5390-9

Wine For Dummies
0-7645-5114-0

Also available:

Bartending For Dummies
(0-7645-5051-9)

Chinese Cooking For Dummies
(0-7645-5247-3)

Christmas Cooking For Dummies
(0-7645-5407-7)

Diabetes Cookbook For Dummies
(0-7645-5230-9)

Grilling For Dummies
(0-7645-5076-4)

Low-Fat Cooking For Dummies
(0-7645-5035-7)

Slow Cookers For Dummies
(0-7645-5240-6)

TRAVEL

Italy For Dummies
0-7645-5453-0

Hawaii For Dummies
0-7645-5438-7

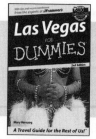

Las Vegas For Dummies
0-7645-5448-4

Also available:

America's National Parks For Dummies
(0-7645-6204-5)

Caribbean For Dummies
(0-7645-5445-X)

Cruise Vacations For Dummies 2003
(0-7645-5459-X)

Europe For Dummies
(0-7645-5456-5)

Ireland For Dummies
(0-7645-6199-5)

France For Dummies
(0-7645-6292-4)

London For Dummies
(0-7645-5416-6)

Mexico's Beach Resorts For Dummies
(0-7645-6262-2)

Paris For Dummies
(0-7645-5494-8)

RV Vacations For Dummies
(0-7645-5443-3)

Walt Disney World & Orlando For Dummies
(0-7645-5444-1)

Available wherever books are sold. Go to www.dummies.com or call 1-877-762-2974 to order direct.

  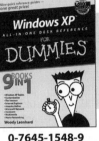

FOR DUMMIES®

The advice and explanations you need to succeed

SELF-HELP, SPIRITUALITY & RELIGION

Sex For Dummies
0-7645-5302-X

Parenting For Dummies
0-7645-5418-2

Religion For Dummies
0-7645-5264-3

Also available:

The Bible For Dummies
(0-7645-5296-1)

Buddhism For Dummies
(0-7645-5359-3)

Christian Prayer For Dummies
(0-7645-5500-6)

Dating For Dummies
(0-7645-5072-1)

Judaism For Dummies
(0-7645-5299-6)

Potty Training For Dummies
(0-7645-5417-4)

Pregnancy For Dummies
(0-7645-5074-8)

Rekindling Romance For Dummies
(0-7645-5303-8)

Spirituality For Dummies
(0-7645-5298-8)

Weddings For Dummies
(0-7645-5055-1)

PETS

Puppies For Dummies
0-7645-5255-4

Dog Training For Dummies
0-7645-5286-4

Cats For Dummies
0-7645-5275-9

Also available:

Labrador Retrievers For Dummies
(0-7645-5281-3)

Aquariums For Dummies
(0-7645-5156-6)

Birds For Dummies
(0-7645-5139-6)

Dogs For Dummies
(0-7645-5274-0)

Ferrets For Dummies
(0-7645-5259-7)

German Shepherds For Dummies
(0-7645-5280-5)

Golden Retrievers For Dummies
(0-7645-5267-8)

Horses For Dummies
(0-7645-5138-8)

Jack Russell Terriers For Dummies
(0-7645-5268-6)

Puppies Raising & Training Diary For Dummies
(0-7645-0876-8)

EDUCATION & TEST PREPARATION

Spanish For Dummies
0-7645-5194-9

Algebra For Dummies
0-7645-5325-9

The ACT For Dummies
0-7645-5210-4

Also available:

Chemistry For Dummies
(0-7645-5430-1)

English Grammar For Dummies
(0-7645-5322-4)

French For Dummies
(0-7645-5193-0)

The GMAT For Dummies
(0-7645-5251-1)

Inglés Para Dummies
(0-7645-5427-1)

Italian For Dummies
(0-7645-5196-5)

Research Papers For Dummies
(0-7645-5426-3)

The SAT I For Dummies
(0-7645-5472-7)

U.S. History For Dummies
(0-7645-5249-X)

World History For Dummies
(0-7645-5242-2)

Available wherever books are sold. Go to www.dummies.com or call 1-877-762-2974 to order direct.

FOR DUMMIES®

We take the mystery out of complicated subjects

WEB DEVELOPMENT

Creating Web Pages For Dummies
0-7645-1643-4

HTML 4 For Dummies
0-7645-0723-0

Dreamweaver MX For Dummies
0-7645-1630-2

Also available:

ASP.NET For Dummies
(0-7645-0866-0)

Building a Web Site For Dummies
(0-7645-0720-6)

ColdFusion "MX" For Dummies (0-7645-1672-8)

Creating Web Pages All-in-One Desk Reference For Dummies
(0-7645-1542-X)

FrontPage 2002 For Dummies
(0-7645-0821-0)

HTML 4 For Dummies Quick Reference
(0-7645-0721-4)

Macromedia Studio "MX" All-in-One Desk Reference For Dummies
(0-7645-1799-6)

Web Design For Dummies
(0-7645-0823-7)

PROGRAMMING & DATABASES

C++ For Dummies
0-7645-0746-X

XML For Dummies
0-7645-1657-4

Access 2002 For Dummies
0-7645-0818-0

Also available:

Beginning Programming For Dummies
(0-7645-0835-0)

Crystal Reports "X" For Dummies
(0-7645-1641-8)

Java & XML For Dummies
(0-7645-1658-2)

Java 2 For Dummies
(0-7645-0765-6)

JavaScript For Dummies
(0-7645-0633-1)

Oracle9i For Dummies
(0-7645-0880-6)

Perl For Dummies
(0-7645-0776-1)

PHP and MySQL For Dummies
(0-7645-1650-7)

SQL For Dummies
(0-7645-0737-0)

VisualBasic .NET For Dummies
(0-7645-0867-9)

Visual Studio .NET All-in-One Desk Reference For Dummies
(0-7645-1626-4)

LINUX, NETWORKING & CERTIFICATION

Red Hat Linux 7.3 For Dummies
0-7645-1545-4

Networking For Dummies
0-7645-0772-9

A+ Certification For Dummies
0-7645-0812-1

Also available:

CCNP All-in-One Certification For Dummies
(0-7645-1648-5)

Cisco Networking For Dummies
(0-7645-1668-X)

CISSP For Dummies
(0-7645-1670-1)

CIW Foundations For Dummies with CD-ROM
(0-7645-1635-3)

Firewalls For Dummies
(0-7645-0884-9)

Home Networking For Dummies
(0-7645-0857-1)

Red Hat Linux All-in-One Desk Reference For Dummies
(0-7645-2442-9)

TCP/IP For Dummies
(0-7645-1760-0)

UNIX For Dummies
(0-7645-0419-3)

Available wherever books are sold.
Go to www.dummies.com or call 1-877-762-2974 to order direct.

Canning and Preserving For Dummies®

Cheat Sheet

Tips for Successful Canning

- Use tried and tested recipes made for modern-day canning (about 1982 or newer).
- Don't double your recipes. If you want more than one recipe produces, prepare the recipe more than once.
- Carry copies of recipes with you. You'll always know how much to buy when you see your favorite, perfectly ripe fruit or vegetables.
- Use only perfect fruit or vegetables, not bruised or over-ripe.
- Measure all ingredients accurately.
- Don't increase or decrease your ingredients or your processing time.
- Don't substitute powdered pectin for liquid pectin or vice versa.
- Use salt without any additives, such as canning and pickling salt.
- Use jars and two-piece caps approved for canning.
- Only use new lids.
- Always wipe the top rim of your jars before placing the hot lid on top.
- Always label and date your product.
- Use all canned items within one year of the date of processing.
- Store your vacuum-sealed jars without the screw band.
- Periodically check your stored, sealed jars for any signs of spoilage such as leaking, bubbles, mold or film, or any unusual discoloration.
- If in doubt about the quality or safety of a preserving product, dispose of it without taking a taste.

Water-Bath Canning Altitude Adjustments

Based on your elevation, add the additional amount of processing time (refer to the following table) to the processing time specified in your recipe.

Altitude (in feet)	Increase in Your Processing Time
1,001 to 3,000	5 minutes
3,001 to 6,000	10 minutes
6,001 to 8,000	15 minutes
8,001 to 10,000	20 minutes

Pressure Canning Altitude Adjustments

For pressure canning at an elevation higher than 1,000 feet above sea level, adjust the pounds of pressure for processing, according to the following table. Your pressure canner processing time remains the same.

Altitude (in feet)	Weighted Gauge	Dial Gauge
0 to 1,000	10	11
1,001 to 2,000	15	11
2,001 to 4,000	15	12
4,001 to 6,000	15	13
6,001 to 8,000	15	14
8,001 to 10,000	15	15

Canning and Preserving For Dummies®

Cheat Sheet

Terms of Preserving

blanching: A process to loosen the skin of soft fruit or halt the ripening process by quickly dipping the food in boiling water.

boiling point of water: 212 degrees at an altitude of 1,000 feet or less above sea level.

butter: A smooth, thick spread made from fruit purée and sugar, cooked for a long period of time.

chutney: An accompaniment to food that contains fruit, vinegar, sugar, and spices. It ranges in flavor from sweet to spicy and mild to hot with a texture from smooth to chunky.

conserves: Contains two fruits mixed with sugar and nuts, cooked to a consistency similar to jam.

dry pack: A method for packing fruit for freezing using no sugar or liquid.

gel point: The point at which jelly becomes firm, 8 degrees above the point of boiling, or 220 degrees.

headspace: The amount of air left between the food, any liquid, and the top of your container.

high-acid food: Foods containing large amounts of acid with a pH of 4.6 or less. They include most fruit and pickled food. Process in a water-bath canner.

hot pack: A process of heating or precooking food before packing it into canning jars or freezer containers.

jam: A cooked combination of fruit (crushed or chopped), sugar, and sometimes pectin and acid. The mixture is cooked until the pieces of fruit are soft and almost lose their shape.

jelly: A sweet transparent mixture made from fruit juice, sugar, and sometimes pectin.

low-acid food: Food that contains very little amounts of natural acid. These include vegetables, meat, fish, and poultry with a pH greater than 4.6. Process in a pressure canner.

marmalade: A soft jelly with pieces of fruit rind, usually citrus fruit, suspended in them.

pickling: A process of preserving food in a strong mixture of water, salt, vinegar, and sometimes sugar.

preserves: Refers to all sweet spreads, but it's also cooked, sweetened fruit with a jam-like consistency and whole or large pieces of fruit.

pressure canner temperature: The internal temperature of a pressure canner is 240 degrees to destroy heat-resistant bacteria.

purée: A food that's been ground or mashed until it's completely smooth.

raw pack: Food packed in canning jars or freezer containers without any preheating or cooking.

relish: A cooked mixture of fruit or vegetables preserved with vinegar. Flavors range from sweet to savory or hot to mild. The texture may be smooth, finely chopped, or chunky.

salsa: Means "sauce" in Spanish. A traditional salsa is made with tomatoes, cilantro, chiles, and onions and served at room temperature.

wet pack: A method used for freezing fruit. Granulated sugar is sprinkled over the fruit before freezing and the natural juices from the fruit dissolve the sugar or adding a sweet syrup to the fruit after it's put into a freezer container.

For Dummies: Bestselling Book Series for Beginners